TAXATION IN INDONESIA

TAXATION
IN
INDONESIA

J.S. UPPAL, Ph. D.
Professor of Economics
State University of New York
Albany, New York, USA

GADJAH MADA UNIVERSITY PRESS

Perpustakaan Nasional : katalog dalam terbitan (KDT)

UPPAL, J. S.
Taxation in Indonesia / J.S. Uppal — Cet.3 — Yogyakarta : Gadjah Mada University Press, 1993.
ix, 343 hal. ; 21 cm.
Bibliografi : hal. 43
ISBN 979-420-020-4

1. Pajak dan perpajakan I. Judul

353.937.24

First printing 1986
Second printing 1991
Third printing 1993

665.72.11.93

Printed in Indonesia by:
GADJAH MADA UNIVERSITY PRESS
Member of IKAPI (Indonesian Publishers Association)
9309171—C1E

ISBN 979-420-020-4

PREFACE

Like several other developing countries formerly under colonial domination, Indonesia inherited an outmoded and highly inefficient tax structure. The chief purpose of the colonial tax system, was to raise revenues to finance the colonial administration. No attention was paid by the colonial government, or even for several years after independence, to restructuring the Indonesian tax structure to meet major goals of economic growth, stabilisation, equity and conform to various aspects of efficiency. It is no wonder then, that the Indonesian tax system was not effective in curbing serious inflation and promoting capital formation for raising the low economic growth rate - the two serious problems confronting the country during the sixties and seventies.

Since recently the New Order Government has been attempting to restructure the Indonesian tax system. The old personal and corporation income taxes have been replaced by a new Income Tax. The Value Added Tax has been introduced in place of the old Sales Tax. New Property Tax has been implemented recently to replace the old similar taxes. The purpose of all these new tax measures is to enhance tax revenues for capital formation for financing developing planning and promoting equity in income and wealth distribution in the society. The need to raise additional revenues from the tax system has become more pressing on account of fall in the international price of oil, which contributed to bulk of the government revenues. To what extent, the restructured

Indonesian tax structure will produce more revenues and also achieve other desired goals, will be subjects of discussion in the next few years. There is, thus, need for literature on the Indonesian tax structure which could enable the students, teachers and others interested in public finance, to understand fully the recent changes in taxes and their outcome.

The few books available on the subject deal mainly with legal aspects of the taxation - what is needed is an economic analysis of the emerging tax structure in Indonesia. This book is an attempt to fill in this gap. In this humble attempt, we have outlined major drawbacks that existed in the old tax system. We have also provided salient features of the new tax measures. The latest data on various taxes: and statements from the Ministry of Finance have been incorporated. Comprehensive bibliography on taxation in developing countries in general and on the Indonesian tax system has been provided. Data on various aspects of taxation have been given in appendices 1—20. To enable the readers to study in depth various components of the new tax lelgislation, original texts of the major tax laws and their elucidation, have also been included as Appendices. We sincerely hope that this effort will be useful to students, teachers and general readers interested in economic analysis of the Indonesian tax structure.

The study was undertaken when the author was a visiting Professor; at the Gadjah Mada University, Yogyakarta. Several faculty members and graduate students assisted in the study. professors Soetrisno Prawirohardjono and M. Suparmoko were kind enough to review the manuscript. My special thanks are due to Drs. Chairul Ichsan, who prepared most of the statistical tables and Drs. Jamaluddin Ahmad for research assistance. The author alone, however, is responsible for any errors and ommissions.

Yogyakarta, Indonesia **J.S. Uppal**
May, 1986.

CONTENTS

Page

Preface v
Table of Statistical Data Appendices viii
Table of Texts of the original: Tax Laws ix
Chapter 1. Introduction 1
Chapter 2. Inter-Governmental Finance 3
Chapter 3. Efficiency in the Tax System 14
Chapter 4. Direct Taxes 23
Chapter 5. Indirect Taxes 31
Bibliography 43
Appendices 51

STATISTICAL DATA APPENDICES

Appendix No.	Heading	Page
1.	Central Government Actual Revenue Receipts 1960—1984/85	53
2.	Central Government Actual Revenue Receipts 1960—1984/85 (cont'd)	54
3.	The Composition of Tax Structures in Indonesia, 1960—1968	55
4.	The Composition of Tax Structure in Indonesia, 1969/70—1973/74	56
5.	The Composition of Tax Structure in Indonesia, 1974/75—1978/79	57
6.	The Composition of Tax Structure in Indonesia, 1979/80—1983/84	58
7.	The Composition of Tax Structure in Indonesia, 1984/85	59
8.	Taxes and other revenues as percentages of the GDP, 1960—68	60
9.	Taxes and other revenues as percentages of the GDP, 1969/70—1973/74	61
10.	Taxes and other revenues as percentages of the GDP, 1974/75—1978/79	62
11.	Taxes and other revenues as percentages of the GDP, 1979/80—1983/84	63
12.	Central Government Domestic Revenue, 1969—1973	64
13.	Central Government Domestic Revenue, 1974—1978	65
14.	Central Government Domestic Revenue, 1979/80—1984/85	66
15.	Tax Revenues as Proportion of the GDP in Selected Underdeveloped Countries	67
16.	Corporation Tax Revenues in Indonesia, 1979/70—1983/84	68

17. Values of Imports and Import Tax Revenues in Indonesia, 1960—1983/84 69
18. Values of Export and Export Tax Revenues in Indonesia, 1960—1983/84 70
19. Actual Receipts of Provinces (First Stage Governments) in Indonesia, 1977/78--1982/83 71
20. Growth of Public Expenditures in Indonesia, 1960—1983/84 72

TEXTS OF THE ORIGINAL: TAX LAWS

Appendix No.	Heading	Page
21.	General Provisions and Procedures on Taxes. Law No. 6, 1983	73
22.	Elucidation on Law No. 6, 1983 regarding General Provisions and procedure on Taxes	98
23.	Income Tax: Law No. 7, 1983	130
24.	Elucidation on Law regarding Income Tax	154
25.	Value Added Tax on Goods and Services and Sales Tax on Luxury Goods: Law No. 8, 1983	218
26.	Elucidation on the Law regarding Value-Added-Tax on Goods & Services and Sales Tax on Luxury Goods	234
27.	Implementation Regulations on the National Tax System: Law 35, 1983	254
28.	Implementation of the Income Tax Law 1984, Law No. 36, 1983	258
29.	Elucidation on the Law No. 36, 1983 on Implementation of the Income Tax Law 1984	268
30.	Tax on Interest on Time Deposits and Other Savings: Law No. 37, 1983	281
31.	Elucidation on Law No. 37, 1983 regarding tax on interest of Time Deposits and Other Savings	283
32.	Implementation of Law on Value-Added Tax 1984: Law No. 38, 1983	285
33.	The Law on Land and Buildings, Law No. 12, 1985	298
34.	Elucidation on Law No. 12, 1985 on the law on Tax on Land and Buildings	312
35.	The Law on Stamp Duty, Law No. 13, 1985	329

CHAPTER I

INTRODUCTION

Taxes are no longer meant only for raising adequate revenues for operation of government. Taxation is now regarded as a powerful fiscal tool to guide the national economy towards achievement of her socio-economic goals. For an underdeveloped economy like Indonesia, embarked on development planning, these objectives are economic growth, fuller employment, stabilisation and more equitable distribution of income and wealth. Economic growth requires host of economic policies particularly, diversion of a proportion of national income to capital formation and investment both in private and public sectors; optimal allocation and efficient use of national resources. Taxation can play a dominant role in promoting savings by discouraging unnecessary consumption, including conspicious consumption and expenditure on wasteful ceremonies. Taxation can also promote a system of incentives to work, risk taking and investment. Through taxes and subsidies, negative externalities can be minimised and positive externalities promoted, both in the fields of investment and consumption, to achieve optimal allocation of resources. Tax structure can also promote creation of job opportunities through investment credits, depreciation allowances and thus, diversion of investment to labor intensive technology in a labor abundant underdeveloped economy like Indonesia. Changes in tax rates can assist in achieving stability through managing aggregate demand. Changes in tax rates can be discretionary *ie* deliberate tax changes according to desired level of stability, or automatic, in which case tax rates are so designed that level of revenues varies automatically with changing levels of national income. while the automatic tax policy is highly preferred for various reasons, particularly for ease of administration and political feasibility, its success, however, depends on the degree of elasticity or built-in-tax flexibility in the tax structure. The important goal of more equitable distribution of income and wealth can be achieved, to some extent, through an appropriate tax policy: Horizontal as well verticle tax equities can assist egalitarian policies and promote justice in taxation. Thus, tax system has an important role to play in achieving a country's socio-economic goals, besides raising adequate revenues for financing public expenditure. Because of the crucial potential of tax system to achieve national goals, economists judge the tax structure of a county with reference to some well known canons of taxation such as: revenue adequacy, administrative ease; built-in-flexibility; optimal allocation of resources and equity. We will analyse the Indonesian tax structure with reference to these tax principles in Chapter III.

CHAPTER II

INTER-GOVERNMENTAL FINANCE

Indonesian fiscal system is based on federal structure: central government, provincial governments (first stage regions), Kabupaten (administrative area below the provincial level), Kotamadya (municipality with the same administrative status as Kabupaten), Kecamatan (administrative area below the Kabupaten or Kotamadya) and desa or Kelurahan (village).

The division of revenue sources between the different levels of governments is governed by several regulations: particularly Law No. 32/1956, Balance of Inter-Governmental Fiscal Relations, Law No. 5/1974, Principles of Regional Government. These laws provide for allocation of some sources of revenues and subsidies to subnational levels of government. Besides their own sources, such as revenues from local taxes, service charges, profits from local enterprises, rental receipts, there are receipts from central government, which fall into two categories: Assigned Revenues and Grants, as discussed below:

(i) Assigned Revenues: Taxes, royalties etc., levied by the central government but assigned wholly or in part to regional governments. These include Ipeda (Iuran Pembangunan Daerah): tax on property - land and urban buildings. 10 percent of Ipeda may be defrayed in assessment and collection costs, 10 percent of revenue net of collection costs, is assigned to privincial governments, and the remaining 90 percent is paid to the Kotamadya (municipalities) and Kabupaten. Ipeda revenues are assigned in development budgets. From the F.Y. 1986—87, however Ipeda has been replaced by a new "property tax" which also includes the wealth tax. Provinces also receive an allocation from duty charged on petrol sales at 1 rupiah per litre sold within the province. In addition, regional authorities receive levies on 70 percent of the royalties on timber extracted from their territories. Royalties and cesses provide 3.7 percent of provincial revenues and 2.6 percent of regional government funds as a whole. However, there are great variations among provinces on the royalties and cess as proportion of provincial budgets. These range from 0.3 percent for D.I. Yogyakarta to 8 percent for Lampung for the 1978/79 budget.

(ii) Grants (Subsidi Daerah Otonom): Grants from the Central government constitute an important source of revenues for regional governments. There are various types of grants which include: (i) subsidi Daerah Otonom, which covers the salaries and responsibility allowances plus 66 percent of the food allowances of civil servants in privincial, Kabupaten and Kotamadya governments; (ii) provincial Development Grant (Bantuan Pembangunan Dati I), also known as Inpres Propinsi or Inpres Dati I, for development projects undertaken by provincial governments; (iii) District Development Grant (Bantuan Kabupaten), given to all Kotamadya and Kabupaten on the basis of their population, with a minimum of 50 million rupiah for each jurisdiction, for use in development projects; (iv) elementary Education Grant (Bantuan Pembangunan Sekolah Dasar), given to Kabupaten and Kotamadya for expenditure on elementary education; (v) Public Health Grant (Bantuan Sarana Kesehatan); (vi) Village Grant (Bantuan Desa) given by central government to each village to be spent on materials—labor to be provided communally and freely by villages. Most of the allocations have been made for small road, bridge and water supply projects; (vii) Several operational and Maintenance Grants.

Following are the major sources of revenue for different levels of government:

Table I
Sources of Revenue for Central Government in Indonesia, 1980/81—1985/86

Revenue Sources	Proportion of Total Revenues			
	1980—81		1984—85	
A. Operating Receipts		78.80		81.1
1. Direct Taxes		63.36		62.7
Income Tax	2.18		13.3[a]	
Non-oil corporations Tax	4.14			
Oil Corporations Tax	51.98		48.7	
Others (wealth tax, stamp duty interest-dividend-royalty tax	5.6		0.7	
2. Indirect Taxes		15.44		18.4
Sales tax-domestic	3.14		7.2[b]	
Sales tax-imports	1.40			
Excise tax	4.22		4.2	
Import Tax	3.04		3.1	
Export Tax	0.57		0.4	
Others	0.23		0.4	
Non Tax Receipts (licence fees, and services)	2.84		3.1	
B. Development Receipts (Program and project aids)		21.20		18.9

Notes : A. Pajak Penghasilan Perseorangan/Private income tax and non-oil corporation tax.
b. Value added tax on goods and services and sales tax on luxury goods.

Source : Biro Pusat Statistik, *Statistik Indonesia 1984,* Jakarta, pp. 572—73 and 1985—86 Budget Report.

Table II
Sources of Revenue for Provincial Government, (First Stage Regions) in Indonesia 1980—81 and 1982—83
(Percent of Total Revenue)

Revenue Sources	1980—81		1983—84	
A. *Revenue From Own Sources*		24.60		23.59
(a) Taxes		11.90		12.00
Household Tax	0.10		0.24	
Transfer Duties on Motor Cars	6.50		6.81	
Tax on Motorized Vehicles	3.40		3.80	
Surcharge on Wealth Tax	0.10		0.00	
Tax on Forestry Products	0.00		0.00	
Tax on Fuel	0.01		0.01	
Tax on Fish Catch	0.01		0.01	
Other taxes	1.78		1.13	
(b) Income from Local Government Enterprises		0.20		0.30
(c) Receipt from Services		1.20		1.50
(d) Rental Receipts (Land, Housing and Buildings, Vehicles)		0.01		0.02
(e) receipts from Official Services Agencies		0.80		0.90
B. *Inter-Governmental Revenues*		75.40		76.14
(a) Assigned Revenues	6.10		3.30	
(b) Grants	69.30		72.84	
C. Miscellaneous (including loans)		10.49		8.87

Sources: Calculated from Biro Pusat Statistik, *Statistik Keuangan Pemerintah Daerah, Daerah Tingkat II,* and *PRISMA* 12, 1985 p. 38—39.

Table III
Sources of Revenue for Municipalities (Kotamadya) and Kabupaten in Indonesia, 1980—81 (Percent of total Revenue)

Revenue Sources	1980—81	
A. *Revenue from Own Sources*		13.04
a. *Taxes*		2.84
1. Entertainment Taxes	1.10	
2. Restaurants and Hotel Taxes	0.68	
3. Radio Tax	0.04	
4. Foreigners Tax	0.15	
5. Slaughter Tax	0.08	
6. Tax on Non-Motorized Vehicles	0.05	
7. Advertisement Tax	0.08	
8. Dog Licenses	0.13	
9. Liquor Tax	0.01	
10. Toll Road	0.15	
11. Enterprise Registration Tax	0.14	
12. Other Taxes	0.23	
b. Tax on Local Services		4.93
c. Receipt from Official Services		0.93
d. Rental Receipts (Land, Houses, and Buildings and Vehicles) and others		1.00
e. Income from Local Government Enterprises		0.26
B. *Inter-Governmental Revenues*		86.96
a. Assigned Revenues	7.30	
b. Grants	79.66	
C. Miscellaneous Receipts		3.08

Sources: Calculated from Biro Pusat Statistik, *Statistik Keuangan Pemerintah Daerah: Daerah tingkat II*, and *PRISMA* 12, 1985 p. 38—39.

The figures in Table 1—3 are averages for all governments at different levels or jurisdictions. However, there are great variations amongst different governmental units even at the same level, particularly on the grants and subsidies from central government. We give below relevant figures for some randomly selected provinces, during the year 1980—81, to illustrate the point:

Table IV
Central Government Contributions to Selected Provincial Governments in Indonesia 1980—81

Provinces	Contribution by the Central Government (Percent of total Provincial Receipts)		
	Current Receipts	Development Receipts	Total
D.I. Yogyakarta	86.28	66.94	82.72
West Sumatra	79.32	73.40	66.63
Aceh	78.35	16.27	63.00
Lampung	74.49	64.68	71.82
Bali	76.80	84.23	78.17
East Kalimantan	64.20	45.03	49.08
South East Sulawesi	93.70	79.36	88.35
East Nusa Tenggara	92.46	98.76	93.56

Sources: Calculated from data in Biro Pusat Statistik, *Statistik Keuangan Pemerintah Daerah, 1980—81,* Jakarta.

Figures in Tables 1—3 and 4 indicate some important aspects of the inter-governmental finance in Indonesia. Firstly and most importantly, a high proportion of provincial revenues: average 76 percent - come from grants, subsidies and assigned revenues form the central government. For the municipal and kotamadya governments, about 87 percent of revenues are contributed by central and provincial governments. This indicates high degree of centralisation in the Indonesian fiscal federalism. Also, since there is a legal requirement of balanced budgets at all levels of government, the provincial and local governments have to apply cuts in their projects or resort to borrowing from banks, in case of reduction in the central assistance. As regards taxes, these constitute a minor part of total local finance—about five percent and also most of them are highly inelastic. Thus, while increasing gross domestic product does not enhance the provincial and local government's tax revenues proportionately, the government outlays register an increase according to the Wagner's law of government expenditure, which indicates a positive relationship between gross domestic product and government expenditure as percent of GDP. This creates fiscal pressure or budget squeeze for provincial and local governments. The Laws governing distribution of central subsidies amongst provincial governments list factors such as population, size of province, economic potential, educational level of population, infrastructural facilities, geographical factors and number of civil servants. But, an analysis of the central aid to various provinces shows that the 'population factor' has been the dominant factor in distribution of central assistance. During 1980—81, Java received 54.5 percent of the total central subsidies, while the share of Sumatra was only 19.1 percent. What is required is a careful study of various factors governing distribution of central grants and subsidies in order to devise a formula for assigning proper weights to various factors such as tax effort, tax capacity and fiscal needs. Another feature of the Indonesian tax structure is, the large number of taxes on the statutes. There are about 50 taxes listed in the laws for local governments, while in most cases, their revenue is negligible. It is very likely that many of these taxes are highly uneconomic, particularly in view of the inadequate tax enforcement capabilities at local levels. Moreover there is considerable overlap between taxes levied by different levels of government. For example, a single building may be subject to property tax (central government) and household tax (province). This overlapping increases administrative costs and creates resentment and non-compliance amongst tax payers. There is a need to evaluate carefully all these local taxes with particular reference to their role in local finance. Table V and VI give figures on revenues from various taxes which would show trend of revenues over time:

Table V
Total Government Receipts (Both Oil and Non-Oil Sources) 1973—74/1983—84
(Rupiah billion)

Revenue Sources	1973—74		1978—79		1983—84	
	Amount	%	Amount	%	Amount	%
I. *Direct Taxes*	*511.1*	*43.2*	*2996.3*	*56.5*	*11605.1*	*63.4*
Income Tax	33.3	2.8	122.2	2.3	398.8	2.2
Corporation Tax	49.3	4.1	226.5	4.3	757.4	4.1
Oil Companies Corporation Tax	346.9	29.3	2308.7	43.5	9520.2	52.0
Other Taxes Including with-holding Tax, Ipeda)	81.6	7.0	338.9	6.4	928.7	5.1
II. *Indirect Taxes*	*421.6*	*35.6*	*1078.4*	*20.3*	*2308.6*	*12.6*
A. Taxes on Domestic Consumption	*168.0*	*14.2*	*491.4*	*9.2*	*1392.1*	*7.6*
Sales Tax	55.6	4.7	221.1	4.2	575.2	3.2
Excise Tax	62.4	5.3	252.9	4.7	773.2	4.2
Other Taxes and Levies	50.0	4.2	17.4	0.3	43.7	0.2
B. Taxes on International Trade	*253.6*	*21.4*	*587.0*	*11.1*	*916.5*	*5.0*
Import Duties	132.4	11.2	295.3	5.6	557.0	3.0
Sales Tax on Imports	51.5	4.3	125.5	2.4	255.5	1.5
Export Tax	69.7	5.9	166.2	3.1	104.0	0.5
III. Non-Tax Receipts	*44.4*	*3.6*	*191.4*	*3.6*	*514.0*	*2.8*
IV. Total Domestic Revenues	*977.1*	*82.5*	*4266.1*	*80.5*	*14432.7*	*78.8*
V. Development Receipts	*207.7*	*17.6*	*1035.5*	*19.5*	*3882.4*	*21.2*
Program Aid	93.6	8.0	48.2	0.9	14.9	0.08
Project Aid	114.1	9.6	987.3	18.6	3867.5	21.12
IV. Total Revenues	1184.8	100.0	5301.6	100.0	18315.1	100.0

Notes : Includes commercial bank and suppliers credits for development Programs/Projects.

Source : Biro Pusat Statistik, *Indonesia, 1984,* - pp. 572—74.

_________, *Economic Indicators,* various issues.

Table VI
Proportion of Non-Oil Revenues from Various Sources 1973/74 — 1983-1984
(Percent of total non-oil revenue sources)

Revenue Sources	1973—74	1978—79	1983—84
I.. *Direct Taxes*	*19.6*	*23.0*	*23.7*
Income Tax	4.0	4.1	4.5
Corporation Tax	5.9	7.6	8.6
Other Taxes	9.7	11.3	10.6
II. *Indirect Taxes*	*50.3*	*36.0*	*26.2*
A. Domestic Taxes on Consumption	*20.0*	*16.4*	*15.8*
Sales Tax	6.6	7.4	6.5
Excise Tax	7.5	8.4	8.8
Miscellaneous Levies	5.9	0.6	0.5
B. Taxes on International Trade	*30.3*	*19.6*	*10.4*
Import Duties	15.8	9.9	6.3
Sales Tax on Imports	6.2	4.2	2.9
Export Tax	8.3	5.5	1.2
III. Non Tax Receipts	*5.3*	*6.4*	*5.9*
IV. Total Domestic Revenues	*75.2*	*65.4*	*55.8*
V. Development Receipts	*24.8*	*34.6*	*44.2*
Program Aid	11.2	1.7	0.3
Project Aid	13.6	32.9	43.9
VI. Total Revenues	100.0	100.0	100.0

Source: Calculated from data in Biro Pusat Statistik, *Economic Indikators for various years.*

Figures in table V are revenues from major taxes and also their proportion to total revenues, while in Table VI we have computed the corresponding figures from the non-oil tax revenues. It will be observed that the exclusion of revenues from oil related taxes, (mainly the corporation tax on oil companies) changes drastically the relative proportions since this one tax alone accounts for more than half of the total revenues. It is, thus, more appropriate to use non-oil revenues as the base for analysing the relative importance of various taxes as well as their trend over time. We can make the following general observations from data in Table VI. Like other developing countries, indirect taxes are more predominant than the direct taxes in Indonesia, though over-time and with economic develoment, the role of indirect taxes is diminishing. Indirect taxes, particularly sales and excise taxes and import duties, are quite substantial as revenue sources. Amongst direct taxes, individual income tax plays a minor role and revenue from it has been more or less constant as a proportion of the gross domestic product since 1973—74. An important component of the government revenues in Indonesia, is development receipts, which includes foreign assistance and borrowing both domestic and foreign. The growth in the proportion of development receipts indicates that domestic revenues do not grow sufficient enough to meet the mounting public expenditure, hence growing fiscal pressure and reliance on outside funds. Though, we will analyse major taxes in Indonesia individually in a latter section, we would now evaluate the tax structure as a whole, with reference to various norms of efficiency.

CHAPTER III
EFFICIENCY IN THE TAX SYSTEM

A. REVENUE ADEQUACY:

Like several other developing countries formerly under colonial domination, Indonesia inherited an outmoded and highly inefficient tax structure. The chief purpose of the colonial tax structure, based manily on the individual income tax Law 1944 and the Corporation Income Tax Law 1925, was to raise revenues to meet government outlays to run the colonial administration. No attention was paid by the colonial government, or even for some years after independence, to restructuring the Indonesian tax structure to meet major goals of economic growth, stabilisation, equity and to conform to various tests of efficiency. It is no wonder, then that the Indonesian tax structure was not effective in curbing serious inflation or raising the low economic growth rate: the twin serious problems confronting the country during the sixties and seventies.

Raising sufficient revenues to finance planned government outlays, is a major prerequisite of an efficient tax system. It is particularly important for a developing economy, with inadequate capital market to enable governments to borrow internally and also difficulties involved in borrowing externally, to meet budget deficits and to finance massive public expenditure for development plans. This criterion is likely to assume greater importance in future as, with increase in per capita income from development planning, government expenditure as proportion of gross national product will increase.[1] The elasticity of government expenditure with respect to GDP ranged from 1.13 to 1.54—(differing in routine and different components of development expenditure)—during 1970—78, and it is likely to grow in future with planned massive public outlays in the Repelita. This will necessitate a big increase in public revenues. There is already a big shortfall in domestic revenues from non-oil sources. Of the total revenues raised in 1983—84, the amount raised from non-oil sources amounted to only 26.8 percent, the rest raised from oil (52.0 percent) and other sources including development aid, etc (21.2 percent). The gravity of revenue inadequacy of the Indonesian taxes, is evident from the inability of the total domestic revenues from non-oil sources to cover even the routine expenditure during 1983—84. In other words, the routine expenditure was being financed from oil revenues, which should better be used for development outlays.

The revenue inadequacy stems essentially from the inability of a country to maximize revenue collection through "tax effort" consistent with her 'tax ability', which is best indicated by per capita income. A cross-country comparison of tax revenues as proportion of GNP, indicates that while Indonesia compares favorably with many developing countries, in terms of total tax revenues (both from oil and non-oil sources) as proportion of gross national product, she fares quite unfavorably with respect to comparable middle income or even lower income countries: *e.g.*, (Indonesia 5.9 percent, Thailand 13.48 percent, Philippines 12.3 percent, Pakistan 14.5 percent, India 14.1 percent and Sri Lanka 22.2 percent) when the tax on oil is excluded from total tax revenues. The relative position of Indonesia with respect to the major taxes for the period 1978—1980, is indicated below:

1. For elaboration of this issue, see Richard Musgrave, *Fiscal Systems,* Part II, New Haven, Conn; Yale University Press, 1969.

Table VII
Tax Revenues by Types of Tax as proportion of Gross Domestic Product, 1978—80

Countries	GNP per capita US $	Income Tax	Sales Tax	Excise Tax	Import Duty	Export Duty	Wealth and property
Indonesia 1980	370	0.42	1.09	0.95	1.01	0.8	0.32
1982	625						
Average of 21 low income countries with per capita income less than $300	206	1.22	1.71	1.63	4.15	1.62	0.26
Average of 43 middle income countries with per capita income US $300 — 600	510	1.90	1.54	2.5	5.80	1.15	0.37

Source: Calculated from World Bank, *Indonesia: Policies, Prospects for Growth 1984*, p. 64.

Clearly, Indonesia, which on the basis of per capita income, belongs to middle income countries, has a low tax revenue ratio—lower than even the low income countries. Studies have shown that Indonesia has rather a poor "Tax Effort" Index, which warrants serious efforts to revamp the tax system for collecting badly needed additional revenues. Some major reasons for poor tax collections would be: Low tax base due to tax avoidance from legal exemptions, and tax evasion or illegal practices. For example, for the income tax, realized net tax receipts have been estimated at only 2.5 percent of the tax source income.[2]

2. Dietrich Lerche, Efficiency of Taxation in Indonesia, *Bulletin of Indonesian Economic Studies*, Vol. XVI, No. 1, March 1980, p. 39. This ratio, according to Lerche is, though illustrative, yet not "too far from the Indonesian situation."

It also means that there is wide gap between the tax potential (i.e. the tax revenues collectable with proper inforcement of tax laws) and actual tax realization. Dietrich Lerche has estimated tax potential and realization for various Indonesian taxes for 1974—1975[3] as in Table VIII.

Table VIII
Tax Potential and Realization for Various Indonesian Taxes for 1974—1975

Tax	Realization as percentage of the Tax Potential 1974—1975
Income Tax (excluding Oil)	
Personal (excluding MPO)	16
Corporate	24
Wealth Tax	14
Sales Tax (Domestic)	33
Excise Tax	34
Import Sales Tax	23
Custom Duties on Imports	31
Ipeda (land tax)	20
All Taxes	28

Source: Dietrich Lerche, *Bulletin Indonesian Economic Studies,* Vol. XVI, No. 1, March 1980, p. 37.

Several causes for this high tax gap or low realization rates relate to difficulties involved in:

(1) Identifying and locating tax payers.
(2) Verifying tax returns in making correct assessments.
(3) Fully collecting taxes due and large unpaid tax arrears.

The difficulty in identifying and locating tax payers is indicated

3. These estimates are for the latest data available, *i.e.,* for 1974—75. According to Lerche, "There is no evidence to suggest that the situation has greatly changed since then."

by the small number of registered tax payers (those registered as liable to pay tax). Whereas the proportion of registered to potential tax payers is very low, (e.g., for personal income tax it is 7 percent: 252,000/3,600,000), the ratio of effective tax payers (Tax payers who actually file tax returns) was only 50 percent of the registered one.[4] In other words, only 3.5 percent of the potential tax payers filed tax returns for personal income Tax. According to a 1985 survey in Jakarta, 30—40 percent of tax obligators avoided paying sales and excise taxes.[5] This, in the words of a tax official, ''paralyzes implementation of new tax laws.''

The tax compromise practice—commonly known as Tawar-Menawar—which characterises relationship between tax payers and the tax collecting authorities, also increases gap between potential and actual tax revenues. Under this system, the actual collected tax is determined by "bargaining," "compromise" through "pull and push" between a tax payer and the tax official, rather than the legal tax liability. The origin of this practice may lie in lack of tax information, unreliable tax payer's records and books, shortage of qualified staff in tax departments and also the traditional 'non conflict' and 'compromise' social attitudes. However, the result of this practice is that tax payers tend to grossly underreport their income knowing fully well that the tax authorities will increase the liability during negotiations. The compromise generally results in 'under payment of the legal liability.' It is estimated that the domestic tax revenue to GDP ratio in Indonesia would be more than triple if all taxes were fully collected according to legal provisions.

B. ECONOMY

Minimizing the cost of tax collection is an important criterion of fiscal efficiency. Due to several administrative

4. *Ibid,* p. 41.
5. *Jakarta Post,* April 1985.

bottlenecks, underdeveloped economies generally have high costs of tax collection. Whereas Indonesia has recently switched to the indirect assessment method of with holding tax (MPO) for personal and corporation income taxes, the collection costs still continue to be high: 15 percent and 10 percent for personal and corporation income taxes respectively.[6] The cost of collection has been as high as 20 percent for the tax on land or Ipeda tax (Pajak Tanah). Dietrich Lerche mentions the case of Jakarta, "where more than 600,000 tax payers were registered on the computer list for Ipeda/Ireda in 1972, one third were assessed at less than $1.00, an amount which did not even cover collection costs".[7] Also, some nuisance taxes, *e.g.*, dog tax (Pajak anjing), tax on radios (Pajak Radio), involving high collection costs relative to minor revenues, continue to be on the tax rolls of local governments.

C. FLEXIBILITY

An efficient tax system should be flexible i.e., tax base and rates should be so set that tax revenues change automatically with changes in GNP, to finance the mounting public expenditures (or the GNP elasticity of tax should be equal to or greater than one). A flexible tax system can also assist stabilization of the economy by acting as an automatic stabilizer: (anti-inflationary or anti-deflationary fiscal tool). Generally, tax structure in underdeveloped countries is less flexible due to several rigidities and also the predominance of inelastic indirect taxes, which generally have lower tax elasticities. In Indonesia, revenues from indirect taxes, where income elasticity is quite low (e.g., 0.91 for sales and excise taxes, 0.81 for import duties and 0.9 for import sales tax) constitute 26.2 percent of total non-oil domestic revenues. On the other hand, direct taxes with higher income

6. Larche, *op. cit.*, p. 43.
7. *Ibid*, p. 44.

elasticities (income tax 1.19, witholding tax 1.30; corporation tax 1.37), form only 23.7 percent of the revenues. A cross country comparison shows that the Indonesian tax structure has lower income elasticity of tax revenues (or lower tax buoyancy) than several developing countries as per figures in Table IX.

Table IX
Tax Buoyancy in Selected Developing Countries, 1976—82

Country	Income Elasticity of Total Tax Revenues
India	2.4
Korea	2.2
Marocco	2.2
Honduras	2.1
Pakistan	1.9
Malaysia	1.9
Indonesia	
Total-taxes	1.8
Non-oil taxes	0.8

Source: world Bank: *Indonesia Policies, Prospects for Economic Growth, 1984,* p. 66 and Raja Chelliah, "Trends in Taxation in Developing Countries," in M. Bird, *Readings on Taxation in Developing Countries,* John Hopkins University Press, 1975.

Even for taxes on income, which traditionally are more elastic, the estimate on elasticity for Indonesia is just about 1.0. The low income elasticity for the Indonesian tax structure indicates its low potential, or fiscal ability, to finance her development plans and its use as a stabilizer. In consequence, in Indonesia, more reliance has been placed on monetary rather than fiscal policies for stabilisation of the economy.

The low elasticity of taxes in Indonesia can be explained by the very low tax base for various taxes. As regards the income tax, as mentioned earlier, realised net tax receipts are estimated at only

2.5 percent of the tax source indicating a wide gap between tax source or base of income, (legal tax base) and actual (or realised) tax base.

Equity: another desired feature of an efficient tax system is its effectiveness to alter income distribution in a society. The impact of various Indonesian taxes on income distribution is not known. However, since the traditionally progressive taxes, e.g., income and corporation taxes, constitute only a minor proportion of the total tax revenues and also, as pointed out earlier, these taxes are relatively inelastic, one could safely infer that the Indonesian tax structure lacks progressivity and equity. Thus, the tax system could not be relied upon to alleviate poverty and redistribute incomes.

D. OVER DEPENDENCE ON OIL AND LNG TAX REVENUES

An efficient tax system should be diversified so that the tax revenues do not fluctuate greatly from changes in particular sectors of the national economy. Another disquieting feature of the Indonesian tax structure is its continued dependence on oil and LNG (Liquefied natural gas) taxes.

Table X
Tax Revenues From Oil and LNG

	1973—74	1978—79	1981—82	1983—84	1985—86[a]
Tax revenues from oil and LNG taxes as percent of total tax revenues	43.2	56.5	70.7	63.4	48.4

a. the fall in the proportion during 1985—86 is due to fall in international oil prices.

Source: world Bank, Indonesia, *Policies and Prospects for Growth,* 1984, p. 68.

With declining world oil prices and also the uncertain prospects for foreign funds, this over dependence constitutes a lopsided fiscal structure. Indonesia must diversify her sources of tax revenues for a balanced fiscal system to collect adequate public revenues in case of decline in income from a particular sector.

Hard pressed for raising adequate domestic revenues to finance her increasing government expenditures, and in the face of falling prices of oil, which forms a substantial part of her gross domestic product with oil related taxes constituting 63.4 percent of total revenues, the Government of Indonesia is in the process of restructuring her tax structure. In the newly emerging tax structure, particular attention is being paid to reduce various inadequacies as explained above. For example, the preamble to the new Value-Added-tax, which has replaced the old sales tax remarks, that the 'state tax collection implementation so far applicable, is not in accordance any more with the socio-economic living standard of the people of Indonesia, both in the aspect of the national mutual aid principle and the already achieved national development growth rate." The preamble states further. "that the tax system, particularly that manifested in the indirect tax provisions so far applicable, has not motivated the participation of all taxable entrepreneur strata to increase the state revenue urgently required to manifest the continuity of state financing and development on the basis of the national development principles." We will now give salient features of the old taxes and also the main provision of the new tax structure emerging in Indonesia. Since the new tax structure is still in the process of being formulated and implemented, it is not feasible to assessfully the impact of new taxes.

CHAPTER IV

DIRECT TAXES

A. THE OLD PERSONAL INCOME TAX

The old personal income tax was regulated by the 1944 Income Tax Ordinance, which was ammended several times with hundred of decrees issued, lastly by the Law 9, in 1970. Due to the absence of any single comprehensive source of income tax law, there was considerable confusion and contradictions in the tax laws. Definitions of the key terms such as income, resident, non-residents, were not clearly stated in the laws. Contradictions, confusions and lack of precise definitions created great amount of uncertainty and selective enforcement with resulting high magnitude of tax evasion. There were 19 marginal tax rates, ranging from 10 percent to 50 percent for various taxable income classes. The old income tax was a schedular tax in which different items of income were taxed at different rates. For example, rental income and honorarium were taxed at the flat rate of 10 percent, while other items of income were taxed at different rates. There was a long list of tax exempt items *e.g.*, allowance from parents to their family, war allowance of armed forces, profit from selling or transfer of inherited property, interest from Tabanas (savings accounts) and Taska (Time deposit) and other types of deposits. Under the old laws, almost all sources of income were technically subject to withholding by the payers, including wages and salaries (PPD Buruh), interest, dividends and royalties (PBDR) and income, from sales (MPO). Because of the large number of such items of income, withholdings were limited to only few enforceable ones from practical view point: wages and salary, interest, dividends and royalties paid by corporations. There was uncertainty on what items on income, withholdings should be made. This lead to limited enforcement of witholding rules.

On account of the uncertainties, loopholes and limited enforcement, revenue from the personal income tax, as proportion of GDP, has been woefully low as indicated from figures in Table XI.

Table XI
Revenue from Personal Income Tax As a Proportion of GDP

Years	Average Ratio
1960 — 1968	0.42
1969 — 1974	0.48
1974 — 1979	0.52
1979 — 1984	0.46

Source: Biro Pusat Statistik, *Statistik Indonesia for various years.*

The buoyancy or flexibility of the old personal income tax was low as mentioned earlier. Also the personal income tax, did not have much impact on the income distribution from the low tax base from very limited enforcement, massive tax evasion as also indicated by low revenue elasticity.

B. THE OLD CORPORATE INCOME TAX

The Corporation income tax was first levied in Indonesia under the Corporation Tax Regulation 1925 and since then it has been revised and modified several times, with the last revision done by the Law No. 8 in 1970. Under the old tax law, the tax was chargeable from a body: Perseroan Terbatas — P.T. (Limited responsibility of the owner to the amount of shares owned): Perseroan Komaditer — C.V. (Unlimited, Liability of the owner); state enterprises or other government enterprises owned by lower levels of government; companies, groups, firms, cooperatives, insitutions. Under the old law, taxable income was defined as gross income, less costs to earn the income, including depreciation, pension funds, contribution losses. There were two rates: general rate and the special rate. The general tax rates were 20 percent, 30 percent and 45 percent for the first Rp 25 million, Rp 50 million and above of the taxable profit respectively. For the special rates, companies were divided into several categories: companies using public accountant services, public companies, cooperatives, liquidated companies and rates ranged from 20 to 45 percent of the taxable income. These varying rates and different company types created great amount of confusion and prevented full implementation of the Law. The system of depreciation allowed was also complicated. There were many different depreciation rates applied to various individual depreciable assets. In certain cases, firms were allowed to take accelerated depreciation or to take 20 percent investment allowance over 4 years. There was also considerable confusion on this account. Also the tax treatment of fringe benefits allowed to emplyees was subject to abuse. The old law counted the values of certain benefits, *e.g.*, housing provided to an employee as income to the employee. Also the values of the fringe benefit were deductible as business expenses to the employer. The method of assigning values to fringe benefit was complicated and it was abused particularly where employer could charge nominal rent to the employees for the use of the benefit provided.

The revenues from the corporation income tax are shown in Table XII for oil and non-oil corporations.

Table XII
Corporation Income Tax Revenues

	1960-61	1969-70	1974-5	1979-80	1983-84
			(Rp billions)		
Oil Companies Corporation Tax	—	48.3	973.1	4259.6	9520.2
		(14.44)	(49.01)	(52.73)	(51.98)
Non-Oil Companies, Corporation Tax	—	15.6	91.2	297.1	757.44
		(4.67)	(4.59)	(3.68)	(4.13)
Corporation Tax	5.2	63.9	1064.3	4556.7	10277.6
	(10.34)	(19.11)	(53.60)	(56.41)	(56.11)

Note: Figures in the paranthesis are proportion of total Tax Revenues.
Source: CBS, *Monthly Statistical Bulletins.*

The big increase in the tax revenues from oil companies, particularly after 1970, is due to sudden increase in the oil prices. It may be noted that the proportion of revenue from oil companies has started decreasing from 1983-84, which is due to declining prices of oil.

C. THE NEW INCOME TAX LAW 1984 (PAJAK PENGHASILAN)

Under Law No. 7, 1983, (Full text of the Law is given in Appendices 22 and 23) the personal income tax and corporation income tax have been integrated into a 'New Income Tax,' which, according to Preamble to the Law, has the objectives: simplicity, progressivity, certainty, closing of loopholes, and tax evasion. The new tax law defines clearly "tax subject," which includes individuals, undivided inheritance or body, bodies such as limited liability companies, limited partnerships, state owned undertakings, regional state owned undertakings, corporations or other associations, firms, partnerships cooperatives or institutions. The reformed income tax will be 'global tax' with all items of income; wages, salaries, honorarium, interest, dividends, royalty, net profit, capital gains, treated alike. It will be no longer necessary to distinguish between different items of income to compute tax liability. All gross income consolidated into one tax return, and taxable income to be computed by subtracting well defined personal exemptions (Rp 960,000 for tax payer, in addition Rp 480,000 for non-working spouse, Rp 960,000 for working spouse and Rp 480,000 for each dependent with maximum of three), exclusions, deductions, including depreciation and cost of generating income. The tax brackets have been reduced to only three: 15 percent, 25 percent and 35 percent. The highest marginal tax rate has been reduced from 50 to 35 percent. The rules on withholding of income have been greatly simplified. Rather than withholding on all forms of income as before, witholding would now be limited to few enforceable items: wages and salaries, interest, dividends and royalties. In the case of a tax payer and other members of tax payer's family, who earn income only subject to witholding from one employer, the tax withheld by an employer will constitute employee's final tax liability. As a result of some of the above provisions: *i.e.*, simplied personal exemptions and withholding rules, it is estimated that 85 to 90 percent of households would no longer be required to file tax returns. This will leave tax authorities to divert attention to check the remaining 10 percent tax returns, which would, evidently, result in stricter tax enforcement. The rules on depreciation, which were subject to great amount of confusion in the old tax laws, have been greatly simplified. The depreciable items have been classified according to their useful lives, into four categories along with clearly stated annual depreciation tariffs ranging from 10 to 50 percent. Tax treatment of fringe benefits has also been simplified. The employers have been disallowed deductions as cost for fringe benefits (housing, automobiles, vacation travel, etc.) provided to employees for their personal use. This should prevent abusing tax laws for deducting from tax liability values of large numbers of expensive goods and services, particularly by business executives of large companies. The investment tax credits and tax holidays allowed to firms under the old tax laws have been eliminated. Normally all business firms are required to maintain detailed accounts for audit by tax assessors. However, smaller firms *i.e.*, those with annual turn over less than Rp 60 million, have now been permitted to follow the system of "calculation norms", to be issued by the tax authorities periodically, in place of detailed accounts. The new tax system is based on self-assessment, with the tax authorities to audit only selected sample of tax returns. Under the old system, the tax authorities were required to audit all tax returns, which was beyond the administrative capability of the tax administration.

The Indonesian government claims that the new tax system would meet the principles of simplicity, certainty and convenience from making the income tax "global" by treating all items of income similar, simplifying depreciation rules, allowing small firms to follow calculation norms. It will make the tax administration easier by making the tax system subject to self assessment with selective audit, making withholding of large number of tax payers as the final assessment. It is claimed that inspite of reducing the marginal tax rate from 50 to 35 percent, the new income tax system would be more progressive and also flexible, on account of several provisions; taxing certain types of income at higher tax rate, *i.e.,* the tax rate on rental income will increase from 10 percent to 15 percent or even higher, long term capital gains, hitherto tax free, will now be fully taxable, tax payers to consolidate their income from all sources taxable at uniform rate (rather than some incomes at lower rates), denying deductions of fringe benefits provided to employees (generally in higher tax brackets) by business firms, stricter tax compliance which should reduce tax evasion. Since the corporations will no longer be entitled to tax credit on capital investment (generally on capital intensive machines), there will be relative preference for the introduction of cheaper labor intensive technology thus promoting employment opportunities in the industrial sector. The new tax system is expected to generate greater tax revenues by plugging several loopholes and also streamlining tax administration. It is claimed that reduction in the marginal tax rates will promote economic growth by increasing relative preference for work and effort, savings and investment and risk taking. It may be pointed out that since the new tax laws have been introduced very recently (from January 1, 1984), it is too early to evaluate fully their impact on the national economy. It is, however, gratifying to note that the initial reactions of business enterpreneurs and general tax payers have been favorable. The number of individual income tax payers increased from 327,547 in 1983 to 554,272 at the end of 1985. Similarly, the number of companies which collect withholding incme tax from, their employees rose from 94,474 to 161,022 during the some period. It is our view that after the new laws have overcome the initial "teething phase," these would assist in restructuring the income and corporate income taxes in Indonesia.

D. NEW PROPERTY TAX (PAJAK BUMI DAN BANGUNAN) AND STAMP DUTY (BEA MATERAI)

The old property tax was governed by seven different acts covering separately taxes on land, roads, wealth including liquid and fixed assets, and several other assets. As a result, the old laws were, in many instances, contradictory, overlapping and created uncertainty for the tax payers. Their administrations was also difficult with consequential very low revenue collections. The new property tax (PBB: Pajak Bumi dan Bangunan: The text of the law is given in Appendices 33 and 34) supersedes all old seven laws governing taxes on land and buildings including Ipeda and would be applicable from January 1, 1986 on land and property. It stipulates a single rate of 0.5 percent of taxable value of properties. The taxable values will be set minimally at 20 percent and maximally at 100 percent of the sale values. The sale values of property would be determined once in three years. However, in areas where property prices tend to rise markedly within a short period of time, the property sales values might be determined every year. The government expects this new tax to be easier for tax payers to understand and comply with and also easier for tax authorities to administer. An element of progressivity has been introduced, in that buildings valued at less than Rp 2 million would be exempt from the property tax. The property tax collections will be entrusted to provincial governments, which would be in a better position to administer because of large number of tax payers (estimated at 30 million) spread all over the country.

The old stamp duty was complex in that it contained over 100 rates of duty chargeable on different types of documents and legal transactions. The new stamp duty (Bea Materai: The text of the law is given in Appendix 35). Act has only two rates Rp 500 and Rp 1,000. The new Law will also be easier to comply with by the tax payers and to administer by the tax authorities. It is expected to generate more revenues and be economical.

CHAPTER V

INDIRECT TAXES

Indonesia had a variety of indirect taxes: sales tax, both on domestic and imported goods, excise tax, import and export taxes, on her tax rolls, but revenue from them has been very small: only 12.1 percent of total revenues during 1984-85. The Preamble to the Tax Law No. 8 of 1983, replacing some of the indirect taxes by a new Tax: Value-Added-Tax remarks that, "indirect tax provision — have not motivated the participation of all taxable entrepreneur strata to increase the state revenues — the currently prevailing sales tax does not comply any more as the means to support the national need for economic development."

A. THE OLD SALES TAX

The old sales tax was first introduced in 1950 as a multistage turn over tax on delivery of goods and services including imports, at the rate of 2.5 percent. Since it was critized as having high burden from cascade effects (*i.e.,* the tax was added to the price of goods at every transaction), it was replaced by a single stage tax at manufacturing level with a special rate of 10 percent for luxury goods. Services were not taxable under this law and to avoid the cascading effect, credit was allowed for the tax paid on raw materials and intermediate goods against the tax liability incurred by manufacturers on the final products. Further important changes were introduced in 1959 and 1960; the basic rates were doubled, though on essential goods the Minister of Finance was empowered to retain 5 percent tax rate. The tax credit arrangement, mentioned above, was abolished and sales tax on imports was repealed. From 1966, the tax rates were again doubled: 20 percent with 50 percent for some luxury goods. In 1968, sales tax on imports was reintroduced and tax rates reduced to 10 percent with 20 percent for luxury goods, while a large number of raw materials, intermediate goods and services, were charged 5 percent tax rate. Government issued a long list of goods and services, with different rates chargeable, and also the exempted items. In its last form, sales tax in Indonesia was a tax on the delivery of goods by producers or manufacturers, on the provision of services and on the entry of goods into custom regions. The sales tax suffered from various problems. Firstly, varying rates on different goods created great amount of confusion, uncertainty and administrative difficulties. This may partly explain why, as pointed out earlier, there was inadequate compliance with sales tax and the resulting tax evasion in the country. Secondly, there were elements of multiple taxation in the old sales tax: tax on raw materials and certain intermediate goods, which affected adversely optimum factor combination, promoting use of tax exempt rather than taxed raw materials. Also, the distinction between different types of raw materials for imposition of sales tax, put higher tax burden on goods using taxed raw materials relative to goods manufactured from low taxed or tax exempt intermediate goods. These were some of the major reasons for replacing the Indonesian sales tax with the Value Added Tax, to be discussed in a later section.

B. IMPORT DUTIES AND EXPORT TAX

The import duties have been used in Indonesia, both for

raising revenues and as a protective device. There have been frequent revisions in the Indonesian tariff structure: the most comprehensive being in January 1973. Recently there were about 34 tariff categories, ranging from 3.05 percent to five percent. Glassburner[8] has calculated that on the basis of 1973 tariff rates, average tariff rates for consumption, intermediate and capital goods were 52.3 percent, 22.5 percent and 18.9 percent respectively. The comparatively lower rate on capital goods, has been criticised for promoting use of capital intensive technology, in the labor abundant Indonesian economy. Import duties provided Rp 351.0 billions in tax revenues or 4.35 percent of the total tax revenues in 1982.

Taxes on exports date back to colonial times; Before 1969, however, the bulk of revenues from this tax was retained by exports producing provinces. In 1969, the proceeds from export tax were to go directly to the central government, which would distribute the proceeds as direct subsidies to the provinces. During 1969—1976, it was levied at the flat rate of 10 percent on large number of non-oil export goods, with bulk of revenues coming from lumber, rubber, tin, palm oil, coffee, tobacco and copra. In 1976, the tax rate was reduced to 5 percent, on most commodities, to promote their exports. In 1978 the export tariff rates where put on ad valorem basis at 0. 5, 10 or 20 percent of the check price or the FOB price. The Minister of Finance was authorised to put additional export tax on certain commodities, based on his assessment of the foreign demand and domestic cost of production. After the 1978 devaluation, additional export tax was imposed on some commodities including coffee, tea, palm oil, copra and coconut oil, varying from 3.6 percent to 19.8 percent. Heavy export taxes of 20 percent were levied on certain raw materials: raw buffalo, sheep, goat and cow hides and unworked rattan. The objective of this high tariff was to promote processing of raw

8. Bruce Glassburner, The January 1973, Tariff Revision, *Bulletin of Indonesian Economic Studies,* Vol. IX, No. 3, Nov, 1973, pp. 103—108.

materials domestically. Exporters in Indoensia, are pressing for reduction in the export tax in view of the difficulties being experienced by the country's non-oil exports on account of the increasing international competition and recessionary economic conditions. In 1985-86, the export tax provided 101.7 billion rupiah which amounted to 0.4 percent of the total government revenues.

C. THE VALUE-ADDED TAX (PPN: PAJAK PERTAMBAHAN NILAI)

Indonesia has recently joined the growing number of countries, which have adopted Value-Added Tax (VAT), as an integral part of tax restructuring plans. Through the ACT No. 8, 1983, and subsequent announcements (Full text of the law is given in the Appendices 24 and 25), Indonesia replaced the Sales Tax by VAT with effect from April 1, 1985. The reasons cited for this policy are: to reduce cascading effects of the sales tax, to improve resource allocations, curb evasion of taxes through non reporting or under-reporting manufacture output, to promote exports by leving zero tax rate on exports and most importantly, to raise additional tax revenues for financing development plans. What is the VAT? Rather than a tax on single stage: production level or use level, in VAT values added at various stages in production and distribution processes by firms are taxed. In this sense, it is a multiple stage tax as against the single stage sales tax. There are different variants of the VAT differing in the matter of calculating the taxable values added. There is an ''addition method'' in which various elements constituting values are added for imposition of the tax. Then, there is a 'subtraction method,' in which net value added is computed by substracting production cost including the cost of purchasing intermediate goods from total receipts of a firm. Tax is applied to thus estimated net value added. The third and the most commonly used method is ''tax credit method'' in which the tax liability is estimated on value of net product by allowing credit on tax paid by a taxable firm on intermediate goods and services. This is the easiest and practicable method to compute the tax liability and also to check tax evasion through cross checking of tax returns filed by different firms involved at different production stages. Indonesia is using the "tax credit method." Also, there are different bases for imposition of VAT. It can be levied on either (a) sum of factors income including profit, with provisions for depreciation of capital - called income type tax or (b) sale price of goods and services or the consumption type tax. The latter is easier to apply than the former, particularly because tax on compensation of labor and profits of companies are levied under the income tax. Theoretically, the size of the tax base and also tax revenues should be the same from both types of VAT since in national income accounting, the sum of spending is equal to factors income. Indonesia has adopted consumption type VAT, so that it does not, in any way, confuse with the income taxes. Other features of the Indonesian VAT are outlined below:

There are two components of the VAT package: first is the VAT tax itself applied to manufacturer, importers and providers of service by a contractor or sub-contractor. VAT is levied at a single rate of 10 percent with zero rate on export goods (*i.e.*, export goods are tax exempt). The second part of the package consists of sales tax on luxury goods-levied only on the sale price by the manufacturers and by the importers on import value of the commodities. The luxury goods subject to the sales tax are also subject to VAT. Thus, luxury goods are subject to VAT initially and the sales tax additionally. The rates differentials between the ordinary and luxury goods have been introduced to mitigate the regressive effect of VAT and also to discourage their consumption. VAT applies equally to all manufactured goods whether manufactured domestically or imported (unlike the old sales tax with different tax rates for different goods).

Taxable items include manufacturing and certain services. Manufacturing is defined as any activities to process by changing the form or nature of good from its original form to a new one.

This could include fabrication, cooking, assembly, packing, bottling and mining. The value added itself arises due to the application of the production factors on each business link in preparing, producing, dealing and trading goods or in rendering services to the consumers. Services have been defined as, any business activity and services rendered on the basis of a commitment or legal act causing goods, facility or right ready for use. However, the only services subject to the VAT are construction services, including contracting, architectural services and other services related to the construction of buildings and other items of real estate. Goods excluded from the imposition of VAT, including planting or harvesting, agricultural produce, breeding cattle, catching or breeding fish, drying or salting food, wrapping or packing, commonly occuring in whole sale or retail trade, serving food and drinks at restaurants, inns/hotels or catering.

For certainty and ease of administration and also for assisting small scale and cottage industries, any firm with a turnover of less than Rp 24 million per year or total capital of less than Rp 10 million, is exempt from the VAT. It is possible that some big firms will find it advantageous to split into smaller units. Besides evading the tax, splitting of the big firms might prevent securing economies of scale, thus forsaking economic efficiency.

As mentioned earlier, the Indonesian VAT is based on input tax credit method in which tax paid on intermediate input by a tax payer is creditable against tax liability on sale value of output, if such purchases are used directly in manufacturing process including capital goods. In order to cross check and also to ensure that tax credit is not fraudulently used, a tax invoice must be issued by a taxable firm for any transaction subject to VAT giving full information: description of transaction including quantity, price, total sale, name and identification numbers of the tax payer and seller. A copy of the tax invoice should be given to the buyer, who shall use it to claim credit for this tax against his tax liability on sale of output. In case of exporters, refund will be given for the tax paid on intermediate products.

For ensuring proper enforcement of the VAT, several administrative steps have been taken. All individuals and firms subject to tax would be assigned identification numbers, which will be computerised to check on their filing tax returns regularly. All taxable firms would keep records of taxable and non-taxable transactions and also all transactions subject to luxury sales tax. Small taxable firms with turnover less than Rp 60 million would be permitted to use "calculation norms" to be issued by the government from time to time. They must, however, maintain records of gross sales and receipts. Stern criminal punishments, including imprisonment, have been set for tax evasion for tax payers as well as for tax officials who would abuse their responsibilities. Government has launched massive educational compaign for educating business firms on the VAT through meetings and distribution of easy to understand literature. Realising that the country is still in the teething phase and it takes time to implement such a complex tax fully, the government has recently issued some modifications. In February 1985, it was announced that for the present the VAT will be limited to only producers, importers, main distributors, patent holders and business ready for the VAT. On April 20, 1985, the government announced deferment of the VAT on capital goods, on application.

What will be the impact of the VAT on the Indonesian tax structure? Since it has had only one year's operation and that too with several modifications and delays of several provisions, it is too early to evaluate its actual operation. The best that we can do is to make an assessment on the basis of our analysis of the tax law and whatever one can learn from one year's experience. There are major questions to answer: Will this tax raise more revenues? Will it be more equitable than the sales tax? What will be impact on prices and effect on resource allocation in the economy?

Raising more revenues was, certainly one of the main objectives to introduce the VAT. More revenues were expected from broadening the tax base, raising tax rates to uniform 10 percent in case of several commodities taxed previously at lower sales tax rate; curbing tax evasion through cross checking of tax returns of firms. In the budget estimates for 1986—87, the government expects the VAT receipts to increase from Rp 1,666,4 billion during 1985—86 (7.2. percent of total budget receipts) to Rp 2,143,3 billion during 1986—87 (10 percent of the total revenues). The actual receipts form the VAT have been running well ahead of the expected revenues. The first semester 1986 receipts were 58 percent of the budgeted amount and collections up till November 1985 had averaged Rp 175 billions per month in the fiscal year. A flat extrapolation for the period from November 1985 to March 1986 yields an estimate of Rp 2200 billions of the fiscal year, which would be 32 percent above the budgeted amount. As regards the question of equity, the government expects VAT to promote 'justice feeling' in the country, but will the tax do so? Though the luxury tax of 20 percent will to some extent, mitigate the regressivity of the VAT, but on the whole, we can expect higher burden on lower and middle income classes because several commodities previously tax exempt, will now be taxable. On many goods, commonly used by these classes, *e.g.*, vegetable products, edible fats and essential oil, rubber, wood cork, straw, and paper products, textile materials, animal products, the tax rate has been increased to 10 percent under the VAT from the previous rate of 5 percent under sales tax. Will the VAT result in increase in prices? The prices will certainly increase from two sources. Firstly, the prices will increase to the extent the hitherto untaxed commodities are taxed and those taxed at previously lower rates are now subjected to higher tax rates, as explained above. During the first years of the imposition of VAT, general price increase of 2.8 percent was attributed to this tax, though price of some individual commodities *e.g.*, fuel, paper products, increased at higher rates. The prices would have increased at higher rates but for the recessionary conditions and depressed domestic demand in general and for some goods *e.g.*, textiles, electronic goods, automobiles, motor cycle, in particular. Secondly, taxable firms will have to incur accounting costs to maintain detailed required accounts. According to the experience from some European countries which adopted VAT, these expenses can amount to as high as 5—10 percent of the total cost. Most of these costs would be shifted forward as increase in prices.

As regards impact of the VAT on resource allocation, it will have less distortion effect than the old sales tax, since the former has uniform tax rate on goods except on luxury goods. However, the VAT in Indonesia will create special problems for farmers and small business firms. Farmers will pay the VAT on some inputs *e.g.,* fertilizers, while they will not be able to get credit for the same, since sales of agricultural product is tax exempt. Small tax exempt forms will be at disadvantage compared to the taxable larger firms, particularly for selling intermediate goods. Producers using these goods will be able to deduct tax credit paid on intermediate goods from their tax liability on final product for buying from taxable large scale rather from the non-taxable smaller firms. Another problem with the V.A.T. will be about the time of payment of the tax liability. Under the salex tax system, the tax had to be paid when the producer received payment for the sale. In the case of VAT, however, the tax is due at the time the sale transaction occurs even though the sellers have not received the payment. Thus, some businesses, particularly those with smaller turn over, might be forced to borrow, which will impose additional financial burden particularly if they have to borrow form the informal market. These are some of the issues which would need to be addressed to as Indonesia learns more from the operation of the VAT.

The experience of other countries in Europa, Asia and Africa from the Value-Added Tax shows that its proper implementation requires competent administration and willing compliance from the tax paying firms. Ultimately, the sucess of the VAT in Indonesia will depend on the extent to which public administration and business firms are made more responsive to this new tax structure.

D. EXCISE TAX

Excise tax, also known as selective or specific tax has a narrow coverage in Indonesia. The total revenue from the excise tax is a only 4.2 percent of the total government revenue and 87 percent of the total revenue from this tax comes from tobacco products (mainly cigarettes), followed by sugar, beer and alcoholic products as in Table XIII.

Table XIII
Excise Tax Revenue 1982

Type of Goods	Revenue (Rp billions)	Tax Rate (in percentage)
Tobacco	565.4	0—40[a]
Sugar	39.8	10[b]
Beer	13.2	50[b]
Alcohol	1.7	70[b]

Source: Direktorat Jenderal Bea dan Cukai.
Notes: a. Depending on the cigarettes produced.
b. Percentage of the base price.

The tax rates on cigarettes vary according to types of cigarettes and the size of the producing firms: lesser rates for clove cigarettes, which are produced mainly in smaller size firms. Using labour intensive technology, than the white cigarettes. The maximum rate of 40 percent is applied to cigarettes which are produced using capital intensive methods in which the producer produces more then 4 billion cigarettes per year. The differential in excise tax rates in different types of cigarettes can be defended on the basis of promoting small scale industries and enhancing use of local goods (eg cloves) and increasing employment opportunities.

Though the excise the tax on alcohol and tobacco products can also be defended on sumptuary considerations *ie* to discourage their consumption, but on equity basis, excise tax tends to be relatively regressive.

BIBLIOGRAPHY

Ardic, F.M. "Poverty and Tax Incidence in West Malaysia", *Public finance Quarterly,* No. 5, 1977, 329—50.

Asher, Mukul G. "Recent Tax changes in ASEAN and their implications", Asian Pacific Tax and Incentive Bulletin, 2, 5, May 1984.

__________, An Economic Analysis of the Indonesian VAT Package, APTIRC-Bulletin, 1984, 201—206.

__________, and Anne Booth, *Indirect Taxation in ASEAN Countries,* Singapore University Press, Singapore, 1984.

Bahl, Roy, "Alternative Methods of Tax Revenue Forecasting in Developing Countries: A Conceptual Analysis", *International Monetary Fund,* Oct. 1972.

Bird, R.M. and Oldman, O. edit., *Readings on Taxation in Developing Countries,* John Hopkins University Press, Baltimore, 1975.

__________, and H.L. de Wulf, "Taxation and Income Distribution in Latin America; A Critical Review of Empirical Studies", *IMF Staff Papers,* No. 2, 1973, 639—82.

Biro Pusat Statistik, *State and Local Government Financial Statistics, 1977-78/1982-83.*

__________, *Statistik Indonesia,* 1982 to 1984, Jakarta.

Booth, A., "The Incidence of Taxation: A Preliminary Analysis," in *Issues in Public Finance.* Edit. M.G. Asher and D. Osborne, Singapore University Press, Singapore, 1980.

__________, Ipeda: Indonesia's Land Tax", *Bulleti of Indonesian Economic Studies,* No. 10, 1974, 55-81.

__________, *Ipeda and Land Tax in Indonesia,* Unpublished Ph.D. dissertation, Australian National University, 1974.

__________, "The Economic Impact of Export Tax in ASEAN", *Malayan Economic Review,* 25, No. 1, 1981, 36—61.

__________, and G.F. Break, "The Incidence and Economic Effects of Taxation," in Blinder *et.al.* Edit., *Economics of Public Finance,* The Brookings Institution, Washington D.C., 1974.

__________, and P. McCawley, "Fiscal Policy", in A. Booth and P. McCawley edit., *The Indonesian Economy During Suharto Era,* Oxford University Press, Kuala Lumpur, 1981.

__________, and Peter McCawley, edit., *The Indonesian Economy During the Suharto Era,* Kuala Lumpur, Oxford University Press, 1981.

Chand, S.K., *Tax Revenue Forecasting: An Approach Applied to Malaysia,* Unpublished, March 1975.

Chelliah, Raja J, *et.al.,* Tax Ratios and Tax Effort in Developing Countries, *IMF* Vol. 22, March 1979.

Chaudhury, N.N., "A Study of the Elasticity of the West Malaysian Income Tax System, 1961—70, *IMF Staff Papers,* Vol. 22, 1975.

Cnossen, S., *The Indonesian Sales Tax,* Kulwer Deventer, 1973.

__________, *Excise Systems,* John Hopkins University Press, Baltimore, 1978.

__________, "The Case for Selective Taxes on Goods and Services in Developing Countries,*World Development,* 6, No. 6, 1978.

De Wulf, Luc., "Fiscal Incidence Studies in Developing Countries: Survey and Critique." *IMF Staff Papers,* 22, No. 1, 1975, 61—131.

Djojosubroto, Dono, *Export Tax in Indonesia. A Study of Taxation in a Developing Country",* Unpublished Ph.D. dissertation, University of Illinois, Urbena, 1977.'

Dris, M.D., Taxation in Indonesia; *Ekonomi dan Keuangan Indonesia,* August 1968, 408—420.

Due, J.F., *Sales Taxation,* Routledge and Kegan Paul, 1957.

__________, *Indirect Taxation in Developing Economies,* John Hopkins University Press, Baltimore, 1970.

Edwards, Clive T., *Public Finances in Malaysia and Singapore,* Australian National University Press, Canberra, 1970.

Garnaut, R.G., and P. McCawley, *Indonesia: Dualism, Growth and Poverty,* Australian National University, Canberra, 1980.

Glassburner, Bruce, "The January 1973 Tariff Revision," *Bulletin of Indonesian Economic Studies,* 9, No. 3, 1973, 103—108.

Hananto Sigit, "Musalah Penghitungan Distribusi Pendapatan di Indonesia, *Prisma*, January, 1980, 45—55.

Heller, Walter, "Fiscal Policies for Underdeveloped Countries," in Bird and Oldman, Eds., *Readings on Taxation in Developing Countries,* John Hopkins University, Baltimore, 1975.

Hinrichs, H., "Determinants of Government Revenue Share amongs Less Developed Countries," *Economic Journal,* Vol. 73, Sept. 1969.

Indonesia, Central Bureau of Statistics, *Economic Indicators,* Monthly-Various Issues.

__________, Department of Finance, *Indonesian Tax Guide for Foreigners,* Jakarta, 1975.

__________, *Nota Keuangan,* various issues.

Kakwani, N.C., "Measurement of Tax Progressvity An International Comparison," *Economic Journal,* 87, 1984, 71—80.

Krongkaew, M., *The Income Redistribution Effects of Taxes and Public Expenditure in Thailand.* Unpublished Ph.D. dissertation, Michigan State University, 1974.

Lakadwala, D.T., "Value-Added-Tax," *Indian Economic Journal,* 24, No. 2, 1976, 183—207.

Lam, N.V., "Incidence of The Rice Export Premium in Thailand," *Journal of Development Studies,* 14, 1977, 1—13.

Lent, G.E., C. Milka and G. Michele, "The Value-Added Tax in Developing Countries, *IMF Staff Papers,* 20, 1973, 318—78.

Larche, D., *Taxation and Tax Administration in Developing Countries,* Unpublished, Jakarta, 1981.

_____________, "The Revenue Potential of the Land Tax for Urban Finance in Indonesia," in J. Wong, Ed., *Cities in Asia,* Singapore University Press, Singapore 1976.

_____________, "Efficiency of Taxation in Indonesia," *Bulletin of Indonesian Economic Studies,* 16, 1, March 1980, 34—51.

Lewis, S.R., Agricultural Taxation in a Developing Economy, in Bird and Oldman, *Readings On Taxation in Developing Countries,* John Hopkins University Press, 1975.

Lotz, J.R. and Morses, E.R., "Measuring Tax Effort in Developing Countries," *Economic Development and Cultural Change,* 18, 3, April 1970.

Lluch, C., "Household Servings in Indonesia, Unpublished Paper, July 1983.

Mann, A.J., "The Fiscal System and Income Distribution: The Case of Puerto Rico," *Public Finance Quarterly, 4, 1976, 339—66.*

Mangkusubroto, Guritno, *Tax Incidance in a Developing Country: The Case of Indonesia,* Ph.D. dissertation, University of Colorado, Boulder, 1986.

McLure, Charles and Thirsk, W.R., "The Inequity of Taxing Inequity," *Economic Development and Cultural Change,* 26, 1978, 487—503.

Mansuary, "General overview of 1984 Indonesian Tax Laws," *APTIR.C, Bulletin,* 1984, 187—191.

Meerman, J. *Public Expenditure in Malaysia. Who Benefits and Why?",* Oxford University Press, New York, 1970.

Nasution, A., Neraca Ekonomi Indonesia, *Prisma,* 11/12, 1983.

Oei, Hong Lan, "Indonesia's Economic Stabilization and Rehabilitation Program," An evaluation," *Indonesia,* 5, 1968, 135—74.

Ojha P.D., and Lent, G., "Sales, Tax in the Countries of the Far East," *IMF Staff Papers,* 16, 1969, 529—79.

Paauw, Douglas, *Financing Economic Development, The Indonesian Case,* Free Press, New York, 1960.

Panglaykim, J., and K.D. Thomas, "The New Order and the Economy," *Indonesia,* 3, 1967, 73—120.

Peacock, A., and Shaw, G.K., "Fiscal Measure to Create Employment: The Indonesian Case," *Bulletin for International Fiscal Documentation,* 27, 1973, 443—54.

Pitt, Mark, M., "Alternative Trade Strategies and Employment in Indonesia," in Anne O. Kreuger, Edit., *Trade and Employment in Developing Countries,* University of Chicago Press, 1981.

Please, S., "Savings through Taxation: Reality or Mirage?", *Finance and Development,* 4, 1, 1967, 24—32.

Reyes, Zenaida, S., *Investment Incentive Laws of ASEAN Countries,* University of Philippines Law Center, Quezon City, 1978.

Sahota, G.S., *Indian Tax Structure and Economic Development,* Asia Publishing House, 1961.

Salleh, I.M., "*Tax Incidence and Incme Redistribution in West Malaysia,*" Ph.D. dissertation, University of Illinois, 1977.

Sundrum, R.M., "Changes in Consumption Patterns in Urban Java, 1970—76," *Bulletin of Indonesian Economic Studies,* 13, 1977, 102—116.

————————, *Development Economics, A Framework for Analysis and Policy,* Wiley, Chichester, 1983.

Suharsono H. and Sajid B., "A Guide to the Indonesian Taxation," *Weekly Review;* Jakarta, 1975.

Suparmoko, M., *Ilmu Keuangan Negara,* BPFE, Yogyakarta, 1984.

Tan, E.A., "Philippine Taxation, Government Spending and Income Distribution", in *Income Distribution, Employment and Economic Development in Southeast and East Asia,* council for Asian Manpowers Studies, Manila, 1975.

Tanzi, V., "Export Taxation in Developing Countries: Taxation of Coffee in Haiti." *Social and Economic Studies,* 25, 1976, 66.

Toye, J.F.J., Edit., *Taxation and Economic Development, Twelve Critical Studies,* Frank Case, London, 1978.

United Nations, *Statistical Year Book 1981,* United Nations, New York, 1982.

___________, *Statistical Year Book for Asia and Far East,* Bangkok, 1980.

___________, *Year Book of National Account Statistics,* 1980, United Nations, New York, 1980.

Uppal, J.S., *India's Economic Problems,* New Delhi Tata, McGraw Hill, 3rd edition, 1983.

___________, *Economic Development in South Asia,* St. Martins Press, New York, 1977.

___________, "Some Recent Trends in Public Finance", *Ekonomi dan Keuangan Indonesia,* 32, 4, 1986.

___________, "Income Distribution, Growth and Poverty in Indonesia", *Ekonomi dan Keuangan Indonesia,* 32, 3, 1985, 229—349.

___________, Improving Efficiency in the Indonesian Tax Structure, Unpublished monograph, Yogyakarta, 1985.

___________, Economic Theory and The Asian Economies, The Question of Relevance, *Indian Journal of Quantitative Economics,* 1, 2, 1985, 100—109.

Usman B., *Ruang Pajak Kompas,* Yayasan Bina Pajak, 1983.

___________, *Ruang Pajak Sinar Harapan,* Yayasan Bina Pajak, Jakarta, 1983.

___________, Pajak-pajak Indonesia, Yayasan Bina Pajak, 1980.

Valaisathien, S., *The Thai Taxation,* SGV-Na, Thailand, Bangkok, 1975.

Van Quinneken, Rural and Urban Inequality in Indonesia, Mexico, Tanzania and Tunisia, International Labor Office, Geneva, 1976.

White, L., "Problems and Prospects of the Indonesian Foreign Exchange System," Indonesia, 14, 1972, 125—55.

Wong, John, *ASEAN Economies in Perspect,* MacMillan, London, 1979.

World Bank, *Indonesia: Policies for Growth and Employment,* Jakarta, 1985.

____________, Indonesia: Policies and Prospect for Economic Growth and Transformation, Jakarta, 1984.

____________, Indonesia, Development Prospects and Policy options, 1981, Jakarta.

APPENDICES

Appendix 1

Central Government Actual Revenue Receipts 1960— 1984-85
(Rp billions Current Prices)

(A)

No.	Kind of Receipts	1960	1961	1962	1963	1964	1965	1966	1967	1968	69/70	70/71	71/72
A.	Routine Receipts	0.0496	0.0520	0.0724	0.1602	0.2798	0.9183	13.14	60.21	149.74	243.70	344.60	428.02
1.	Direct tax	0.0088	0.0119	0.0178	0.0333	0.0703	0.2658	1.79	16.82	51.03	91.47	121.67	180.99
a.	Income tax	0.0031	0.0032	0.0061	0.0128	0.0284	0.0433	0.64	3.13	9.43	12.06	13.38	17.39
b.	Corporation tax[1]	0.0052	0.0084	0.0114	0.0201	0.0410	0.0852	0.61	3.42	9.50	15.64	20.68	25.41
c.	Oil corporation tax	—	—	—	—	—	—	—	7.39	25.50	48.33	68.82	112.50
d.	MPO	—	—	—	—	—	—	—	0.68	6.37	15.27	18.59	24.61
e.	Ipeda	—	—	—	—	—	—	—	—	—	—	—	—
f.	Other[2]	0.0004	0.0003	0.0003	0.0004	0.0009	0.1374	0.54	2.19	0.23	0.17	0.20	1.08
2.	Indirect tax	0.0152	0.0206	0.0297	0.0573	0.1126	0.3116	10.53	42.10	93.96	149.07	209.82	219.54
a.	Sales tax (dom)[3]	0.0033	0031	0.0050	0.0096	0.0246	0.1012	1.72	4.20	9.17	15.10	18.29	24.01
b.	Sales tax (import)	—	—	—	—	—	—	—	—	6.04	15.87	22.10	22.40
c.	Excises tax	0.0068	0.0075	0.0108	0.0272	0.0405	0.1332	2.22	7.00	16.57	32.09	38.88	40.39
d.	Import tax	0.0029	0.0051	0.0042	0.0125	0.0339	0.0517	3.69	16.90	37.30	57.67	70.70	69.42
e.	Export tax	0.0015	0.0032	0.0025	0.0018	0.0008	—	1.97	10.60	13.92	7.45	25.03	28.10
f.	Others	0.0008	0.0017	0.0072	0.0063	0.0128	0.0256	0.94	3.40	10.96	20.90	34.82	35.21
3.	Non tax receipts	0.0257	0.0195	0.0249	0.0696	0.0969	0.3409	0.82	1.30	4.75	3.17	13.11	27.49
B.	Development Rec.	0.0007	0.0102	0.0025	0.0020	0.0036	0.0051	—	24.69	57.90	91.06	120.43	135.53
1.	Program aids[4]	0.0007	0.0017	0.0007	0.0003	0.0012	—	—	24.69	57.90	65.76	78.95	90.53
2.	Project aids	—	—	—	—	—	—	—	—	—	25.30	41.48	45.00
3.	Other	0.0000	0.0086	0.0018	0.0017	0.0024	0.0051	—	—	—	—	—	—
	Total Receipts	0.0503	0.0622	0.0749	0.1622	0.2834	0.9234	13.14	84.90	207.64	334.76	465.03	563.55

Sources: 1. Central Bureau of Statistics (CBS), *Monthly Statistical Bulletins.* 2. Bank of Indonesia (B.I.), Report for the years 1960—65.

Note : 1. For 1960—66 included oil corporation tax. 2. For 1965—67 included Ipeda. 3. For 1960—67 included sales tax (import). 4. For 1960—68 included project aids.

Appendix 2

Central Government Actual Revenue Receipts 1960—1984-85
(Rp billions Current prices)
(continued from Appendix 1)

(B)

No.	72/73	73/74	74/75	75/76	76/77	77/78	78/79	79/80	80/81	81/82	82/83	83/84	84/85
A	590.6	967.7	1,753,7	2,241.9	2,906.0	3,535.4	4,266.1	6,696.8	10,227.0	12,212.6	12,418.3	14.432.7	16.149.4
1	302.2	505.0	1,228.7	1,592.1	2,046.6	2,511.3	2,996.3	5,129.3	8,230.3	10,100.3	10,009.9	11,605.1	13.043.7
a	23.7	34.4	43.3	61.7	84.2	104.6	122.2	148.1	164.2	207.2	288.8	398.9	577.6[5]
b	30.6	44.2	91.2	128.2	127.2	169.5	226.5	297.1	447.6	559.1	674.5	757.4	1.873.5
c	198.9	344.6	973.1	1,249.1	1,619.4	1,948.7	2,308.7	4,259.6	7,019.6	8,627.8	8,170.4	9,520.2	10.366.6
d	30.2	56.8	83.3	97.3	148.4	201.7	232.5	291.3	433.5	513.0	641.9	628.1	—
e	15.2	19.5	28.0	34,6	42.2	52.5	63.1	71.4	87.2	94.5	105.2	132.4	—
f	3.6	5.5	9.8	21.2	25.2	34.3	43.3	61.8	78.2	98.7	129.1	168.1	—
2	253.8	412.9	458,4	539.4	740.9	880.5	1,078.4	1,380.2	1,681.0	1,775.9	1,972.8	2,308.6	2.490.7
a	34.5	54.6	84,9	119.2	162.3	203.4	221.1	192.2	265.6	310.7	476.6	575[6]2	
b	27.8	50.7	68,9	72,5	102.2	114.6	125.5	137.2	195.1	223.3	231.0	255.2	958.2
c	47.3	61.7	74.4	97.3	130.7	181.9	252.9	326.4	437.9	544.2	620.1	773.2	727.5
d	73.2	128.2	160.6	174.0	257.4	286.9	295.3	316.7	448.0	536.2	521.9	557.0	681.4
e	32.7	68.6	70.3	61.6	61.7	81.2	166.2	389.1	305.0	128.4	82.5	104.0	123.6
f	38.3	49.1	—0,7	14,8	26.6	12.5	17.4	18.6	29.4	33.1	40.7	43.7	—
3	34.6	49.8	66.6	110.4	118.5	143.6	191.4	187.3	315.7	336.4	435.6	519.0	615.0
B	157.8	203.9	232.0	491.6	783.3	773.4	1,035.5	1,381.1	1,493.9	1,709.0	1,940.0	3,882.4	4:411:0
1	95.5	89.8	36.1	20.2	10.2	35.8	48.2	64.8	64.1	45.1	15.1	14.9	39.5
2	62.3	114.1	195.9	471.4	773.6	737.6	978.3	1,316.3	1,429.8	1,663.9	1,924.9	3,867.5	4.371.5
TR	748.4	1,171.6	1,985.7	2,733.5	3,689.8	4,308.8	5,301.6	8,077.9	11,720.9	13,921.6	14,358.3	18,315.1	20,560.4

Sources: Central Bureau of Statistics (CBS). *Monthly Statistical Bulletins,* B.I. report for the year 1960—65.

Notes: 1. For 1960—66, include oil corporation tax. 2. For 1965—67, included Ipeda. 3. for 60—67, included sales tax (input). 4. For 1960—68, included project aids. 5. Private Income Tax. 6. Value Add. d Tax.

Appendix 3.

The composition of tax structures in Indonesia
1960—1968 (in millions of Rp. current prices)

Taxes	1960	1961	1962	1963	1964	1965	1966	1967	1968	Total 1960—68	%
1. Direct taxes	*8.8*	*11.9*	*17.8*	*33.3*	*70.3*	*265.8*	*1,790.0*	*16,820.0*	*51,030.0*	*70,047.9*	*22.80*
a. Personal income tax	3.1	3.2	6.1	12.8	28.4	43.3	640.0	3,130.0	9,430.0	13,290.9	4.33
b. Corporation income tax	5.2	8.4	11.4	20.1	41.0	85.2	610.0	10,810.0	35,000.0	46,591.3	15.16
c. Other (Ipeda, etc)	0.4	0.3	0.3	0.4	0.9	137.4	54.0	2,870.0	6,600.0	10,165.7	3.31
2. Indirect taxes	*15.2*	*20.6*	*29.7*	*57.3*	*112.6*	*311.6*	*10,530.0*	*42,100.0*	*93.960.0*	*147,137.0*	*47.89*
a. Sales tax	3.3	3.1	5.0	9.6	24.6	101.2	1,720.0	4,200.0	15,210.0	21,276.8	6.93
b. Excise tax	6.8	7.5	10.8	27.2	40.5	133.2	2,220.0	7,000.0	16,570.0	26.016:0	8.47
c. Import tax	2.9	5.1	4.2	12.5	33.9	51.7	3,690.0	16,900.0	37,300.0	58.000:3	18.88
d. Export tax	1.5	3.2	2.5	1.8	0.8	0.0	1,970.00	10,600.0	13.920.0	26.499.8	8.62
e. Other	0.8	1.7	7.2	6.3	12.8	25.6	940.0	3,400.0	10,960.0	15,344.1	4.99
3. Total taxes (1 + 2)	*24.0*	*32.5*	*47.5*	*90.6*	*182.9*	*577.4*	*12,320.0*	*58,920.0*	*144,990.0*	*217,184.9*	*70.69*
4. Total revenue	*50.3*	*62.2*	*74.9*	*162.2*	*283.4*	*923.4*	*13,140.0*	*84,900.0*	*207,640.0*	*307,236.4*	*100.00*

Sources: CBS, *Monthly Statistical Bulletins,* several numbers.
Bank of Indonesia (B.I.), *Report for the year 1960—65.*

Appendix 4.

The composition of tax structure in Indonesia 1969/70—1973/74, (Rp billions, current price)

Taxes	1969/70	1970/71	1971/72	1972/73	1973/74	Total 1969/70 1973/74	%
1. Direct taxes	*91.47*	*121.67*	*180.99*	*302.2*	*505.0*	*1,201.33*	*36.59*
a. Personal income tax	12.06	13.38	17.39	23.7	34.4	100.93	3.07
b. Corp. income tax	15.64	20.68	25.41	30.6	44.2	136.53	4.16
c. Oil corp. income tax	48.33	68.82	112.50	198.9	344.6	773.15	23.55
d. With holdings	15.27	18.59	24.61	30.2	56.8	145.47	4.43
e. Other	0.17	0.20	1.08	18.8	25.0	45.25	1.38
2. Indirect taxes	*149.07*	*209.82*	*219.54*	*253.8*	*412.9*	*1,245.13*	*37.92*
a. Sales tax	30.97	40.39	46.41	62.3	105.3	285.37	8.69
b. Excise tax	32.09	38.88	40.39	47.3	61.7	220.36	6.71
c. Import tax	57.67	70.70	69.42	72.2	128.2	399.19	12.16
d. Export tax	7.45	25.03	28.10	32.7	68.6	161.88	4.93
e. Other	20.90	34.82	35.21	38.3	49.1	178.33	5.43
3. Total taxes (1 + 2)	*240.54*	*331.49*	*400.53*	*556.0*	*917.9*	*2,446.46*	*74.51*
4. Total revenue	*334.76*	*465.03*	*563.55*	*748.4*	*1,171.6*	*3,283.34*	*100.00*

Source: CBS, *Monthly Statistical Bulletins*, several years.

Appendix 5.

The composition of tax structure in Indonesia 1974/75—1978/79,
(Rp billions, current price)

Taxes	1974/75	1975/76	1976/77	1977/78	1978/79	Total 1974/75 1978/79	%
1. Direct taxes	1,228.7	1,592.1	2,046.6	2,511.3	2,996.3	10,375.0	57.58
. Personal income tax	43.3	61.7	84.2	104.6	122.2	416.0	2.31
b.Corp. income tax	91.2	128.2	127.2	169.5	226.5	742.6	4.12
c.Oil corp. income tax	973.1	1,249.1	1,619.4	1,948.7	2,308.7	8,099.0	44.95
d. With holdings	83.3	97.3	148.4	201.7	232.5	763.2	4.24
e. Other	37.8	55.8	67.4	86.8	106.4	354.2	1.96
2. Indirect taxes	*458.4*	*539.4*	*740.9*	*880.5*	*1,078.4*	*3,697.6*	*20.52*
a.Sales tax	153.8	191.7	264.5	318.0	346.6	1,274.6	7.07
b.Excise tax	74.4	97.3	130.7	181.9	252.9	737.2	4.09
c.Import tax	160.6	174.0	257.4	286.9	295.3	1,174.2	6.52
d.Export tax	70.3	61.6	61.7	81.2	166.2	441.0	2.45
e.Other	—0.7	14.8	26.6	12.5	17.4	70.6	0.39
3. Total taxes (1 + 2)	*1,687.1*	*2,131.5*	*2,787.5*	*3,391.8*	*4,074.7*	*14,072.6*	*78.10*
4. Total revenue	*1,985.7*	*2,733.5*	*3,689.8*	*4,308.8*	*5,301.6*	*18,019.4*	*100.00*

Source: CBS, *Statistics of Indonesia,* Various years.

Appendix 6

The composition of tax structure in Indonesia, 1979/80 — 1983/84 (Rp billions - current - prices)

YEAR	1979/ 80	1980/ 81	1981/ 82	1982/ 83	1983/ 84	Total 1979/ 80—1983/84	%
1. Direct taxes	*5,129.0*	*8,230.3*	*10,100.3*	*10,009.9*	*11,605.1*	*45,074.9*	*67.89*
a. Personal income tax	148.1	164.2	207.2	288.8	398.9	1,207.2	1.82
b. Corpor. income tax	297.1	447.6	559.1	674.5	757.4	2,735.7	4.12
c. Oil corpor. inc. tax	4,259.6	7,019.6	8,627.8	8,170.4	9,520.2	37,597.6	56.63
d. Withholdings	291.3	433.5	513.0	641.9	628.1	2,507.6	3.78
e. Other	133.2	165.4	193.2	234.3	300.5	1,026.6	1.54
2. Indirect taxes	*1,380.2*	*1,681.0*	*1,775.9*	*1,972.8*	*2,308.6*	*9,118.5*	*13.73*
a. Sales tax	329.4	460.7	534.0	707.6	830.7	2,862,4	4.31
b. Excise tax	326.4	437.9	544.2	620.1	773.2	2,701.8	4.07
c. Import tax	316.7	448.0	536.2	521.9	557.0	2,379.8	3.58
d. Export tax	389.1	305.0	128.4	82.5	104.0	1,009.0	1.52
e. Other	18.6	29.4	33.1	40.7	43.7	165.5	0.25
3. Total taxes (1 + 2)	*6,509.5*	*9,911.3*	*11,876.2*	*11,982.7*	*13,913.7*	*54;193.4*	*81,62*
4. Total revenues	*8,077.9*	*11,720.9*	*13,921.6*	*14,358.3*	*18,315.1*	*66,393.8*	*100.00*

Source: CBS, *Statistics of Indonesia,* Various years.

Appendix 7

The composition of tax structure in Indonesia, 1984/85 (Rp billions - current - prices)

TAXES	Semester I	Semester II	Total	%
1. Direct taxes	*5,915.0*	*6,792.9*	12,707.9	*65.56*
a. Income tax	875.0	1,246.0	2,121.0	10.94
b. Oil corpor. tax	4,971.8	5,458.0	10,429.8	53.81
c. Other	68.2	88.9	157.1	0.81
2. Indirect taxes	*1,122.4*	*1,387.9*	*2,510.3*	*12.95*
a. Sales tax	398.1	480.0	878.1	4.53
b. Exercises tax	375.5	497.2	872.7	4.50
c. Import tax	276.5	253.6	530.1	2.73
d. Export tax	38.8	52.2	91.0	0.47
e. Other	33.5	104.9	138.4	0.72
3. Total taxes (1 + 2)	*7,037.4*	*8,180.8*	*15,218.2*	*78.51*
4. Total revenue	*8,546.6*	*10,836.9*	*19,383.5*	*100.00*

Source: CBS, Monthly Statistical Bulletins, various issues.

Appendix 8

Taxes and Other revenues as percentages of the GDP, 1960—68

YEAR	GDP Rp. Billions (current prices)	As percentages to GDP (%)					
		Personal Income tax	Direct taxes	Indirect taxes	Total taxes	Other Revenues	Total Revenues
1960	0.39	0.79	2.26	3.90	6.16	6.74	12.90
1961	0.47	0.68	2.53	4.38	6.91	6.32	13.23
1962	1.34	0.46	1.33	2.22	3.55	2.04	5.59
1963	3.21	0.40	1.04	1.79	2.83	2.22	5.05
1964	7.13	0.40	0.99	1.58	2.57	1.40	3.97
1965	23.71	0.18	1.12	1.31	2.43	1.43	3.86
1966	315.90	0.20	0.57	3.33	3.90	0.26	4.16
1967	847.80	0.37	1.98	4.97	6.95	3.06	10.01
1968	1,993.90	0.47	2.56	4.71	7.27	3.14	10.41
Total/ averages	3,193.85	0.42	2.19	4.61	6.80	2.82	9.62

Source: CBS, *Statistik of Indonesia,* various years.

Appendix 9

Taxes and Other revenues as percentages of the GDP, 1969/70 — 1973/74

YEAR	GDP Rp. Billions (current prices)	As percentages to GDP (%)						
		Personal Income tax	Direct taxes	Indirect taxes	Total taxes		Other revenue	Total revenue
					w/o oil	w/ oil		
1969/70	2,718.0	0.44	3.37	5.48	7.07	8.85	3.47	12.32
1970/71	3,238.0	0.41	3.76	6.48	8.11	10.24	4.12	14.36
1971/72	3,672.0	0.47	4.93	5.98	7.84	10.91	4.44	15.35
1972/73	4,564.0	0.52	6.62	5.56	7.82	12.18	4.22	16.40
1973/74	6,753.4	0.51	7.48	6.11	8.49	13.59	3.76	17.35
Total	20,945.4							
Averages		0.48	5.74	5.94	7.99	11.68	4.0	15.68

Source: CBS, *Statistik of Indonesia,* various years.

Appendix 10

Taxes and Other revenues as percentages of the GDP, 1974/75 — 1978/79

YEAR	GDP Rp. Billions (current prices)	As percentages to GDP (%)						
		Personal Income tax	Direct taxes	Indirect taxes	Total taxes		Other revenues	Total revenue
					w/o oil	w/ oil		
1974/75	10,708.0	0.40	11.48	4.28	6.67	15.76	2.78	18.54
1975/76	12,642.5	0.49	12.59	4.27	6.98	16.86	4.76	21.62
1976/77	15,466.7	0.54	13.23	4.79	7.55	18.02	5.84	23.86
1977/78	19,030.0	0.55	13.20	4.62	7.58	17.82	4.82	22.64
1978/79	22,746.0	0.54	13.17	4.74	7.76	17.91	5.40	23.31
Total	80,593.2							
Averages		0.52	12.87	4.59	7.41	17.46	4.90	22.36

Sources: CBS, *Statistik of Indonesia,* various years.

Appendix 11

Taxes and Other revenues as percentages of the GDP, 1979/80 — 1983/84

YEAR	GDP Rp. Billions (current prices)	As percentages to GDP (%)						
		Personal Income tax	Direct taxes	Indirect taxes	Total taxes		Other revenues	Total revenue
					w/o oil	w/ oil		
1979/80	32,625.4	0.46	16.02	4.31	7.03	20.33	4.89	25.22
1980/81	45,445.7	0.36	18.11	3.70	6.36	21.81	3.98	25.79
1981/82	54,027.0	0.38	18.69	3.29	6.01	21.98	3.79	25.77
1982/83	59,632.5	0.48	16.79	3.31	6.39	20.10	3.98	24.08
1983/84	71,214.7	0.56	16.30	3.24	6.17	19.54	6.18	25.72
Total	262,345.3							
Averages		0.46	17.18	3.48	6.33	20.66	4.65	25.31

Source: CBS, *Statistiks of Indonesia,* various years.

Appendix 12

Central Government Domestic Revenue 1969—1973
(as percentage of total revenues)

Type of Revenue	Years				
	1969/70	1970/71	1971/72	1972/73	1973/74
Direct Taxes	*27.86*	*26.16*	*32.12*	*40.38*	*43.1*
Individual Income Tax	4.73	2.88	3.09	3.17	2.8
Corporate Taxes	4.58	4.45	4.51	4.09	4.1
Oil Corporate Taxes	14.87	14.80	19.96	26.58	29.3
MPO (Withholding Tax)	3.51	3.99	4.37	4.03	4.84
Other Direct Taxes[a]	0.15	0.04	0.19	2.52	2.13
Indirect Taxes	*41.02*	*45.11*	*38.96*	*33.91*	*35.6*
Sales Tax	3.66	3.93	4.26	4.61	4.7
Import Sales Tax	3.05	4.75	3.97	3.72	4.3
Excise Tax	8.61	8.36	7.17	6.32	5.3
Import Duties	18.33	15.20	12.32	9.78	11.2
Export Taxes	2.14	5.38	4.99	4.37	5.9
Other Oil Receipts	—	—	—	—	—
Other Indirect Taxes	0.92	1.06	1.24	0.89	4.2
Non-Tax Revenues	*0.76*	*2.82*	*4.88*	*4.62*	*3.6*
Development Receipts	*30.36*	*25.91*	*24.05*	*21.08*	*17.6*
Total Revenue	*100.00*	*100.00*	*100.00*	*100.00*	*100.00*

Source: Biro Pusat Statistik, *Statistik Indonesia*, Jakarta, various issues.

Note: a. Includes Ipeda.

Appendix 13

Central Government Domestic Revenue 1974—1978
(as percentage of total revenues)

Type of Revenue	1974/75	1975/76	Years 1976/77	1977/78	1978/79
Direct Taxes	*61.88*	*58.24*	*55.47*	*58.28*	*56.5*
individual Income Tax	2.18	2.25	2.28	2.42	2.3
Corporate Taxes	4.59	4.69	3.45	3.93	4.3
Oil Corporate Taxes	49.01	45.70	43.39	45.23	43.5
MPO (Withholding Tax)	4.19	3.56	4.02	4.68	4.41
Other Direct Taxes[a]	0.49	0.78	0.68	0.80	0.82
	0.14	1.27	1.14	1.22	1.20
Indirect Taxes	*23.08*	*19.73*	*20.08*	*20.43*	*20.3*
Sales Tax	4.28	4.36	4.40	4.72	4.2
Import Sales Tax	3.47	2.65	2.77	2.66	2.4
Excises Tax	3.75	3.56	3.54	4.22	4.7
Import Duties	8.09	6.36	6.98	6.66	5.6
Export Taxes	3.54	2.25	1.67	1.88	3.1
Other Oil Receipts	—0.80	—0.04	0.43	—	—
Other Indirect Taxes	0.76	0.06	0.29	0.29	0.3
Non-Tax Revenues	*13.43*	*4.04*	*3.21*	*3.33*	*3.6*
Development Receipts	*11.68*	*17.98*	*21.25*	*17.95*	*19.5*
Total Revenues	*100.00*	*100.00*	*100.00*	*100.00*	*100.00*

Source: Biro Pusat Statistik, *Statistik Indonesia,* Jakarta, various issues.

Note: a. Includes Ipeda.

Appendix 14

Central Government Domestic Revenue 1979-80/1984-85
(as percentage of total revenues)

Type of Revenue	1979-80	1980-81	1982-83	1984-85
			Years	
Direct Taxes	*59.3*	*70.32*	*71.20*	*62.7*
Individual Income Tax	2.1	1.65	1.64	13.3[a]
Corporate Taxes	3.3	3.37	5.27	
Oil Corporate Taxes	48.2	60.80	58.44	48.7
MPO (Withholding Tax)	4.2	4.10	4.35	—
Other Direct Taxes	1.5	1.40	1.48	0.7
Indirect Taxes	*16.7*	*13.76*	*14.42*	*15.3*
Sales Tax	4.0	2.38	2.83	7.2[b]
Import Sales Tax	1.6	1.38	1.91	
Export/import Tax	2.4	3.21	4.34	3.5
Excises	4.3	3.32	3.96	4.2
Other Indirect Taxes	4.4	3.47	1.38	0.4
Non Tax Revenues	*2.4*	*1.70*	*2.51*	*3.1*
Development Receipts	*21.6*	*14.22*	*11.87*	*18.9*
Total Revenues	*100.0*	*100.00*	*100.00*	*100.0*

Source: Biro Pusat Statistik, *Statistik Keuangan,* 1983—84, Jakarta, 1985.

a. Income Tax

b. Value Added Tax.

Appendix 15

Tax Revenues as Proportion of the GDP in Selected Underdeveloped Countries

	Year	GNP per capita (1979)	Total Taxes	Income Tax		Domestic Taxes on Goods and Services		Foreign Trade		Wealth and Property
				Individual	Corporate	Sales/VAT	Excises	Import Duties	Export Duties	
India	1978—1980	210	14.05	1.19	1.26	0.12	5.39	2.46	0.12	0.19
Srilanka	1978—1980	230	22.19	0.74	2.03	2.49	3.63	4.06	8.15	0.13
Pakistan	1978—1980	270	14.53	0.94	1.07	0.97	4.20	4.93	0.18	0.09
Kenya	1978—1980	390	20.87	n.a.	n.a.	5.22	2.24	4.72	0.28	0.19
Egypt	1977—1979	400	27.90	1.58	2.96	—	1.91	7.44	0.34	0.58
Thailand	1979—1981	600	13.44	1.12	1.54	2.74	2.88	2.96	0.48	0.12
Philippines	1978—1980	640	12.30	1.74	1.19	1.88	2.67	2.84	0.25	0.67
Nigeria	1975—1977	910	20.61	0.03	16.77	—	0.42	3.36	0.01	—
Korea	1978—1980	1,510	17.05	2.37	2.19	3.84	2.80	3.11	—	0.49
Brazil	1978—1980	1,770	23.19	0.18	1.02	6.79	4.39	0.63	0.34	0.43
Mexico	1978—1980	1,880	13.92	2.53	3.13	2.44	1.77	0.92	1.73	0.02
Venezuela	1978—1980	3,440	19.99	0.72	14.46	—	0.92	n.a.	n.a.	0.07
Indonesia	1978—1980	370	18.74	0.42	13.02	1.09	0.95	1.01	0.8	0.32
Average of low income countries[1]		206	13.23	1.22	1.54	1.71	1.63	4.15	1.62	0.26
Average of middle income countries[2]		510	18.55	1.90	3.02	1.54	2.05	5.80	1.15	0.37

1. Sample of 21 countries with GNP per capita of less than $300 per year.
2. Sample of 43 countries with GNP per capita of between $300 and $650 per year.

Source: IMF, Fiscal Affairs Department, "Quantitative Characteristics of the Tax System of Developing Countries" DM/83/79.

Appendix 16

Corporation Tax Revenues in Indonesia 1969—70/1983—84
(Rp millions Current Prices)

Year	Corporation Tax Revenues			AS % of Total Revenues		
	Oil Companies	Non Oil Companies	Total	Oil Companies	Non Oil Companies	Total
1969/70	48,330.0	15,640.0	63,970.0	14.44	4.67	19.11
1970/71	68,820.0	20,680.0	89,500.0	14.80	4.45	19.25
1971/72	112,599.0	25,410.0	,137,910.0	19.96	4.51	24.47
1972/73	198,900.0	30,600.0	229,500.0	26.58	4.09	30.67
1973/74	344,600.0	44,200.0	388,800.0	29.42	3.77	33.19
1974/75	973,100.0	91,200.0	1,064,300.0	49.01	4.59	53.60
1975/76	1,249,100.0	128,200.0	1,377,300.0	45.70	4.69	50.39
1976/77	1,619,400.0	127,200.0	1,746,900.0	43.88	3.46	47.34
1977/78	1,948,700.0	169,500.0	2,118,200.0	45.23	3.93	49.16
1978/79	2,308,700.0	226,500.0	2,535,200.0	43.55	4.27	47.82
1979/80	4,259,600.0	297,100.0	4,556,700.0	52.73	3.68	56.41
1980/81	7,019,600.0	447,600.0	7,467,200.0	59.89	3.82	63.71
1981/82	8,627,800.0	559,100.0	9,186,900.0	61.97	4.02	65.99
1982/83	8,170,400.0	674,500.0	8,844,900.0	56.90	4.70	61.60
1983/84	9,520,200.0	757,400.0	10,277,600.0	51.98	4.13	56.11

Source: CBS, *Monthly statistical Bulleltins.* Various Issues.

Appendix 17.

Values of Imports and Import Tax Revenues in Indonesia, 1960—1983/84

Year	Values of Import			Import Tax Revenues		
	Millions of US $	US$ — Rp Rate (Rp)	Billions of Rp	Billions of Rp	AS Percentages of	
					TR (%)	Import (%)
1960	577.7	0.165	0.0953	0.0029	5.76	3.04
1961	796.2	0.305	0.2428	0.0051	8.20	2.10
1962	647.0	1,100	0.7117	0.0042	5.61	0.59
1963	544.1	1.400	0.7617	0.0125	7.71	1.64
1964	679.9	7.200	4.8953	0.0339	11.96	0.69
1965	694.7	36.000	25.0092	0.0517	5.59	0.21
1966	526.7	122.000	64.2574	3.6890	28.07	5.74
1967	649.2	185.125	120.1832	16.9010	19.91	14.06
1968	730.2	388.750	283.8653	37.3000	17.96	1.31
1969/70	780.7	386.067	301.4025	56.6700	16.96	18.80
1970/71	1,001.5	382.125	382.6982	70.7000	15.20	18.47
1971/72	1,102.8	405.750	447.4611	69.4200	12.32	15.51
1972/73	1,561.7	417.417	651.8801	73.2000	9.78	11.23
1973/74	2,729.1	417.250	1,138.7170	128.2000	10.94	11.26
1974/75	3,841.9	420.583	1,615.8378	160.6000	8.09	9.94
1975/76	4,769.8	421.157	2,008.8347	174.0009	6.37	8.66
1976/77	5,673.1	420.646	2,386.3668	257.4000	6.98	10.79
1977/78	6,230.3	420.687	2,621.0062	286.9000	6.66	10.95
1978/79	6,690.4	447.135	2,991.5120	295.3000	5.57	9.87
1979/80	7,202.3	631.762	4,550.1395	316.7000	3.92	6.96
1980/81	10,834.4	633.218	6,860.5371	448.0000	3.82	6.53
1981/82	13,272.1	643.765	8,544.1135	536.2000	3.85	6.16
1982/83	16,858.9	676.477	11,404.1523	521.9000	3.63	4.50
1983/84	16,351.8	987.578	16,148.6779	557.0000	3.04	3.45

Sources: 1. CBS, *Monthly Statistical Bulletins.* Various Years.
2. Bi, *Monthly Financial and Banking Reports.* Various Issues.

Appendix 18.

Values of Export and Export Tax Revenues in Indonesia, 1960—1983/84

Year	Values of Export			Export Tax Revenues		
	Millions of US $	US$ — Rp Rate (Rp)	Billions of Rp	Billions of Rp	AS Percentages of TR (%)	AS Percentages of Export (%)
1960	840.8	0.165	0.1387	0.0015	2.98	1.08
1961	788.2	0.305	0.2404	0.0032	5.14	1.33
1962	663.7	1.100	0.6971	0.0025	3.34	0.36
1963	697.9	1.400	0.9771	0.0018	1.11	0.18
1964	724.2	7.200	5.2142	0.0008	0.28	0.02
1965	707.7	36.000	25.4772	0.0000	0.00	0.00
1966	678.7	122.000	82.8014	1.9660	14.96	2.37
1967	665.4	185.125	123.1822	10.6010	12.49	8.61
1968	688.5	388.750	267.6544	13.9200	6.70	5.20
1969/70	853.7	386.067	329.5854	7.4500	2.23	2.26
1970/71	1,108.1	382.125	423.4327	25.0300	5.38	5.91
1971/72	1,233.6	405.750	500.5332	28.1000	4.99	5.61
1972/73	1,777.7	417.417	742.0422	32.7000	4.37	5.41
1973/74	3,210.8	417.250	1,339.7063	68.6000	5.86	5.12
1974/75	7,426.3	420.583	3,123.3755	70.3000	3.54	2.25
1975/76	7,102.5	421.157	2,991.2676	61.6000	2.25	2.06
1976/77	8,546.5	420.646	3,595.0510	61.7000	1.67	1.72
1977/78	10,852.6	420.687	4,565.5477	81.2000	1.88	1.78
1978/79	11,643.2	447.135	5,206.0822	166.2000	3.13	3.19
1979/80	15,590.1	631.762	9,849.2328	389.1000	4.82	3.95
1980/81	23,950.4	633.218	15,165.8244	305.0000	2.60	2.01
1981/82	25,164.5	643.765	16,200.0243	128.4000	0.92	0.79
1982/83	22,328.3	676.447	15,103.9116	82.5000	0.57	0.55
1983/84	21,145.9	987.578	20,883.2256	104.0000	0.57	0.50

Sources: 1. CBS, *Monthly Statistical Bulletins.* Various Issues.
2. Bank of Indonesia, *Monthly Financial and Banking Reports.* Various Issues.

Appendix 19

Actual Receipts of Provinces (First Stage Governments) in Indonesia 1977-78/1982-83
(Rp. Billions - Current Prices)

Classification	1977—78	1978—79	1979—80	1980—81	1981—82	1982—83
A. Current Receipts	618,135.5	698,991.5	872,750.9	1,291,945.9	1,569,410.5	1,715,128.9
1. Local Taxes	77,624.6	105,315.0	131,565.9	196,804.6	233,464.9	259,803.3
Household Tax	1,377.2	1,611.3	1,636.8	2,105:3	2,652.5	5,196.1
Motor Car Transfer duties	33,540.5	44,530.8	60,424.3	107.512.9	140.317.6	147,433.3
Tax on motorized vehicle	22,626.2	36,732.3	44,923.1	55,771.8	68,263.9	82,234.4
Surcharge on Wealth Tax	—	0.2	26.6	49.2	59.6	744.5
Tax on Lottery, gambe, etc.	—	—	—	—	—	—
Radio Tax	25.8	20.4	18.5	13.8	10.6	7.9
Foreigners Tax	643.9	772.6	580.3	1,233.2	1,357.9	1,228.5
Entertainment, Recreation, Fair	—	—	—	—	—	9,312.2
Tax on Fuel	2,968.8	17.5	20.5	—	—	—
Tax on Fish Catch	3,625.1	45.7	49.3	36.9	175.9	31.4
Restaurant and Hotel Taxes	—	—	—	—	—	11,760.7
Other taxes	12,826.9	21,584.2	23,887.0	30,081.5	20,626.6	1,854.4
2. Receipt from services	9,498.7	10,856.5	15,103.8	19,630.5	26,694.6	31,669.5
3. Receipt from Official Services	9,104.7	9,373.0	10,077.3	14,237.4	16,552.8	20,043.2
4. Current Receipts from higher level of Governments	471,685.6	518,198.8	657,138.9	963,583.2	1,172,996.6	1,282,187.9
5. Rental Receipts	195.8	31.2	53.3	100.1	22.9	572.3
6. Net Profits of Local Government Enterprises	1,221.4	1,954.5	2,469.2	3,921.4	5,253.8	7,106.8
7. Other Mischellaneous Receipts	48,804.5	53,262.2	56,342.3	93,031.0	112,630.9	41,976.9
B. Development Receipts	143,458.8	188,141.5	241,687.9	363,692.8	432,823.8	450,236.4
Total Receipts A + B	761,594.3	887,132.9	1,114,438.8	1,655,638.8	2,002,234.3	2,165,365.4

Sources: Biro Pusat Statistik, *State and Local Government Financial Statistics,* 1977-78/1982-83.
____________, *Statistik Indonesia,* 1983 & 1984 Issues, Jakarta.

Appendix 20.

Growth of Public Expenditures in Indonesia
(1960—1983/1984 Current Prices)

Year	% of GDP	Per capita (Rp)	Total (billion) Rp	Precent Increase
1960	15.89	6.59	0.62	—
1961	11.91	5.60	0.56	—9.67
1962	8.73	11.70	1.17	108.92
1963	9.53	30.00	3.06	161.54
1964	7.25	49.71	5.17	68.95
1965	10.67	23.87	2.53	—51.06
1966	9.33	270.00	29.43	1,063.24
1967	10.33	788.73	87.55	197.48
1968	10.41	1,837.52	207.64	137.16
1969/70	12.31	2,885.00	334.67	61.18
1970/71	13.71	3,879.91	457.83	36.80
1971/72	11.97	4,504.13	545.00	19.04
1972/73	16.19	5,986.34	736.32	35.10
1973/74	10.87	9,240.16	1,164.26	58.11
1974/75	15.65	15,332.79	1,977.93	69.88
1975/76	17.65	20,684.09	2,730.30	38.04
1976/77	19.70	27,290.66	3,684.24	34.94
1977/78	19.76	31,200.72	4,305.70	16.8[illegible]
1978/79	23.30	37,583.82	5,299.32	23.08
1979/80	25.22	55,314.72	8,075.98	52.39
1980/81	25.77	78,107.53	11,716.13	45.07
1981/82	25.76	90,965.62	13,917.74	18.79
1982/83	24.07	91,348.98	14,355.92	3.15
1983/84	25.71	114,443.56	18,310.97	27.55

Source: CBS, *Statistik Indonesia,* for Various Years.

Appendix 21

LAW OF THE REPUBLIC OF INDONESIA
NO. 6 YEAR 1983

R E

GENERAL PROVISIONS AND PROCEDURE ON TAXES

BY THE GRACE OF GOD
PRESIDENT OF THE REPUBLIC OF INDONESIA,

Considering : a. that the State of the Republic of Indonesia is a legislative State on the basis of Pancasila and the 1945 Constitution highly appriciating the rights and obligations of the citizens, it therefore positions tax as one of the manifestations of the Stateship obligation of the citizens constituting the means of participation in financing the state and national development ;

b. that the tax system constituting the basis of the state taxes collection implementation so far applicable is no more complying to the socioeconomic living standard of the people of Indonesia both in the aspects of national mutual aid principle and the already achieved national development growth rate:

c. that the system manifested in the provisions applicable so far has not motivated the participation of all strata of the tax subjects playing important role in increasing the domestic revenues extremely required for materializing the continuity and improvement of the national development;

d. that it is therefore, also pursuant to the message contained in the Outline of the State Policy (Act of the People's Deliberative Assembly of the Republic of Indonesia No. II/MPR/1983) necessary to renew the prevailing tax system with that giving certainty to the tax subject to execute his obligations and meet his rights in tax sector so as to materialize the expansion and improve the awareness of tax obligation as well as to equitably distribute the income of the community ;

e. that to reach the aforementioned objectives, it is deemed necessary to renew and substitute the prevailing tax legislative regulations so far;

In view of

1. Article 5 paragraph (1), Article 20 paragraph (1), and Article 23 paragraph (2) of 1945 Constitution;
2. Act of the People's Deliberative Assembly of the Republic of Indonesia No. II/MPR/1983 re Outline of State Policy ;
3. Regeling van het Beroep in Belastingszaken (State Gazette year 1927 No. 29 (as already several times amended, lastly by Law No. 5 Year 1959 (State Gazette No. 13; Supplement to State Gazette No. 1748) ;
4. Law No. 19 Year 1959 re State Taxes Collection by Coercion Letter (Gazette Year 1959 No. 63; Supplement to state Gazette No. 1850);
5. Law No. 8 Year 1981 re Criminal Code Procedure (State Gazette Year 1981 No. 76; Supplement to State Gazette No. 3209);

With the approval of

THE PARLIAMENT OF THE REPUBLIC OF INDONESIA

HAS DECIDED :

By revoking :

1. 1925 Corporate Tax Ordinance (State Gazette year 1925 No. 319) as already several times amended, lastly by Law No. 8 Year 1970 re Amendment on and Addition to 1925 Corporate Tax Ordinance (State Gazette year 1970 No. 43, Supplement to State Gazette No. 2940);

2. 1944 Income Tax Ordinance (State Gazette Year 1944 No. 17) as already several times amended, lastly by Law No. 9 Year 1970 re Amendment on and' Addition to 1944 Income Tax Ordinance (State Gazette Year 1970 No. 44, Supplement to State Gazette No. 2941);
3. Law No. 8 Year 1967 re Amendment on and Improvement of 1944 Income Tax, 1932 Property Tax and 1925 Corporate Tax Collection Procedure (State Gazette year 1967 No. 18, Supplement to State Gazette No. 2827); except the provisions on the Property Tax collection procedure ;
4. Law No. 10 Year 1970 re Tax on Interest, Dividend and Royalty 1970 (State Gazette Year 1970 No. 45, Supplement to State Gazette No. 2942).

To Stipulate : LAW RE GENERAL PROVISIONS AND PROCEDURE ON TAXES

CHAPTER I
GENERAL PROVISION

Article 1.

In this Law, the meaning of :

a. Tax payer shall be an individual or body according to the tax provision is stipulated to execute the tax obligations ;

b. Body shall be the limited liability company, limited partnership, state owned undertaking body and state-owned regional undertaking body under any name form, association. Corporation or other organizations, firm, partnership, cooperatives, foundation or institution and permanent undertaking form ;

c. Tax period shall be that used as the basis for calculating the indebted tax ;

d. Fiscal year shall be that in one calender year or book year;

e. Part of fiscal year shall be the part of that of one fiscal year ;

f. Tax Return shall be that used by the Tax Payer to report the calculation and payment of the indebted tax according to the taxes law ;

g. Period Tax Return shall be that used by the Tax Payer to inform the indebted tax in a tax period or at a certain time ;

h. Annual tax Return shall be that used by the Tax Payer to inform the indebted tax in a fiscal year ;

i. Tax Deposit Document shall be that used by the Tax payer to pay the indebted tax at the State Treasury or other designated by the ministry of Finance to receive the payment of tax and/or report to the Directorate General of Taxes ;

j. Tax Collection Letter shall be that to collect the tax and/or sanction in the form of interest and administrative fine;

k. Tax Assessment Letter shall be the Decree stipulating the amount of the indebted tax, tax payment reduction deficiency of tax principal, sanction, and amount of tax to be paid ;

l. Additional Tax Assessment Letter Shall be the decree adding the amount of the already assessed tax ;

m. Tax Payment Excess Decree shall be that stipulating the reimbursement of tax payment excess already paid and/or deducted and/or collected, due to the amount of the already paid tax;

n. Notification letter shall be that informing the Tax Payer that the amount of the indebted tax is equal to the already paid, deducated or collected tax ;

o. Indebted tax shall be that still to be paid on, during the tax period, in the fiscal year or in the part of the fiscal year according to the provisions of law on taxes ;

p. Coercion Letter shall be the order to pay the tax and collection related to tax, giving competence to the implementor to make direct execution without any judge's verdict, to the current and Fixed assets belonging to the Tax Payer and/or tax bearer, with sanction of detention without judge's verdict, in compliance with Law No. 19 Year 1959 re Collection of State's Taxes with Coercion Letter (state Gezette Year 1959 No. 63; Supplement to state Gazette No. 1850);

q. Tax credit shall be the amount of tax to be paid by the Tax payer himself, plus the tax deducted or collected by other party deducated from the total indebted tax including, if any, the amount of the indebted Income Tax abroad;

r. Free Employment shall be that conducted by a person having special expertise as an effort to gain income without any work/ employment relation ;

s. Auditing shall be the action conducted by the tax officer in the framework of examining the Tax Payer to obtain the input to calculate the amount of the indebted tax and the tax to be paid.

CHAPTER II
TAX PAYER REGISTRATION NUMBER , TAX RETURN AND PROCEDURE OF TAXES PAYMENT

Article 2.

Every Tax Payer shall be obligated to register himself at the Directorate General of Taxes and to him shall be given the Tax Payer Registration Number.

Article 3.

(1) Every Tax Payer shall be obligated to fill in the Tax Return, sign and submit it to the Directorate General of Taxes, within the region of the Tax Payer as residence or domicile.

(2) The Tax Payer as referred to in paragraph (1) shall take the Tax Return on his own at the place determined by the Director General of Taxes.

(3) The time limit for submitting the Tax Return shall be :
   a. for the Periodical Tax Return, no later than 20 (twenty) days after the expiry of the tax period ;

   b. for Annual Tax Return no later than 3 (three) months after the expiry of the fiscal Year.

(4). The Director General of Taxes on the request of the Tax Payer can extend the time for submitting the Annual Tax Return as referred to in paragraph (3) letter b.

(5). The application as referred to in paragraph (4) shall be in writing accompanied by the statement concerning the provisional calculation of the indebted tax in one fiscal year and receipt of the payment of the indebted tax deficiency.

(6) The Tax Return as referred to in paragraph (1) shall be completed with the required attachments in compliance with the requirements stipulated in the provisions of the relative legislative regulation taxes.

Article 4.

(1) The Tax Payer shall fill in and submit the Tax Return correctly, completely, clearly, and sign it.

(2). In case the Tax Payer is a body, the Tax Return shall be signed by the executive or management.

(3) In the case the Tax Return is filled in and signed by a person other than the Tax Payer, shall be attached by a special power of attorney.

(4) The completion of the Annual Tax Return of Income Tax by the Tax Payer obligated to keep accounting record, shall be with the financial statement in the form of balance sheet and profit/loss statement, as well as the other necessary information calculate the taxable income.

Article 5.

To submit the Tax Return the Director General of Taxes in certain cases can determine a place other than that as referred to in Article 3 Paragraph (1)

Article 6.

(1) The Tax Return directly submitted to the Directorate General of Taxes by the Tax Payer shall bear the date of receipt by the official designated therefore, whereas for the Annual Tax Return shall also have the receipt.

(2) The Tax Return sent via the Post Office s. .ll be by registered mail, and the receipt and the date of delivery shall be considered the evidence and date of receipt.

Article 7.

If the Tax Return is not submitted or submitted not in time as referred to in Article 3 paragraph (3) shall be subject to administrative fine of Rp. 10,000.00 (ten thousand rupiahs).

Article 8.

(1) The Tax Payer may self correct the Tax Return by submitting written statement, as long as the Director General Taxes has not started any auditing.

(2) In the case the Tax Payer self corrects the Tax Return Resulting the bigger tax debt, to him shall be sanctioned by the interest of 2% (two per cent) per month on the amount of the deficiency, calculated from the expiry of the Tax Return submission to the date of payment due to the correction of the Tax return.

(3) Though auditing has been conducted, as long as there has not been any investigation on the improperness conducted by the Tax Payer as referred to in Article 38, the improper correct in of the Tax Payer shall not be investigated, if the Tax Payer on his own free will reveals said improper conduct accompanied by the payment of deficiency of the actually indebted tax and the administrative fine of twice the tax deficiency.

Article 9.

(1) The Minister of Finance shall determine the due date of payment and deposit of indebted tax for a period or tax period for the respective types of tax, no later than fifteen days ofter the expiry of the indebted tax or tax period.

(2) The payment deficiency of the indebted tax on the basis of the Annual Tax Return shall be fully paid within three months

after the expiry of fiscal year or part of fiscal year, prior to the submission of the Tax Return.

(3) The Tax Collection Letter, Tax Assessment Letter, or Additional Tax Assessment Letter shall be fully paid within one month after the date of issuance thereof.

(4) The Director General of Taxes on the request of the Tax Payer can approve the Tax Payer to instal or postpone the tax payment.

Article 10.

(1) The Tax Payer shall be obligated to pay or deposit the indebts tax to the State Treasury Office or other places determined by the Minister of Finance.

(2) The procedure of payment, tax deposit and reporting thereof as well as the procedure to instal and postpone the Tax payment shall further be regulated by the Minister of Finance.

Article 11.

(1) On the request of the Tax Payer, the tax payment excess as referred to in Article 17 paragraph (1) letter a shall be reimbursed, or if it is found that the Tax Payer has the other indebted taxes, can directly be calculated to first pay up the indebted tax.

(2) The reimbursement of the tax payment excess as referred to in paragraph (1) shall be conducted within one month after the stipulation of the Payment Excess Decree as referred to in Article 17 paragraph (1) Letter a.

(3) If the reimbursement of the tax payment excess is conducted after two months, the Government shall pay the interest of 2% (two percent) permonth on the delay of the tax payment excess, calculated as from the validity of the expiry as referred to in paragraph (2) up to the time of the excess payment.

(4) The procedure of calculation and reimbursement of tax payment, excess shall further be regulated by the Minister of Finance.

CHAPTER III
TAX ASSESSING AND ASSESMENT

Article 12.

Every Tax Payer shall be obligated to pay the indebted tax on the basis of the provisions of the legislative regulation on taxes without depending on the existence of Tax Assessment Letter.

Article 13.

(1) Within five years after the tax indebting period or expiry of Tax period, Part of Fiscal Year or Fiscal Year, the Director General of Taxes can issue the Tax Assessment Letter in the following cases :

a. if on the basis of auditing or other information it is found that the amount of the indebted tax is less or not paid ;

b. if the Tax Return is not submitted within the given time as referred to in Article 3 paragraph (3) and after being given written warning is not submitted in time as provided in the Warning Letter ;

c. if on the basis of the auditing on the Value Added Tax on Goods and Services and Sales Tax on Luxury Goods it is found that it should not compensate the tax excess discrepancy, not impose the tariff of 0% (zero percent), or give the tax reimbursment.

d. if the obligation is not met as referred on in Articles 28 and 29 so that the amount of the indebted tax is not known.

(2) The amount of the indebted tax deficiency in the Tax Assessment Letter as referred to in paragraph (1) letter a plus the administrative sanction in the form of interest of 2% (two per cent) a month for no later than twenty four months, shall be calculated as from the indebted tax time or expiry of Tax Period, Part of Fiscal Year or Fiscal Year to the issuance of The Tax Assessment Letter.

(3) The amount of tax in the Tax Assessment Letter as referred to in paragraph (1) letters b, c and d is added by the administrative sanction in the form of increase of :

a. 50% (fifty percent) of the deficient Income Tax or that not paid within one FiscallYear ;

b. 100% (one hundred percent) of the Income Tax which is not or not sufficiently deducted, collected, deposited or collected but not or not adequately deposited ;

c. 100% (one hundred percent) of the Value Added Tax on Goods and Services and Sales Tax on Luxury goods which is not or not sufficiently paid.

(4) The amount of the deducted and collected Income Tax by the third party for one Fiscal Year, the amount of the self paid Income Tax, the tax collected in the Tax Collection Letter for said Fiscal Year, as well as the tax on Income paid or indebted abroad for the relative fiscal year, shall be credited from the amount of the indebted Income Tax in the Tax Assessment Letter.

(5) The administrative sanctions in the form of interest, administrative fine and increase shall not be credited from the amount of the indebted tax.

(6) The amount of the indebted tax in one Fiscal Year imformed by the Tax Payer in the Annual Tax return shall be certain according to the provisions of law on taxes, if within the time as referred to in paragraph (1) the Tax Assessment Letter is not Issued.

(7) If the five years' period as referred to in paragraph (1) has been over, the Tax Assessment Letter shall remain issuable in the case that the Tax Payer after said five years' period is sanctioned due to communitting criminal act in tax concerning the tax the collection of which has been expired on the basis of the Court Verdict having obtained certain legal enforcement.

Article 14.

(1) The Tax Collection Letter shall be issued if :

a. The tax in the current year is not or not sufficiently paid;

b. the Tax Payer is sanctioned administratively by administrative fine and/or interest ;

c. from the verification of the Tax Return it is found that thereis a tax payment deficiency due to miswriting and/or miscalculation.

(2) The Tax Collection Letter as referred to in paragraph (1) shall have the same legal enforcement as that of the Tax Assessment Letter.

Article 15.

(1) The Director General of Taxes can issue an Additional Tax Assessment Letter within five years after the indebted Tax period, expiry of Tax Period, Part of Fiscal Year or Fiscal Year if he finds new data and/or data initially not yet revealed causing the addition of the indebted tax amount.

(2) The amount of the indebted tax deficiency in the Additional Tax Assessment Letter shall be added by the administrative sanction in the form of 100% (one hundred percent) increase of said tax deficiency amount.

(3) The increase as referred to in paragraph (2) shall not be imposed/ if the Additional Tax Assessment Letter is issued on the basis of the written information from the Tax Payer on own free will, as long as the Director General of Taxes has not conducted any auditing.

(4) If the five years' period as referred to in paragraph (1) has been over, the Additional Tax Assessment Letter shall remain issuable in the case that the Tax Payer after said five years' period is sanctioned due to committing criminal act in tax concerning the tax the collection of which has been expired on the basis of a court Verdict having obtained the certain legal inforcement.

Article 16.

Miswriting, miscalculation, or error in applying the legislative provisions on taxes available in the tax assessment letter can be corrected by the Director General of Taxes due to function or on the request of the Tax Payer.

Article 17.

(1) The Director General of Taxes after verifying or auditing shall issue :

a. The Payment Excess Decree in no later than twelve months after the receipt of the application, if the amount of the tax paid or the amount of the Income Tax Deducted or collected is found bigger than that of the indebted tax or the tax payment which actually should not be indebted ;

b. The Tax Return of the amount of the Tax paid or the amount of the Income Tax deducted or collected is equal to that of the indebted tax .

(2) If after the expiry as referred to in paragraph (1) letter a the Director General for Taxes does not give any decision, the application for said tax payment excess shall be considered granted.

CHAPTER IV
TAX COLLECTION

Article 18.

(1) The Tax Collection Letter, Tax Assessment Letter and Additional Tax Assessment Letter constitute the basis of tax collection.

(2) The implementation procedure of tax collection shall further be regulated by the Minister of Finance.

Article 19.

(1) If on the indebted tax, on the due date of the payment it is not or insufficiently paid, on the unpaid or insufficiently paid tax amount shall be imposed with the interest of 2% (two percent) per month for the whole period calculated as from the due date

to the pay day and part of the month shall be calculated as one full month.

(2) In the case that the Tax Payer is allowed to instal or postpone the tax payment, shall also be imposed with 2% (two percent) interest per month.

(3) In the case that the Tax Payer is allowed to postpone the submission of the Tax Return and found that the provisional calculation of the tax payment as referred to in Article 3 paragraph (5) is less than the actual amount of indebted tax, the deficiency of said tax payment shall be imposed with 2% (two percent) interest per month calculated as from the expiry of the obligation to submit the Tax Return as referred to in Article 3 paragraph (3) letter b to the pay day of said payment deficiency.

Article 20.

Deviating from the provision as referred to in Article 9, the amount of the indebted tax on, the basis of the Tax Collection Letter, Tax Assessment Letter, or Additional Tax Assessment Letter shall be collected at once, in the case that ;

a. The Tax Payer or his representative as referred to in Article 32 paragraph (2) will leave Indonesia for good or has the intention to do that ;

b. The Tax Payer or his representative as referred to in Article 32 paragraph (2) ceases or obviously reduces his business operation or work conducted in Indonesia or transfers the movable or immovable goods he possesses or controls;

c. Liquidation of a body or to Liquidate it, declarationof lbankruptcy, likewise in the case of confiscation on movable or immovable goods belonging to the Tax Payer or his representative as referred to in Article 32 paragraph (2).,

Article 21.

(1) The State shall have the previlege to collect the tax on the goods belonging to the Tax Payer likewise on that to his representative, as well as any person or Body which according to Article 32 paragraph (2) and the other tax legislative regulations to be responsible personally and/or successively.

(2) The provisions on the previlege as referred to in paragraph (1) shall cover the tax principal, interest, administrative fine, increase and collecting cost.

(3) The previlege to collect tax shall be more superior than the other rights, except to that of the parties as referred to in Article 1139 numbers 1 and 4, Article 1149 number 1 of Civil Code and Articles 80 and 81 of Commercial Code.

(4) The previlege shall be void after passing two years as from the date of the issuance of the Tax Collection Letter, Tax Assessment Letter, or Additional Tax Assessment Letter except if within the Validity period of the coercion Letter to pay is officially declared or the payment postponement is granted.

(5) In case the Coercion Letter to pay is officially informed, the period of two years as referred to in paragraph (4) shall be calculated as from the date of coercion Letter notification or in the case of granting the payment postponement said two years' period shall be added by the payment postponement period.

Article 22.

The right to collect tax, including the interest, administrative fine, increase, and collecting cost shall be void after passing five years as from the relative indebted tax period or expiry of the Tax Period, part of Fiscal year on Fiscal year, except if the Tax Payer commits the criminal act in tax sector as referred to in Article 13 paragraph (7) and Article 15 paragraph (4).

Article 23

The amount of the indebted tax on the basis of the Tax Collection Letter, Tax Assessment Letter, and Additional Tax Assessment Letter not paid in time can be collected by a Coercion Letter.

Article 24.

The procedure of eliminating the receivable tax and assessment of elimination shall be regulated by the Minister of Finance.

CHAPTER V
OBJECTION AND APPEAL

Article 25

(1) The Tax Payer can submit his objection to the Director of Taxes on a :

a. Announcement
b. Tax Assessment Letter
c. Additional Tax Assessment Letter
d. Deduction or collection by the third party on the basis of the legislative regulations on taxes.

(2) The objection shall be submitted in writing in Indonesian Language by stating the reasons clearly.

(3) The objection shall be submitted within three months as from the date of the Letter, or deduction or the collection as referred to in paragraph (1), except if the Tax Payer can indicate that the period can not be fulfilled due to beyond his capability.

(4) The Receipt on Objection given by the official of the Directive General of Taxes designated therefor or receipt of Objection Letter despatch via the registered mail shall become the receipt of said Objection Letter for the interest of the Tax Payer.

(5) If requested by the Tax Payer for the interest of proposing the objection, the Director General of Taxes shall be obligated to give, in writing the things becoming the basis of imposition, deduction or collection of tax.

(6) The submission of objection shall not delay the obligation to pay the tax.

Article 26.

(1) The Director General of Taxes in no Later· than twelve months as from the date of the receipt of the Objection Letter shall decide the proposed objection.

(2) Prior to the issuance of the decree, the Tax Payer can submit the additional reasons or written explanation.

(3) The Decesion of the Director General of Taxes on the Objection can be in the form of total or partial acceptance, refusal or addition of the amount of the indebted tax.

(4) In case the Tax payer proposes his objection on the tax assessment provided under Article 13 paragraph (1) Letters b and d, the relative Tax Payer shall prove the incorrectness of said tax assessment.

(5) If the period as referred to in paragraph (1) has passed and the Director General of Tax does not make any decision, said proposed objection shall be considered accepted.

Article 27.

(1) The Tax Payer can make an appeal to the tax justice body on the decision of the Director General of Taxes concerning his objection within three months as from the date of stipulation of the decree by enclosing the copy of said Decree.

(2) The application for an appeal shall be submitted in writing in Indonesian Language.

(3) The submission of the application for an appeal shall not delay the obligation to pay the tax.

CHAPTER VI
ACCOUNTING AND AUDITING

Article 28.

(1) A person or Body operating his business or free employment in Indonesia shall have an accounting able to present the adeguate information to calculate the Taxable Income or aquisition price and delivery of goods or services in order to calculate the amount of the indebted tax on the basis of the legislative regulations on taxes.

(2) For the Tax Payer who according to the legislative Regulation on taxes is exempted from the obligation to make the an accourding as referred to in paragraph (1) shall at least make records for the basis of the indebted tax imposition.

(3) Said accounting or recording shall be conducted by due observance of the good will and reflect the actual business condition or activity.

(4) The accounting as referred to in paragraph (1) shall at least consist of the records regularly conducted concerning the condition of cash and bank, List of payable-receivable accounts and stocks, and at every expiry of Fiscal year the Tax Payer shall close his accounting by producing a balance sheet and profit/loss statement on the basis of the accounting principles allowed by the Minister of Finance.

(5) the accounting or recording and documents becoming the basis thereof as well as the other documents related to the business activities or free employment of the Tax Payer shall be kept for ten years.

Article 29.

(1) The Director General of Taxes shall be competant to audit to assess the amount of the indebted tax and for other purposes

in the framework of executing the legislative Regulations on taxes.

(2) For the purpose of auditing the auditor shall be provided with Auditing Warrant and show it to the audited Tax Payer.

(3) The audited tax Payer shall :

a. show and lend his accounting or recordis, documents becoming the basis thereof, and other documents related to the business operation or free employment of the Tax Payer;

b. give opportunity to enter places or rooms considered necessary and assistance for the smoothness of the auditing;

c. give necessary information.

(4) If in the accounting item, recordis or document as well as the required information, the Tax Payer bound by an obligation to keep it confidential, said obligation shall be eliminated on request for the interest of auditing as referred to in paragraph (3) in compliance with the prevailing legislative regulations.

Article 30.

The Director General of Taxes shall be competent to seal a certain place or room, if the Tax Payer does not fulfil his obligation as referred to in Article 29 paragraph (3) Letter b.

Article 31.

The procedure of auditing shall further be regulated by the government regulation.

CHAPTER VII
SPECIAL PROVISIONS

Article 32.

(1) In executing the rights and fulfilling the obligations according to the legislative regulations on taxes, the Tax Payer shall be represented in the case of.

a. Body by the management/executives ;
b. Body in liquidation or bankruptcy by a person or Body responsible for the settlement ;
c. not yet distributed heritage by any of the heirs/heirerses, testimonial implementer or that arranging his heritage;
d. immaturs child or a person under the guardian of someone or his guardian.

(2) The representative as reterred to in paragraph (1) shall be responsible personally and /or successively for the payment of the indebted tax , except if able to prove and assure the Director General of taxes that they in their position are really inable to responsible for said indebted tax.

(3) A person or Body can appoint a proxy by the special power of attorney to execute the rights and fulfil the obligations according to the legislative regulation on taxes.

Article 33.

The buyer or service recipient as referred to in Value Added Tax on Goods and Services and Sales Tax an Luxury Goods shall be successively responsible for the tax payment, as long as unable to produce the tax payment receipt.

Article 34.

(1) Any official shall be prohibited to inform any mentitled party anything he knows or informed to him by the Tax Payer in the framework of his function or work to execute the legislative regulations on taxes.

(2) The prohibiton as referred to in paragraph (1) shall also apply to the experts designated by the Director General of Taxes to assist the execution of the legislative regulations on taxes.

(3) The Minister of Finance shall be competent to order in writing the official as referred to in paragraph (1) and the experts as referred as referred to in paragraph (2) to give information, produce written evidence of the Tax Payer to the Auditor for

the purpose of State Finance auditing . Said Warrant shall bear the name of the Tax Payer whose information is required and the auditor.

(4) For the purpose of trial in the court in a criminal suit, on the request of the Judge as referred to in Article 180 of Law No. 8 Year 1981 re Criminal Code Procedure, the Minister of Finance can grant written permission to request the tax officers as referred to in paragraph (1) and the experts as referred to in paragraph (2), for written evidence and information of the Tax Payer available with him.

(5) The request of the Judge as referred to in paragraph (4) shall mention the name of the defendant, the required information as well as linkage between the relative criminal suit and said required information.

Article 35.

(1) If in executing the legislative regulations on taxes it is required the information or evidence from the third party having relation to the trialed Tax Payer, on the request of the Director General of Taxes said third party shall produce the required information or evidence.

(2) In case the relative third party is bound by an obligation to keep it confidential, said obligation shall be eliminated on request for the purpose of auditing in compliance with the prevailing Legislative regulations.

Article 36.

(1) The Director General of Taxes can :

a. reduce or eliminate the administrative sanction in the from of interest, fine and decrease indebted according to the legislative regulations on taxes in case said sanction is taken due to the mistake of the Tax Payer or not because of his fault.

b. reduce or annual the incorrect tax assessment.

(2) The procedure for reducing, elimmating or annulling the tax debt as referred to in paragraph (1) shall be regulated by the Minister of Finance.

Article 37.

The amendment of the amount of administrative sanction in the form of interest, administrative fine, and increase shall be regulated by the Government Regulation.

CHAPTER VIII
SANCTION

Article 38.

Any body whosoever, due to his negligence

a. not submitting the Tax Return; or

b. submitting the Tax Return but the content thereof is not correct or incomplete or enclosing incorrect information.

so that it inflicts loss to the State, shall be sanctioned by imprisonment of one year and/or fine of twice the indebted tax at the most.

Article 39.

(1) Anybody whosoever deliberately.

a. not registering himself or misusing or using without Tax Payer Registration number as referred to in Article 2; or

b. not submitting the Tax Return; and/or

c. submitting the Tax Return and/or information bearing incorrect or incomplete content; and/or.

d. showing accounting, recording, or document which is false or falsified as if it is corect; and/or

e. not showing or lending the accounting, records or other documents; and/or.

f. not depositing the already deducted or collected tax.

so that it inflicts loss to the state, shall be sanctioned by imprisonment of three years and/or fine of four times the deficient or not paid indebted tax at the most

(2) The sanction as referred to in paragraph (1) can be doubled if

again one commits the criminal act in tax prior to passing one year, as from the accomplishment of part or total of the sentenced imprisonment.

Article 40.

The criminal act in tax can not be sued after passing ten years as from the relative period of the indebted tax, expiry of tax period, expiry of part of Fi..al year or expiry of Fiscal year

Article 41.

(1) Any official due to his negligence does not keep the matter regulated under Article 34 confidencial shall be sanctioned by imprisonment of six months and/or fine of Rp. 1,000,000,00 (one million rupiahs) at the most.

(2) Any official deliberately does not meet his obligation or anyone causing the nonfulfilment of the obligation of the official as referred to in Article 34 shall be sanctioned by the imprisonment of one year and/or fine of Rp. 2,000,000.00 (two million rupiahs) at the most.

(3) The prosecution to the criminal act as referred to in paragraphs (1) and (2) shall only be conducted on he report of one whose confidentiality is violated.

Article 42.

(1) The criminal act as referred to in Article 38 and Article 41 paragraph (1) shall be a violation;

(2) The criminal act as referred to in Article 39 and Article 41 paragraph (2) shall be a crime.

Article 43.

The propisions as regulated under article 38 and 39 shall also apply to the representative, proxy or employee of the Tax Payer.

CHAPTER IX
INVESTIGATION

Article 44.

(1) A certain civil servant official within the Directorate General of Taxes shall be given special competence as the Investigator of tax criminal act, as referred to in Law No. 8 year 1981 re Criminal Code Procedure.

(2) The Investigator as referred to in paragraph (1) shall be competent to :

a. verify the correctness of the report or information regarding the criminal act in tax ;

b. examine the person suspected committing the criminal act in tax ;

c. ask for information and evidence from a person or Body in respect to the criminal act in tax ;

d. audit the accounting, records and other documents in respect to the criminal act in tax ;

e. examine on a certain place suspected to have the evidence of accounting, recording and other document as well as confiscate the object which can become the evidence in the criminal act in tax ;

f. request the assistance of the export in the framework of the investigation of criminal act in tax.

CHAPTER X
TRANSITIONAL PROVISIONS

Article 45.

To the taxes indebted in a certain period, for the Tax Period, Part of Fiscal Year or Fiscal Year expired prior to the effectiveness of this

Law shall remain applicable the former legislative regulations on taxe: through December 31, 1988.

Article 46.

By the coming into force of this Law all former implementing regulations in taxes shall remain applicable as long as not violating this law.

Article 47.

To the taxable income received or obtained in the sector of Mineral Oil and Natural Gas as well as other mining in respect to the Work Contract and Production Sharing Contract still applicable on the coming into force of this Law shall be imposed with tax on the basis of the provisions of the 1925 Corporate Tax Ordinance and Law of Tax on Interest, Dividend and Royalty 1970 as well as all implementing regulations thereof.

CHAPTER XI
CONCLUDING PROVISIONS

Article 48.

Anything not yet sufficiently regulated herein shall further be stipulated by the Government Regulation.

Article 49.

The provisions herein shall also apply to other laws on taxes except if otherwise stipulated.

Article 50.

This Law shall come into force as from January, 1984. For the public knowledge this law shall be promulgated in the state Gazette of the Republic of Indonesia.

Enacted in Jakarta
On December 31, 1983

THE PRESIDENT OF THE
REPUBLIC OF INDONESIA

SOEHARTO.

Promulgated in, Jakarta
On December 31, 1983

THE MINISTER/SECRETARY OF STATE OF
THE REPUBLIC OF INDONESIA,

SUDHARMONO SH.

STATE GAZETTE OF THE REPUBLIC OF INDONESIA YEAR 1983 No. 49.

Appendix 22

ELUCIDATION

ON

LAW NO. 6 YEAR 1983 RE

GENERAL PROVISIONS AND PROCEDURE ON TAXES

I. GENERAL

1. The legislative regulations on taxes so far being the basis of the prevailing tax collection are mostly the heritage of the colonial era then making them merely accumulate the fund for the colonial Government to maintain and enlarge her conquest in our father land.

   Therefore the tax collection then was considered a heavy burden by the people as both the tax amount assessment, types of tax and the collection procedure thereof were found beyond the justice without considering the capability and adding burden and being far from the consideration and appreciation to the human right.

   Tax merely constitutes the obligation to be obediently conducted by the people.

   The legislative regulations on taxes drawn up during the Dutch occupation were inter alia: 1921 Stamp Duty regulation, 1925 Corporate Tax Ordinance, 1932 Property Tax Ordinance, 1944 Income Tax Ordinance

   though to various.legislative regulations on taxes inherited from the colonial era have been conducted several amendments and adjustments, due to the different philosophy becoming the background thereof, as long as the taxes are based on said legislative regulations, they have not been functioning as the means to support the wish of the nation and national development currently being carried out.

2. Entering the independent era, from August 17 1945 Proclamation, to various legislative regulations on taxes have been conducted amendments, additions and adjustment so as to adjust

them to the condition and demand of the people of a country already gaining her independence. However, the amendment then was partial, where the one rather basic was conducted via Law No. 8 year 1967 re Procedure for collecting the Income Tax, Property Tax and Corporate Tax of which the implementation was regulated by the Government Regulation No. 11 year 1967 further known as "MPS and MPO (Withholding Tax) System."

Said system constitutes the tax system pursuant to the socio-economic development level of Indonesia.

Nevertheless, the efforts already conducted to amend said various legislative regulations on taxes have not fundamentally answered the demand and needs of the people for the basic act of legislative regulations on taxes. The legislative regulations on taxes as referred to shall be based on the philosophy of Pancasila and 1945 Constitution in which is manifested the provision to highly appreciate the rights of Citizen and place the tax obligation as the citizenship obligation and constituting the means of participation of the people in the citizenship sector.

The indication on the needs for the basic amendment has actually been manifested as the People's message, as written. and implied in the Outline of State Policy inter alia reading: "Taxes system shall continuously be improved, the taxes collection shall be intensfied and the taxes apparatus shall be more able and cleaner."

3. This Law therefore as a low on taxes on the philosophy of Pancasila and 1945 Constitution shall be different from those drawn up in the Colonial era.

   Said difference will be very obvious in the system and mechanism as well as the insight to the Tax Payer, not considered as the "object," but a subject to be continuously promoted and directed so as to and able to meet the tax obligation as the citizenship obligation.

   In another aspect the community's demand for the existence of "the more able and cleaner tax officials," is manifested in various provisions having the nature to control herein.

   The difference of philosophy and principle becoming the

background of and basis for formulating this law is reflected in the provisions regulating the system and mechanism of the tax collection. In turn said system and mechanism will become a unique characteristic and motive in the tax system in Indonesia as the position of this law will become the "general provisions" for the other legislative regulations on taxes.
The unique characteristic and motive of said tax collection system is :

a. that the tax collection constitutes the manifestation of the dedication of obligation and participation of the Tax payer to directly and jointly execute the tax obligation required for financing the state and national development;

b. the responsibility for the tax execution obligation, as the reflection of the obligation in tax is with the members of the tax: payers community themselves.
The Government, in this case the tax apparatus pursuant to their function shall be obligated to promote, study and supervise the execution of the tax obligation of the Tax Payer on the basis of the provisions underlined in the legislative regulations on taxes ;

c. the members of the Tax Payers community are intrested to execute the national mutual aid via the self calculation , self accounting and self assessment system so that in this way the tax administration is expected to be able to executed tidier, more controlable and easier to be understood by the members of the Tax Payers community.

On the basis of those three principles of tax collection, the Tax Payer shall be obligated to calculate the amount of tax actually indebted in compliance with the legislative regulations on taxes, so that the assessment of the amount of the indebted tax will be with the Tax Payer himself.
In addition, the Tax Payer shall also be obligated to regularly report the tax indebted and already paid as provided in the legislative regulations on taxes.

By this system expectedly the execution of the complicated and bureaucratic tax administration can be mininated.
The characteristic and motive of said tax collection system is very different from the former one inheritted from the colonial era, inter alia.

a. the responsibility for the tax collection is fully with the authority as reflected in the tax assessment system totally becoming the competence of the tax administration.

b. the execution of the tax obligation, in many cases very much depends on the execution of the tax administration conducted by the tax apparatus causing the members of the Tax Payers community obtain less promotion and guidance to the tax obligation and less participation in bearing the state's burden in maintaining the national development.

It is obvious that the tax collection system stipulated by this Law gives more trust to the members of the Tax Payers community to execute their tax obligation.

In addition, the legal security and certainty on the tax rights and obligations of the Tax Payer obtain more attention, therefore able to encourage the awareness improvement of and responsibility for tax of the community.
The tax administration task is no more like that in the past when the tax administration tried to settle/assess the Tax Return to determine the amount of the indebted tax and the actual amount to be paid but according to this Law it actively plays role in executing the tax collection administration control covering the tasks such as promotion, study, supervision and application of administrative sanction. The tax Payers community promotion can be conducted via various efforts, inter alia providing extention on the tax knowledge both via mass media and direct information to the community.

4. By the principle as aforementioned, as on overall and whole description , as well as pursuant to the message written and implied in the Outline of State Policy, there will be a renewal in the system and Legislation of taxes in Indonesia, manifested

Air the Law re General Provisions and Procedure on Taxes. Said amendment is expected to be able to fully support the growth rate. and accelerate the materialization of the equitable income distribution of the community, improvement and expansion of tax obligation awareness, equity and expansion of taxable object and increase of state revenue in line with the national development growth rate so as to accelerate the materialization of the wish of the August 17, 1945 Proclamation.

II. ARTICLE BY ARTICLE

Article 1.

This article contains the formulation of the definition of tax terminology used in this law.
By the existence of said definition it is possible to prevent the misunderstanding or misinterpretation in executing the relative articles so as to enable to smoothen and make easy the Tax Payer and the apparatus in executing their obligation and eventually achieve the administrative orderliness in tax.
These definitions are essential as they contain the technical and standard particularly in tax.

Article 2.

Any Tax Payer on the basis of the self assessment system shall register himself at the Directorate General of Taxes to be recorded as Tax Payer and at the sametime given the Tax Payer Registration Number (NPWP). Said Tax Payer Registration Number will constitute a means for the tax administration used as the identity of the Tax Payer. By obtaining the Tax Payer Registration Number, it means that the Tax Payer has been registered at the Directorate General of Taxes.

The function of said Tax Payer Registration Number in addition to know the identity of the actual Tax Payer is also for maintaining order in the tax payment and controlling the tax administration. Any Tax Payer in any case related to the tax document shall be obligated to state/include his Tax Payer Registration Number. Any Tax Payer not registering to obtain the Tax Payer Registration Number (NPWP) shall be sanctioned.

Article 3.

Paragraph (1)

The function of the Tax Return (hereinafter called the SPT) is the means of the Tax Payer to Report and account the actually indebted tax calculation and the report on the fulfillment of the tax payment which is self conducted in a fiscal year or part of Fiscal Year and payment report from the deductor or collector concerning the tax deduction/collection of other person or Bodies in a Tax Period determined by the legislative regulations on taxes.

Every Tax Payer shall be obligated to obtain on his own the SPT already provided by the Directorate General of Taxes, fill, calculate and compute the indebted tax for a Tax Period in the SPT, and submit the already completed and signed SPT to the Directorate General of Taxes within the given time.

By filling the SPT we mean to complete the SPT form correctly, clearly, completely pursuant to the directives provided for calculating the indebted tax on the basis of the legislative Regulations on taxes . The incorrect SPT completion inflicting loss to the state shall be sanctioned on the basis of Articles 38 and 39 herein. Likewise, the delay or failure to submit the SPT shall be sanctioned by an administrative fine.

Paragraph (2)

In the framework of the service and facility to the Tax Payer the SPT form will be provided at the offices within the Directorate General of Taxes, Post & Giro Offices, Auxiliary Post Offices and other places determined by the Directorate General of Taxes and considered reachable by the Tax Payer..

Paragraph (3)

This paragraph regulates the time limit for submitting the SPT, the SPT can be grouped into two, namely Periodical SPT to report the Periodical payment conducted by the Tax Payer, and Annual SPT to inform the amount of the indebted tax of the income obtained by the Tax Payer in one fiscal Year. The time limit as referred to in Article 3 paragraph (3) Letters a and b shall be the final time limit. Said time limit is considered sufficient for the Tax Payer to prepare anything related to the tax payment as well as the accounting settlement.

Paragraph (4)

If the Tax Payer both a person and a Body is found unable to settle/prepare the annual financial statement or balance sheet of the company as well as the profit/loss statement within three months and due to the extensiveness of the operation and technical aspect of preparing the balance sheet or financial statement he finds it dificult to meet the time, limit for settlement and requires the prolongation of time, the Tax Payer shall be entitled to apply for the extension of Income Tax Annual SPT submission.

Paragraph (5)

To prevent self evasion and/or extension of the indebted tax payment in a fiscal year to be full paid prior to the expiry of the Annual SPT submission, it is necessary to stipulate special Requirements and administrative sanction in the form of the interest collection for the Tax Payer desiring to extend the Income Tax Annual SPT submission.

Said special requirements constitute the obligation to submit a written statement on the amount of tax to be paid on the basis of the provisional calculation in a Fiscal Year, as the attachment to the Aplication for postponenment of obligatory submission of the Income Tax Annual SPT.

Paragraph (6)

As the SPT constitutes a means to verify the correctness of the indebted tax calculation informed by the Tax Payer, said attachment shall be a part of the SPT and an absolute condition to be fulfilled by the Tax Payer.

Article 4.

Paragraph (1)

Self explanatory

Paragraph (2)

Self explanatory

Paragraph (3)

Self explanatory

Paragraph (4)

Self explanatory

Article 5.

Self explanatory

Article 6.,

Paragraph (1)

Self explanatory

Paragraph (2)

Self explanatory

Article 7.

For the purpose of the tax administration orderliness and maintaining the discipline of the Tax Payer, to the Tax Payer not observing the formal obligation of the SPT submission complying with the given time limit, shall be sanctioned with the administrative fine amounting to Rp. 10,000.00 (ten thousand rupiahs).

Article 8.

Paragraph (1)

To the error in filling in the SPT conducted by the Tax Payer there will still be oportunity for him to self correct it, provided that the Director General of Taxes has not known the existence of incorrectness in the SPT already submitted or has not assigned any of his officials to audit.

Paragraph (2)

By the existence of said SPT self correction it makes the calculation of the indebted tax and tax payment calculation different from the initial amount to the deficiency due to said correction shall be imposed with administrative sanction in the form of 2% (two percent) interest per month.

The interest indebted on the tax payment deficiency shall be calculated as from the expiry of the SPT submission to the date of payment due to said SPT correction. If there is any tax payment excess in said correction, the Tax Payer can apply for the reimbursement of the tax payment excess as referred to in Article 11 of this Law.

Paragraph (3)

Any Tax Payer violating as referred to in Article 39 herein, as long as not investigated by the tax officers, thought already audited and the Tax Payer has revealed his fault and simultaneous ly settle the actually indebted tax as well as the administrative fine of twice of the deficiency of tax, to him theres shall be no investigation. However, if the investigation is conducted and the commencement thereof is notified to the Public Prosecutor, the opportunity for the Tax Payer to make correction is closed.

Article 9.

Paragraph (1)

The time limit of the Periodical Payment shall be stipulated by the Minister of Finance in no more than fifteen days after the indebted time or expiry of the Tax Period. Any delay on said periodical payment shall be subject to administrative sanction in the form of interest of 2% (two percent) per month.

Paragraph (2)

As referred to in Article 3 paragraph (3) Letter b, the Tax Payer shall be obligated to submit the annual SPT within three months after the expiry of the Fiscal Year. If on completing said SPT it is found that there is still a deficiency of the indebted tax payment available, said tax payment deficiency shall be settled prior to the submission of the Annual SPT, for instance the SPT should be submitted on March 31, the indebted tax payment deficiency or the final deposit shall have been settled prior to the submission of SPT.

Paragraph (3)

Self explanatory

Paragraph (4)

The Director General of Taxes can permit the postponement of the indebted tax payment, though the due date of the payment has been determined. Said facility shall be carefully granted and limited to the Tax Payer who undergoes the problem of liquidity. To gain said facility, the Tax Payer shall be conditioned to appy in writing together with the accountable and convincing reasons.

Article 10.

Paragraph (1)

The Directorate General of Taxes shall not receive any deposit from a Tax Payer. Any deposit of the state taxes shall be to the State Treasury office or other places designated by the Minister of Finance such as so far stipulated, namely Post and Giro Office and some State–owned Banks. The expansion of the Places of the tax payment reachable by the Tax Payer is intended to facilitate the Tax Payer to fulfill his obligation, simultaneously to avoid the reluctance in paying the tax.

Paragraph (2)

By the existence of the procedure for paying tax, depositing tax and reporting to be stipulated by the Regulation of the Minister of Finance, likewise, that for installing and postposing the tax payment, expectedly it will facilitate the tax payment and administrative accomodation.

Article 11.

Paragraph (1)

If After the calculation of the actual indebted tax with the already paid tax it indicates the excess (the tax already paid is bigger than the indebted one in amount), the Tax Payer shall be entitled for the reimbursement of the tax payment excess, provided that said Tax Payer has no other tax liabilities. In case the Tax Payer still has the other tax liabilities which are not yet settled, said payment excess shall first be calculated with said tax liabilities and if there is still an excess, it will be reimbursed to the Tax Payer. To obtain said payment excess, the Tax Payer shall apply in writing to the Director General of Taxes or other designated officials.

Paragraph (2)

To guarantee the existence of the legal certainty for the Tax Payer and secure the administrative orderliness the time limit for the reimbursement of the Director General of Taxes shall be within one month after the Tax Payment Excess Decree has been stipulated by the Director General fo Taxes.

Paragraph (3)

To create the balance of right and obligation for the Tax Payer

with the service quickness by the Directorate General of Taxes, this paragraph stipulates that on any delay of tax payment excess, reimbursement from the time limit as referred to in paragraph (2), to the relative Tax Payer shall be granted the remuneration by the Government in the from of interest of 2% (two percent) permonth, calculated as from the coming into force of the one month's time limit to the payment.
By the payment time of the tax payment excess we mean the issuance of the Tax Payment Excess Reimbursement Order (SPMKP).

Paragraph (4)

Self explanatory.

Article. 12.

Principally the tax is indebted on the occurrence of the taxable tax object. The time of said indebted tax shall be :

a. At a certain pont of time, for the Income Tax deducted by a third party.;

b. at the expiry of Period, for the employee's Income Tax deducted by the employer, or other parties on the business activity or by an Entrepreneur on the collection of Value Added Tax on Goods and Services and Sales Tax on Luxury Goods;

c. At the end of the Fiscal Year for the Income Tax.

The amount of the indebted tax already deducted, collected or to be paid by the Tax Payer himself after reaching the time or period of settlement as referred to in Article 9 and Article 10 paragraph (2), shall be deposited by the Tax Payer to the state Treasury office or the designated places.

Article 13.

Paragraph (1)

The provision of paragraph (5) gives competence to the Director General of Taxes to issue the Tax Assessment Letter essentially only to certain cases as referred to in this paragraph, or strictly only to certain tax Payers wno are obviously or on the basis of the verification and auditing do not meet their formal and material obligations.

The competence given by the legislative regulations on taxes to the Director General of Taxes to correct said fiscal is limited to only a five years' period. According to the provisions in paragraph (1) letter a, the Tax Assessment Letter is issued if the Tax Payer does not pay the tax properly as provided in the legislative regulations on taxes. The knowledge indicating that the Tax Payer does not adequately pay the tax is from the auditing to the relative Tax Payer and the result thereof indicates that the Tax Payer does not Sufficiently pay the actually indebted amount. The auditing can be conducted at the place of the Tax Payer in the nature of complete auditing or via the tax administration verification.

The Tax Assessment letter can also be issued in the case that the Director General of Taxes possesses the date other than that submitted by the Tax Payer himself, from which can be known (not assumed) that the Tax Payer does not meet his tax obligation properly. To ensure the correctness of the data, auditing to the Tax Payer shall be conducted.

The SPT not submitted in time, though already warned in writing it is not submitted within the given time, based on the provision in paragraph (1) letter b it can make the Director General of Taxes issues the Tax Assessment Letter functionally. To such a case administrative sanction in the form of increase as referred to in paragraph (3) will be given.

The warning is, inter alia, intended to give opportunity to the Tax Payer having the good will to submit the reasons why he fails to submit his SPT if it is due to force mayeur.

If the SPT is submitted within the time stated in the Warning Letter and the indebted tax is properly settled, the Tax Assessment Letter shall not be issued under the assumption that said SPT has been correctly completed complying with the legislative regulations on taxes.

To the Tax Payer deliberately violating the Tax obligation concerning the Value added tax on Goods and Services and Sales Tax on Luxury Goods such as compensation of the tax payment excess, the tariff of 0% (zero percent) which should not be it, reimbursement of tax payment which should not occur as referred to in paragraph (1) letter c, shall be administratively sanctioned by issuing the Tax Assessment Letter plus the increase of 100% (one hundred percent).

For the Tax Payer not making his accounting according to the provision under Article 28 of this law or on auditing not giving what is reguired as stipulated under article 29 paragraph (2) so that the Director General of Taxes does not know the actual condition of the Tax Payer's business and fails to calculate the amount of the actually indebted tax, the Director General of Taxes shall be competent to issue the Tax Assessment Letter functionally, namely the tax calculation not only based on the data obtained by the Tax Payer. Consequently the burden of evidence of the calculation bread down becoming the basis of calculation functionally by the Director General of Taxes shall be the responsibility of the Tax Payer, inter alia such as :

1) the accounting as referred to in Article 28 paragraph (4) is not complete so the profit/loss statement or circulation is not clear;
2) the accounting documents are not complete so that the figures therein can not be tested ;
3) from the verification and facts known it is highly suspected that there are documents or other proofs hidden in a certain place so that it obviously indicates the ill will of the Tax Payer not to make the auditing smooth.

Paragraph (2) :

This paragraph regulates the administrative sanction of tax imposed to the Tax Payer due to violating the tax obligation as referred to in paragraph (1) letter a the tax administrative sanction in this paragraph is the interest manifested in the Tax Assessment Letter.

Example

An Income Tax Payer having the same book year with the calender year submits the Annual SPT in time completed with the final deposit. In April 1987 is issued a Tax Assessment Letter indicating the indebted tax deficiency of Rp. 1,000,000.00 On the basis of this paragraph the deficiency will be imposed with 2% (two percent) interest per month. Though the Tax Assessment is issued two years after the expiry of the Fiscal, the interest imposed shall only be for two years with the calculation as follows:

– Deficiency of indebted tax	Rp. 1,000,000.00
– 2 years interest = 2%, x 2, x 12 x Rp. 1,000,000.00	Rp. 480,000,00
Amount to be paid	Rp. 1,480,000.00

If said Tax Assessment Letter is issued in May 1986 the calculation shall be as follows :

– Deficiency of indebted tax	Rp. 1,000,000.00
– 17 months interest= 2% x 17 Rp. 1,000,000.00	Rp. 340,000.00
Amount to be paid	Rp. 1,340,000.00

Paragraph (3)

This paragraph regulates the administrative sanction of a Tax Assessment due to violating the tax obligation as referred to in paragraph (1) letter b, c dan d.
Such administrative sanction is an the form of in "increase", a proportional amount to be added to the tax to be collected.

The amount thereof constitutes different increase by the kind of tax, namely, for Income Tax paid by the Tax Payer himself will be the increase of 50% (fifty percent), for the Income Tax deducted by other person/body is the increase of 100% (one hundred percent), whereas for the Value Added tax on Goods and Services and Sales Tax on Luxury goods will be the increase of 100% (one hundred percent).

Paragraph (4)

By the "credited" tax we mean the amount of deduction consisting of :

1. the tax deducted by a third party
2. the tax collected by a third party
3. the tax paid on his own
4. the tax collected in the Tax Collection Letter (SPT)
5. the tax indebted abroad.

Said deduction will be substracted from the indebted tax.

Example :

Income Tax Assessment Letter (SKPPPH).

1. The indebted tax		Rp. 1,000,000.00
2. Deductions		
a. Tax deducted by employer	Rp 150,000.00	
b. Tax paid on his own (periodical deposit)	Rp. 400,000,00.	
c. Tax collected in STP excluding interest and fine)	Rp. 75,000.00	
d. Tax collected abroad	Rp. 100,000.00	
The amount of the credited tax		Rp. 725,000.00
3. The tax still to be collected		Rp. 275,000.00

Paragraph (5)

The Administrative sanction in the form of interest, administrative fine and increase can not be calculated or credited to the amount of the indebted tax. So in the calculation or reimbursement of the tax payment excess, the amount of the already paid tax administrative sanction shall first be credited from the payment excess to be received by the Tax Payer.

Paragraph (6)

To give legal certainty and security for the Tax Payer in relation to the tax collection by the self assessment system, if within five year since the indebted tax period, the expiry of a Tax Period, Part of Fiscal Year or Expiry of Fiscal Year the Directorate General of Taxes has not issued any tax Assessment Letter, the amount of the tax payment in the Periodical or Annual SPT is essentially fixed or certain due to the legal aspect of the legislative regulations on taxes. This, the relative Tax Payer's SPT has become the fixed assessment and shall not be changed (settled).

Paragraph (7).

If the Tax Payer is sanctioned due to commiting criminal act in tax of which the collection has been overdue, on the basis of the court verdict having obtained the permanent legal enforcement the Tax Assessment Letter can still be justified to be issued

though the five years' period as referred to in paragraph (1) has been passed.
By the existence of Court verdict having obtained said permanent legal enforcement, it will reveal the fiscal data so far deliberately not reported by the Tax Payer.

Article 14.

Paragraph (1)

Self explanatory

Paragrapht (2)

The Tax Collection Letter according to this paragraph has similar legal force with the Tax Assessment Letter, so that in the collection the coercion Letter can also apply.

Article 15.

Paragraph (1)

To accomodate the possibility of the issuance of a Tax Assessment Letter found already stipulated lower or having the improper tax reimbursement, or on the assessment in the form of Tax Payment Excess Decree, or the issuance of the Notification Letter, this Law Still gives competence to the Director General of Taxes to issue the Additional Tax Assessment within five years after the indebted tax period, expiry of Tax Period, Part of Fiscal year or Fiscal Year.

The Additional Tax Assessment Letter constitutes the correction of the former Tax Assessment Letter. The new Additional Tax Assessment Letter will be issued if there has been a Tax Assessment letter before. In other words the Additional Tax Assessment Letter is impossible to be issued prior to the Tax Assessmen Letter issuance.
This paragraph only conditions the availability of new data (novum) in the issuance of the Additional Tax Assessment Letter. If there is still unrevealed data found on the issuance of the Additional Tax Assessment Letter or if it is just known, the Director General of Taxes can still issue another Additional Tax Assessment Letter.

Paragraph (2)

Self explanatory

Paragraph (3)

Self explanatory

Paragraph (4)

In case the Tax Payer is sanctioned due to committing the crime in tax concerning that the collection of which has been overdue on the basis of the court verdict having obtained the permanent legal enforcement, the Additional Tax Assessment Letter is stil justifield to be issued, though the period of five years as stipulated under Article 13 paragraph (1) has been passed. By the court verdict having obtained the permanent legal force, the fiscal data so far deliberately not reported by the Tax Payer will be revealed.

Article 16.

If there is any miswriting, miscalculation or error in the tax assessment letter such as mistyping, misaddition, tariff misapplication, the Director General of Taxes can functionally or on the request of the Tax Payer correct said Tax Assessment Letter/ Additional Tax Assessment Letter. The definition to correct in this paragraph can be to add or reduce or delete depending on the mistake or error thereof.

Article 17.

Paragraph (1) Letter a.

The Payment Excess Decree (SKKP) can be issued after the Director General of Taxation verify or audit to ensure and assure that there is a payment excess on the indebted tax.
Said Tax Payment Excess Decree shall be issued within no more than twelve months after the receipt of application.
By said time limit, in addition to taking into account the in terest of legal certainty for the Tax Payer, it is also intended to the tax administrative purpose.

Paragraph (1) Letter b.

The Notification can be issued after the Director General of Taxes has verified and audited to ensure and assure that the amount of tax paid by the Tax Payer has been collected/deducted by the third party at the amount equal to the indebted tax.

Paragraph (2)

Self explanatory

Article 18.

Paragraph (1)

Principally the amount of the tax debt is self calculated by the Tax Payer. If it is then found that there is an error or mistake of the Tax Payer in calculating the indebted tax or the Tax Payer Violates the provisions regulated in the legislative regulations on taxes, the Director General of Taxes can issue the Tax Collection Letter, Tax Assessment Letter or Additional Tax Assessment Letter. The three letters constitute the administrative means for the Director General of Taxes to collect the tax. If the tax collection is not paid on the due date, it will be conducted by a Coercion Letter.

Paragraph (2)

For the Orderliness and uniformity of the tax collection the Minister of Finance shall regulate the procedure thereof including the administrative aspect concerning both the collection and payment of tax.

Article 19.

Paragraph (1)

This paragraph regulates the interest imposition on tax which is not or not sufficiently paid on the due date or paid late.
To make it clear, the example on the interest calculation is giving hereunder :

1. On the less paid tax.
   Income Tax Assessment Letter (SKPPPH)
   Indebted or collected tax (considered no credited tax) :
   Rp. 100,000.00
   The SKP is issued on October 10, 1985.

To be settled no later than November 10, 1985, but just paid at Rp. 60,000.00 on November 1, 1985.
Up to the due date (November 10, 1985) the collection balance is not paid anymore by the Tax Payer.
On November 18, 1985 is issued the Tax Collection Letter by the following calculation :

Indebted tax	Rp. 100,000.00
Paid in time	Rp. 60,000.00
Deficiency of payment	Rp. 40,000.00

Interest

Calculated for a month of 1 x 2% x Rp. 40,000.00 = Rp. 800.00
Said interest is collected by STP.

2. On the amount of tax paid late.
   The basis is as that in number 1. Fully paid but late, for instance on November 20, 1985. On November 24, 1985 STP is issued. The indebted interest in the Tax collection Letter is calculated for a month = 1x2%xRp. 100,000.00 = Rp. 2,000.00

3. On the amount of tax paid less and late.
   The basis is as that in number 1. Paid at Rp. 60,000.00 on November 20, 1985.
   On November 24, 1985 STP is issued.
   The indebted interest is calculated for 1 month = 1 x 2% x Rp. 100 000.00 = Rp. 2,000.00

Paragraph (2)

Self explanatory

Paragraph (3)

Self explanatory

Article 20

In the case of a condition as referred to in this Article, to take precaution of something making the indebted tax uncollectable, without waiting the payment due date in the Tax Collection Letter, Tax Assessment Letter or Additional Tax or Additional

Tax Assessment Letter, the collection thereof can be conducted at once and simultaneously.

Article 21.

Paragraph (1)

This paragraph regulates the position of the state as the preferential creditor stating to have the previlege on the properties belonging to the Tax Payer and those to his representative to be auctioned publicly as referred to in Article 32 paragraph (2). If the collection and active collection have been conducted, then the public auction of the Tax Payer's properties, but the proceeds has not been sufficient to settle his tax liability, Then those belonging to his representative as long as the is responsible therefor in his position, will be is responsible therefor in his position, will be confiscated and publicly auctioned to settle the tax liability of the Tax Payer.

After settling the tax liability then the payment to the other creditors is conducted. This paragraph intends to give the state to obtain the share from the public auction proceed of the properties belonging to the Tax Payer or his representative to cover or settle his tax arrears.

Paragraph (2)

Self explanatory

Paragraph (3)

This paragraph clarifies that the previlege is beyond any other rights, which means stronger than others except to the parties as referred to in :

1. Article 1139 number 1 of Civil Code reading: "the law suit change merely due to a sentence to auction a movable or immovable goods," from which the proceeds thereof shall be the first of any other liabilities given previlege even mortgage and pledge.
2. Article 1139 number 4 of Civil code reading: "cost already incurred to save the property."
3. Article 1149 number 1 of Civil Code reading: "Law suit charge merely due to auction and settlement of a heritage shall be

given priorty even of pledge ana mortgage.

4. Article 80 and 81 of Commercial Code concerning collection right of a commissioner.

Paragraph (4)

Self explanatory

Paragraph (5)

Self explanatory

Article 22.

Principally the tax collection will be expired after five years, but it can exceed that if :

1. Warning Letter and Coercion Letter have been issued;
2. direct or inderect admittance of the Tax Payer, inter alia :
   a. payment of the tax liability ;
   b. application for payment postponement; or
   c. payment installment.

In such a case the expiry of the tax receivable collection shall be calculated as from the aformentioned occurrence.

Article 23.

Self explanatory.

Article 24.

The minister of Finance shall regulate the procedure and stipulate the amount of the uncollectable tax receivable account. In this may it is possible to effectively estimate the tax receivable balance which is collectable and liquidatable.

Article 25.

Paragraph (1)

The word "a" in this paragraph means that one objection shall be proposed for one kind of tax and one fiscal year, for example: the Income Tax of 1985 and 1986 Fiscal Years. The objection to the Income Tax Notification Letter of 1985 and 1986 shall respectively be proposed in different Objection Letters. For said two fiscal years shall be proposed two Objection Letters.

Paragraph (2)

Self explanatory

Paragraph (3)

The time limit for proposing the Objection Letter is determined for three months as from the issuance of the Tax Assessment letter or SKP as provided under paragraph (1), with the intention that the Tax Payer will have a sufficient time to prepare his Objection Letter and the Reasons thereof. If it is found that said three months' time limit can not be fulfilled by the Tax Payer, due to force mayeur, said three months' grace period can still be considered to be extended by the Director General of Taxes.

Paragraph (4)

The Evidence/Receipt of the Objection Letter is extremely necessary to meet the formal requirements, Whether or not the Objection Letter is accepted depends on the fulfilment of the time limit as referred to in paragraph (3) calculated as from the issuance thereof to the acceptance of said Objection Letter.
Said evidence or receipt can be used as a means to control by the Tax Payer to Know the expiry of the twelve months' period as referred to in Article 26 paragraph (1).
The evidence or receipt is required to ensure that his objection is granted, if within said period the Tax Payer does not accept any reply from the Director General of Taxes on the proposed objection. This is the meaning of the word "interest" in this paragraph.

Paragraph (5).

In order that the Tax Payer can prepare the objection with the strong reasons, the Tax Payer shall be entitled to ask for the basis of imposition, deduction or collection of the assessed tax, on the other hand the Director General of Taxes shall be obligation to meet said request.

Paragraph (6)

To prevent the evasion or postponement of tax via the proposal of obligation Tax, the proposal shall not prevent the collection. This provision should be included so that the Tax Payer with his objection still pays the assessed tax to avoid the loss of the State Revenue.

Article 26.

Paragraph (1)

For the Objection Letter proposed by the Tax Payer the settlement competence at the first instance is given to the Director General of Taxes provided that the settlement on the objection of the Tax Payer is stipulated in no more than twelwe months after the receipt date of the Objection Letter. In this may, legal certainty for the Tax Payer can be obtained in addition to the tax administration.

Paragraph (2)

Self explanatory

Paragraph (3)

Self explanatory

Paragraph (4)

This paragraph obligates the Tax Payer to prove the incorrectnes of the tax assessment if the Tax Payer proposes his objection to the taxes assessed functionally. Said Tax Notification Letter issued functionally is issued as the Tax Payer does not submit the Annual Tax Return though having been given written warning, or does not met the obligation to make accounting or refuse the auditor to enter curtained places considered necessary in the framework of assessing the indebted tax. If the Tax Payer can not prove the incorrectness of the Tax Assessment Letter functionlly assessed, the objection letter will be refused.

Paragraph (5)

Self explanatory

Article 27.

Paragraph (1).

If the Tax Payer is not satisfied the decree of the Director General of Taxes on the proposed objection, the Tax Payer is given opportunity to appeal to the Tax Justice Body in this case as that is currently known as the Tax Appeal Council within three months as From the date of said objection decision so the Tax Payer has been given sufficient fine to prepare the Appeal Letter and the reasons and evidences required by said tax justice body.

Paragraph (2) : See elucidation on Article 25 paragraph (20)
Paragraph (3) : See elucidation on Article 25 paragraph (6).

Article 28.

Paragraph (1)

Self explanatory

Paragraph (2)

Principally every person/Body conducting business or free employment shall make and accounting. However, the Tax Payer due to his insufficient capabiltity may be exempted from the obligation to make an accounting.
By "exempted" from the accounting making in this paragraph we do not mean that the Tax Payer shall not improve his capability to make an accounting completely and well so that he has not accounting at all to run his business.
As long as said capability his not been possessed the Tax Payer he is justified to only make records consitituting a simple accounting system containing the principal data usable to calculate the indebted tax for the relative Tax Payer.

Paragraph (3)

Self explanatory

Paragraph (4)

Self explanatory

Paragraph (5)

Self expalanatory

Paragraph (6)

The accounting and documents related to the business operation or the company shall be kept for ten years, so than within said period if the Director General of Taxes will issue a Tax Assessment, the accounting data required is still available.
The ten years, period for keeping the accounting and documents becoming the basis of the accounting shall be consestant to the

provisions under Article 40 of this law concerning the fall of tax criminal prosecution.

Article 29.

Paragraph (1)

The Director General of Taxes in the framework of the tax collection is competent to audit to assess the indebted tax and other purpose to execute the legislative regulations on taxes the intention of auditing is mainly to obtain/collect materials to be the basis for :

a. issuing the Tax Assessment;
b. issuing the Notification letter ;
c. issuing the Tax Payment Excess decree;
d. others related to the tax administration.

The definition of "other purposes" in this paragraph means the auditing to the following :

a. Preparing the Calculation Norm;
b. matching the data and informativ means ;
c. assessing the amount of tax payment in a Tax Period for a new Tax Payer ;
d. others related to the execution of the legislative regulations on taxes.

Paragraph (2)

Self explanatory

Paragraph (3)

As the accounting, records, documents related to the business operation and other required information play very important role in assessing the indebted tax, if required by the auditor, the Tax Payer shall show or lend them.
If the accounting, records and documents which are required can not be given by the Tax Payer only to avoid it, on the basis of this paragraph the auditor is deloved to enter the places or rooms guessed to be the places to keep them.

Paragraph (4)

To provent the reason binding to the confidentiality, so that the accounting, records, documents and other required information can not be given by the Tax Payer, his paragraph clarifies that the confidentiality can be eliminated.

Article 30.

To any person or body on the auditing unwilling to given opportunity to the auditor to enter certain places/rooms guessed to be the place to keep them so that they can not be obtained the Tax Payer will be considered hindering the tax collection.
In such a case, the Director General of Taxes is competent to seal certain places or rooms considered to be the place to keep there or to prevent the lost of them.

Article 31.

For the interest of uniformity, orderliness, and unification of auditing, it is necessary to regulate the provisions and procedure thereof by a Government Regulation.

Article 32.

Paragraph (1)
This law determines who becomes the representative to execute the tax right and obligation of the Tax Payer against a Body, a Body in liquidation, undivided heritage and a child who has not been adults or a person under guardian, for said Tax Payer it is necessary to determine who will be his representative proxy to commit legal action, execute the tax right and obligation as they are unable or impossible to commit said legal action on their own.

Paragraph (2)

The exception as referred to in this paragraph shall be with the evidence that in his position as the representative according to the reasonableness and feasibility it is imposible to ask for his responsibility personally and/or successively.

Paragraph (3)

This paragraph gives relief and opportunity to the Tax Payer to request for assisstance from anyone understanding this tax subject matter as his proxy to and on his behalf to execute his tax right and obligation said assistance shall cover the formal and material obligation as well as the fulfilment of the right of the Tax Payer stipulated in the legislative regulations on Taxes.

Article 33.

The tax burden principle for the Value Added Tax on Goods and Services and Sales Tax on Luxury Goods shall be given to the buyer or consumer of goods or Services Recipient, it should therefore be the buyer or consumer of goods or services recipient who is Desponsible successively for the payment of the indebted tax if it is found that said indebted tax is not paid.

Article 34.

Paragraph (1)
Every officer both tax officer or that having the tasks in tax shall be prohibited to reveal the secret of the Tax Payer concerning tax. The secret shall be protected so privent misusage in the business competition or divulge the origin of the property or income gained essentially becoming the personal secret complying with the tax legal principle.

Paragraph (2)
The exports, such as linguists, accountants, attorneys etcetera designated by the Director General of Taxes to assist in the implementation of the Legislative regulation on taxes are essentiatlly the same with the tax officers prohibited to reveal the secret of the Tax Payer as referred to in paragraph (1).

Paragraph (3)

To safeguard the state finance conducted by the auditor assigned therefor from the Finance Auditing Board, Finance and Development Control Board, the Minister of Finance can give permission to said Boards to see the evidences as referred to in paragraphs (1) and (2) in the framework of auditing and controlling the state finance related to tax.

Paragraph (4)
To execute the trial of the criminal law suit related to tax, for the interest of justice, the Minister of Finance can grant the exemption from the confidentiality obligation to the tax officer including that assigned in the tax justice body or Tax Appeal Council and the exports as referred to in paragraphs (1) and (2) on the written request of the Court chirman of the Board of judges.

Paragraph (5)

This paragraph definess and clarifies that said required tax information only concernis the criminal law suit on the act or event inolving the tax and only limited to the relative defendant

Article 35.

Paragraph (1)

To execute the legislative provisions on taxes, the third parties having relation to the audited Tax Payer such as the Tax Consultant, public Accountant, Notary and other persons related to the act or business activity of the Tax Payer shall give the imformation and evidences required by the Directorate General of Taxes in the Framework of auditing the relative Tax Payer. They are required to complete the tax information/data to calculate and Assess the actual amount of indebted tax of the audited Tax Payer. In additions, the provision in this paragraph is also intended to prevent the effort to conceal the information or evidences on tax in other' place.

Paragraph (2)

Self explanatory

Article 36.

Paragraph (1)

In practice it may occur that the administrative sanction imposed to the Tax Payer due to the carelessness of the tax officer can burden the innocent tax payer or that who does not understand the regulations on taxes. In such a case the administrative sanction in term of interest, fine and increase already assessed can be eliminated or reduced by the Director General of Taxes.

Likewise, the Director General of Taxes due to his function and on the basis of justice can reduce or annual/cancel the Tax Assessment which is incorrect, for instance the tax Payer whose objec--tion proposal is refised due to not meeting the formal requirements (not submitting the Objection Letter in time) though the material requirements are fulfilled.

Paragraph (2)

Self explanatory

Article 37.

In compliance with the financial economic condition, the value of money may change. The law therefore gives competence to the Government if required to issue a Government Regulation amending and adjusting the amount of the administrative sanction in the form of interest, administrative fine and increase complying with the financial economic condition.

Article 38.

Any violation to the tax obligation conducted by the Tax Payer as long as concerning the tax administrative act shall be administratively sanctioned, whereas that related to the criminal act in tax shall be sanctioned criminally. By the existance of said sanction, expertedly there will be awareness of the tax Payer to observe execute the tax obligation as provided in the Law on taxes.

Any negligance as referred to in this Article meant not deliberately., negligent, careless and paying no attention to his obligation, so that it inflicts loss to the state.

Article 39.

Paragraph (1)

Any conduct or act as referred to in this paragraph deliberately done does not constitute an administrative violation anymore but crime. Therefore it is sanctioned heavier than negligence which is only a violation in nature.

Paragraph (2)

To prevent the re occurrence of the criminal act in tax, for those committing it again prior to one year as from the settlement of part of or the total imprisonment shall be sanctioned heavier namely twice as much as that provided in paragraph (1).

Article 40.

The criminal act in tax shall be expired after ten years as from the relative indebted tax period, expiry of Tax period, Part of Fiscal Year and Fiscal year, It is intended to give a legal certainty to the Tax Payer, Public Prosecutor and Judge.

Said ten years' period is to adjust to the expiry of the tax document safe keeping becoming the basis for calculating the indebted tax for ten years.

Article 41.

Paragraph (1)

To guarantee that the tax confidentiality will not be informed to other parties, and in order that the Tax Payer does not hesitate in giving information and data, in the framework of the tax Law execution, there shall be a criminal sanction for the relative tax officer causing the Violation by revealing said secret. The Violation of confidentiality conducted by this paragraph, will be due to negligence, carelessnessess or not paying any attention so that the obligation to keep a condition, information or evidences with the Tax Payer confidential which is protected by law is violated. Said Violation may be subject to the proper sanction.

Paragraph (2)

The provisions regulated in this paragraph indicates the diliberateness causing the revelation of secret as referred to in Article 35. Therefore the sanction is heavier than that provided in paragraph (1). Said deliberateness leads to crime and the sanction shall therefore be properly given.

Paragraph (3)

The criminal prosecution to the secrecy violation at referred to in paragraphs (1) and (2) complying with the nature thereof shall involve the personal interest of a person or Body as a Tax Payer and therefore it will become a charge criminal act.

Article 42.

Paragraph (1)

Self explanatory

Paragraph (2)

Self explanatory

Article 43.

The criminal provisions in tax one not only intended to the Tax. Payer but also to another party designated as the representative, proxy or emloyed of the Tax Payer given responsibility or successive responsibility for implementing the tax obligation of the Tax Payer entrusted or authorized to him.

Article 44.

Paragraph (1)

The tax investigation is a chain of investigating actions to find out and collect the required evidence so as to clarify the criminal act occuring in tax and to find the suspect of criminal in tax, and to find the suspectand to know the amount of the indebted tax guessed embezzled. The investigator in tax is a certain civil servant within the Directorate General of Taxes appointed by the Minister of Justice in compliance with the prevailing legislative regulations.

The criminal act investigation in tax is conducted according to the provisions regulated in Law No. 8 Year 1981 re Criminal Code Procedure and the Implementing Regulations.

Paragraph (2)

Self explanatory

Paragraph (3)

Self explanatory

Article 45.

Though the previous laws on taxes have been revoked by the promulgation of this Law to accomodate the settlement of the indebted tax assessment in the tax period or Fiscal year prior to the effectiveness of this Law the implementation of which shall be based on the former legislative Regulations on taxes, this Law stipulates the effectiveness of them through December 31, 1988. The determination of said five years' period shall be adjusted to the expiry of the tax collection.

Article 46.

Self explanatory

Article 47.

The 1925 Tax Ordinance, and Tax on Interest, Devident and royalty 1970 as well as all implementing regulations thereof shall remain applicable to the taxable income received or gained in the oil and gas mining and other mining sector conducted in the framework of. Contract of Work and Production Sharing Contract, as long as the Contract of Work and Production Sharing contract are still valid on the coming into force of this law.

The provisions in this will be applicable to the taxable income received or gained in oil and gas mining conducted in the from of Contract of work and Production Sharing Contract if they are drawn up after the effectiveness of this Law.

Article 48.

To accomodate anything not yet sufficiently regulated concerning the procedure or the completeness of the material thereof which has been included in this Law shall further be stipulated by the Government Regulation. If will be casier to adjust the implementation of this Law and the required procedure.

Article 49.

Self explanatory

Article 50.

Self Explanatory.

SUPPLEMENT TO STATE GAZETTE OF THE REPUBLIC OF INDONESIA NO. 3262

Appendix 23

LAW OF THE REPUBLIC OF INDONESIA
NO.: 7 YEAR 1983
R E
INCOME TAX

BY THE GRACE OF GOD
THE PRESIDENT OF THE REPUBLIC OF INDONESIA,

Considering :
a. that the Republic of Indonesia is a legislative state on the basis of Pancasila and the 1945 Constitution highly appreciating the rights and obligations of the citizens, she therefore positions tax as one of the manifestations of the obligation of every citizen constituting the participation in financing the state and national development;

b. that the tax system constituting the basis of the state taxes collection implementation so far applicable, is not in accordance anymore with the socioeconomic living standard of the people of Indonesia, both in the aspect of the national principle of mutual aid and financing the development;

c. that the tax system manifested in the tax provisions applicable so far, has not yet been able to motivate the participation of all strata of the tax subjects in increasing the domestic revenues, which are urgently required for materializing the continuity and improvement of the national development in the framework of strengthening the national resilience;

d. that tax constitutes one of the sources of the State Revenues which should always be developed and increased in compliance with the development of the real capability of the community and the national development growth rate;

e. that the system and legislative regulations on taxes constituting the basis for the collection of the state taxes currently applicable should be renewed and adjusted to Pancasila and 1945 Constitution;

f. that it is therefore the system and legislative regulations on taxes in general, corporate tax, Income tax, tax on interest, dividend and royalty currently applicable in particular should be renewed and adjusted so as to give more legal, certainly, be simpler and easier to implement, as well as more just and equitable;

g. that to reach the aforementioned objectives, it is deemed necessary to prepare a Law on Income Tax.

In view of : 1. Article 5 paragraph (1), Article 20 paragraph (1) and Article 23 paragraph (2) of the 1945 Constitution;

2. Act of the People's Deliberative Assembly of the Republic of Indonesia No. II/MPR/1983 re Outline of State Policy of the Republic of Indonesia;

3. Law No. 6 Year 1983 Re General Provisions and Procedure on Taxes: (State Gazette Year 1983 No. 49 Supplement to State Gazette No. 3262).

with the approval of
THE PEOPLE'S HOUSE OF REPRESENTATIVES
OF THE REPUBLIC OF INDONESIA

HAS DECIDED:

By revoking : 1. Article 15 4th and 5th, and Article 16 of Law No. 1 Year 1967 re Foreign Investment (State Gazette Year 1967 No. 1, Supplement to State Gazette No. 2818) as already amended by Law No. 11 Year 1970 re Amendments on and Additions to Law No. 1 Year 1967 re Foreign Investment (State Gazette Year 1970 No. 46, Supplement to State Gazette No. 2943);

2. Article 9, Article 12 4th and 5th, Article 13, and Article 14 of Law No. 6 Year 1968 re Domestic Investment (State Gazette Year 1968 No. 33, Supplement to State Gazette No. 2853) as already amended by Law No. 12 Year 1970 re Amendments on and Additions to Law No. 6 Year 1968 re Domestic Investment (State Gazette Year 1968 No. 47, Supplement to State Gazette No. 2944).

To stipulate : LAW ON INCOME TAX.

CHAPTER I
GENERAL PROVISION

Article 1

Income Tax shall be imposed on any person on individual and body in respect to the income received or obtained in one fiscal year.

CHAPTER II
TAX SUBJECT

Article 2

(1) The tax subject shall be :

a. 1) any individual or person

2) undivided inheritance as a unit, replacing those entitled to it;

b. A Body/Entity comprising limited liability companies, limited partnerships, state owned undertaking bodies and Regional State owned Undertaking Bodies under any name and form whatsoever, associations, corporations or other associations, firms, partnerships, cooperatives, foundations or institutions and permanent undertaking forms.

(2) The tax subject shall comprise domestic and foreign tax subjects.

(3) The Domestic Tax Subject shall be :

a. anyone residing in Indonesia for more than 183 (one hundred and eighty three) days within a period of twelve months, cr anyone who within a fiscal year, resides in Indonesia and has the intention to stay in Indonesia.

b. Body/entity established or domiciled in Indonesia;

c. a permanent undertaking form shall constitute an undertaking form or agent those are used to operate business activities regularly in Indonesia, by a body or company those are not established in or domicile in Indonesia taking the form as branch office, Representative, agent, office building, factory, workshop, construction project, mining, natural resource exploration, fishery, expert, services giving in anyform by employee or other person, person or body with the unfree status that act on behalf body or enterprise that are not established in or domicile in Indonesia and insurance company that are not established in or domicile in Indonesia that receives insurance premium or bearing the task in Indonesia.

(4) The meaning of a foreign Tax Subject shall be a Tax Subject not residing, established nor domiciling in Indonesia able to receive or obtain income in Indonesia;

(5) A person or body/entity resides, domiciles in Indonesia shall be stipulated according to the actual condition;

(6) The Director General of Taxes shall be competent to stipulate whether a person or body/entity is staying, residing or domiciling.

Article 3

Excluded from the Tax Subjects as referred to in Article 2 shall be :

a. the officials of the Diplomatic Representation, Consulate other officials from foreign countries, and anyone assigned to assist those working for and residing together with them, provided that they are not of Indonesian nationality, and in Indonesia not performing any other works or activities, and the relative countries grant a reciprocal treatment;

b. the officials of representatives of the international organizations as stipulated by the Minister of Finance;

c. Government Agency Companies on the basis of a Decree of the Minister of Finance;

CHAPTER III

TAX OBJECT

Article 4

(1) The Tax Object shall be the income, namely, every economic benefit received or obtained by a Tax Payer, originating from Indonesia and abroad, which can be used for consumption or adding the wealth of the relative Tax Payer, under any name and in any form whatsoever, included therein :

a. salary, wage, commission, bonus or gratuity, pension or other remunerations for the work performed;

b. honorarium, lottery prize and reward;

c. undertaking gross profit;

d. profit due to sale or transfer of property, including profit obtained by a Limited Liability Company, association and any other body/entity due to the transfer of property to shareholders, partners, members as well as due to liquidation;

e. re-imbursement of tax payment already calculated as cost;

f. interest;

g. dividend under any name and in any form whatsoever, paid by a limited liability company, divided payment from an insurance company to a policy holder, and Distribution of Return of Undertaking Proceeds of a cooperative to the executives and members;

h. Royalty;

i. rent of property;

j. receipt or acquisition of perodical payment;

k. profit due to debt exemption;

(2) The tax imposition on the interest of the time deposit and other savings shall further be regulated by the Goverment Regulation.

(3) Excluded from the Tax Objects shall be :

a. granted property or aid having no relation to the undertaking/ operation or work of the relative party;

b. inheritance;

c. payment from an insurance company due to accident, sickness or the decease of an insured person and payment of scholarship insurance;

d. remuneration in respect to work or service, obtained in kind, provided that the party granting the remuneration is the Government or a Tax Payer according to this Law, and the Tax Payer granting said remuneration in compliance with the provision in Article 9 paragraph (1) letter d, shall not deduct said remuneration as a cost;

e. profit due to the transfer of property of an individual person, members of a firm, limited partnership or partnership, to limited liability company in the home country as a substitute of the shares thereof, provided that :

   1. the party transferring or the parties collectively transferring it shall own at least 90% (ninety percent) of the paid up capital.
   2. said transfer shall be notified to the Director General of Taxes.
   3. future tax imposition on said profit is guaranteed.

f. Assets received by a limited liability company, association or any other body/entity as substitute of shares or capital participation;

g. dividend received by a domestic limited liability company, other than banks and financial institutions, from another limited liability company in Indonesia, provided that the limited liability company receiving said dividend at least owns 25% (twenty five percent) of the paid up shares value of the body/entity paying the dividend, and both bodies/entities having an economic connection in their line of business;

h. constributions received or obtained by pension funds approved by the Minister of Finance, both paid by the employer and employee, and revenues of the similar pension funds from the capital invested in certain sectors, on the basis of a Decree of the Minister of finance;

i. profit of a foundation or association from operations exclusively intended for public interest;

j. profit of a foundation from the capital as long as intended to public interest;

k. distribution of profits of a limited partnership, of which the capital is not divided into shares, firm, partnership and association to its members, except if otherwise stipulated by the Minister of Finance, due to abuse.

Article 5

(1) Thé Tax Objects of a permanent undertaking form, shall be :

a. income from the operations of said permanent undertaking form and from property controlled or owned by it;

b. income of a parent company and other bodies/entities, not constituting a domestic tax payer having a special relationship with paid parent company, from the operations or sale of goods and/or rendering of services in Indonesia, of the same type with the operations or sale of goods and/or rendering of services conducted by a permanent undertaking in Indonesia, except the income as referred to in paragraph (2).

(2) If the parent company of a permanent undertaking form in Indonesia or another body/entity not constituting a domestic Tax Payer, having a special relationship with said parent company, receives or obtains income from Indonesia, on the basis of Article 26, then :

a. the calculation of the income of said permanent undertaking form shall not be deducted by the costs related to the income of said parent company or said body/entity, and

b. tax of the parent company or said other body/entity shall not be credited with the tax of the permanent undertaking form.

Article 6

(1) The amount of the taxable income shall be determined by the gross income deducted by :

a. the costs to obtain, collect and maintain said income, covering the costs for purchasing the material, wage and salary of employees, including bonus or gratuity, honorarium, interest, rent, royalty, travel expenses, uncollectable receivables, insurance premium, administration cost and tax, except income tax.

b. depreciation cost on expenditures to obtain the company's assets and amortization on expenditures to obtain the rights and/or other costs having the beneficial period of more than one year as referred to in Article 11.

c. constributions to pension funds approved by the Minister of Finance.

d. Lossess suffered due to the sale or transfer of goods and/or rights possessed and used in the company to obtain, collect and maintain said income;

e. balance of a cooperatives in relation to the operation from and for members;

(2) To an individual person as a domestic Tax Payer, a reduction shall be granted in the form of a non taxable income as referred to in Article 7 of this Law.

(3) If the gross income after the cost deduction as referred to in paragraph (1) shows a loss, then said loss can be compensated by the income in :

a. 5 (five) years, or

b. more than 5 (five) year but not exceeding 8 (eight) years expecially for certain types undertaking, on the basis of a Decree of the Minister of Finance,

as from the first year after suffering said loss.

Article 7

(1) To any individual person as a domestic Tax Payer a reduction shall be granted in the form of a non taxable income of :

a. Rp. 960,000.00 (nine hundred sixty thousand rupiahs) for the Tax Payer himself;

b. Rp. 480,000.00 (four hundred eighty thousand rupiahs) as an addition for a married Tax Payer;

c. Rp. 960,000.00 (nine hundred sixty thousand rupiahs) as an addition for a wife receiving income from her work not related to the husband's other family members;

d. Rp. 480,000.00 (four hundred eighty thousand rupiahs) as an addition for each person of bloodrelation family, and a parent in vertical line, as well as adopted children, constituting full dependants, for 3 (three) children at the most.

(2) The application of paragraph (1) shall be determined by the condition in the begining of the fiscal year, or when initially becoming a domestic Tax Subject.

(3) The amount of the non-taxable income as referred to in paragraph (1) above, shall be adjusted with the adjusting factor as stipulated by a Decree of the Minister of Finance.

Article 8

(1) The income or loss for a married woman at the begining of a fiscal year, likewise the loss originating from the previous years not yet compensated as referred to in Article 6 paragraph (3), shall be considered as the income or loss of her husband, except the income of a wife from a work after tax deduction, on the basis of Article 21 herein and that having no relation to the work of the husband or other family member.

(2) The income of a child not yet adult, not originating form the work and income from the work having relation to that of the other members of the family will be combined with the parents' income.

Article 9

To determine the amount of the taxable income, it shall not be deducted with :

a. payment of dividend or other distribution of profit of a company or another body/entity to the shareholders, associates or members under any name and in any form whatsoever, including the distribution of the operational proceeds balance of a cooperative not constituting the return of operational proceeds in relation to the services of the members, dividend paid by an insurance company to the policy holders and costs incurred for the interest of the shareholders, associates or member;

b. the establishment or accumulation of a reserve fund, except in matters as stipulated a Government Regulation;

c. premium of life insurance, health insurance, bifunctional insurance and scholarship insurance, except if paid by the employer, and such a premium is considered the income of the Tax Payer;

d. granting of convenience of leave trip, recreation and other conveniences intended for the interest of the employees of the Tax Payer, including the convenience, to use the company's motor vehicles, and housing, except housing in an isolated area, on the basis of a Decree of the Minister of Finance.

e. payment exceeding the reasonableness as a remuneration for work performed, paid to the shareholders, or parties having a special relationship;

f. granted property, aid and inheritance as referred to in Article 4 paragraph (2) letters a and b;

g. income tax;

h. cost incurred for the personal interest of the Tax Payer or persons constituting his dependants;

i. donations.

Article 10

(1) In the depreciation and amortization of assests and profit or loss calculation in the case of sales not influenced by a special relationship, the acquisition price thereof shall be the amount of the actual expenditure, whereas in case of transfer of property, the acquisition value shall be the amount which should be incurred, except :

a. in case of an exchange as referred to in Article 4 paragraph (3) letter e, the basis of evaluation of the share or other participation received by the party conducting said transfer, shall be equal to the value of the property transferred, according to the accounts of the transferring party.

b. in case of a property transfer as referred to in Article 4 paragraph (3) letter f, the basis of the transferred property evaluation shall be according to the accounts of the transferring party.

c. in case of the delivery of granted property, the tax free aid, and inheritance, the basis of evaluation used by the delivery recipient shall be equal to the evaluation basis for the delivery party.

(2) Property already utilized by the Tax Payer to receive or obtain income, the acquisition price thereof shall be adjusted to the depre-

ciation and/or amortization, addition, correction or revision conducted.

(3) A stock evaluation shall only be conducted on the basis of the acquisition price, on the basis of the stock utilization to calculate the basic price on the average or by giving priority to the stock firstly obtained.

Article 11

(1) The assets which can be depreciated shall be those tangible owned and used in a company or owned to obtain, collect and maintain the income, with a beneficial period of more than one year, except land.
The profit or loss due to transfer of depreciable properties/assets shall be calculated with the method as referred to in paragraph (7) letter b.

(2) The depreciation which can be conducted in one fiscal year shall be the amount of the depreciation of each category of assets as referred to in paragraph (3), and the depreciation for each category of assets shall be stipulated by multiplying the depreciation basis of the category as referred to in paragraph (4) at the depreciation tariff as referred to in paragraph (9).

(3) To calculate the depreciation, the depreciable properties/assets are divided into properties/assets categories as follows :

a. category 1 :
depreciable properties/assets and those not included into the category of buildings having a beneficial period of more than 4 (four) years;

b. category 2 :
depreciable properties/assets and those not included into the category of buildings having a beneficial period of more than 4 (four) years and less than 8 (eight) years.

c. category 3 :
depreciable properties/assets and those not included into the category of buildings a bineficial period of more than 8 (eight) years.

d. category of buildings :
any building or other fixed assets, including additions repairs or changes conducted.

(4) The Basis of depreciation of each category of property/assets in a fiscal year shall be equal to the initial amount in the fiscal year for the category of property/assets plus the additions, repairs or changes, and deducted with the reduction as referred to in paragraph (7).

(5) The initial amount of the respective categories 1, 2 and 3 for a fiscal year, shall be equal to the depreciation basis in the preceeding fiscal year, deducted with the allowable depreciation in the preceeding fiscal year.

(6) The initial amount of the category of buildings for one fiscal year, shall be equal to the depreciation basis in the preceeding fiscal year, namely at the public or value of acquisition.

(7) In case of a property/assets withdrawal from usage :

a. due to an extraordinary cause as a consequence of a disaster or discontinuation of the major part of operations, an amount equal to the book balance value shall be deducted from the initial amount to obtain the depreciation basis, and an amount at the book balance shall constitute the loss in the relative fiscal year, whereas the sales proceeds or insurance indemnification thereof shall constitute the taxable income;

b. due to an ordinary cause, namely other than those as mentioned in letter a, the net income of the relative property/assets shall be deducted from the initial amount to obtain the depreciation basis.

(8) If the deduction as referred to in paragraph (7) in a fiscal year yields a depreciation basis of below zero, then the depreciation basis shall be increased to zero, and an amount equal to the increase shall be added to the income in the relative fiscal year.

(9) Depreciation tariffs per year for :

a. Category 1 : 50% (fifty percent)
b. Category 2 : 25% (twenty five percent)
c. Category 3 : 10% (ten percent)
d. Category of buildings : 5% (five percent).

(10) The acquisition price of intangible assets used in the company to obtain, collect and maintain the income, including other expenditures having a beneficial period of more than one year, such as the rent of tangible assets, will be amortized with a depreciation tariff based on the beneficial period as referred to in paragraph (9) letter a, b or c. or at the tariff of Category I as referred to in paragraph (11) or by means of the production unit method as referred to in paragraph (12) or (13).

(11) The establishment cost and capital expansion cost of a company shall be amortized with the depreciation tariff rate of category 1, except if the tax payer considers it a cost as referred to in Article 6 paragraph (1) letter a, in compliance with his accounts.

(12) The cost or value to obtain a mining other than oil and gas, shall be amortized with the production unit method of 20% (twenty percent) per year at the most.

(13) The cost to obtain right and/or other cost having the beneficial period of more than one year in oil and gas mining sector shall be amortized with the production unit method.

(14) The Minister of Finance shall issue a decree to determine the types of assets/properties included in the respective categories of assets/properties as referred to in paragraph (3) by due observance of the beneficial period of the relative type of assets/properties.

Article 12

(1) The fiscal year shall be the calendar year, except if the Tax Payer employs a book year which is not the same as the calendar year.

(2) A Tax Payer shall not change the fiscal year, without the consent of the Director General of Taxes.

Article 13

(1) A Tax Payer receiving or obtaining, income from an undertaking and/or free employment, shall be obligated to keep an accounting in Indonesia, so that from said accounting the amount of the taxable income can be calculated based on this Law.

(2) At the end of each fiscal year, the Tax Payer shall close his accounts, by preparing a balance sheet and profit/loss statement on the basis of accounting principles consistent with those of the previous year.

Article 14

(1) The calculation norms shall be guideline used to determine the gross turn over or income and to determine the net income on the basis of the line of business or type of free employment, which shall be made and continuously improved and published by the Director General of Taxes on the basis of the guidelines as stipulated by the Minister of Finance.

(2) A tax payer whose business turn over or gross income from his free employment amounts to less than Rp. 60,000,000.00 (sixty million rupiahs) a year, can calculate the net income by applying the Calculation Norms, as long as it is notified to the Director General of Taxes within the first 3 (three) months grace period of the relative fiscal year.

(3) The amount of Rp. 60,000,000.00 (sixty million rupiahs) shall be adjusted with an adjusting factor as stipulated by a Decree of the Minister of Finance.

(4) A Tax Payer as referred to in paragraph (2) who does not notify the Director General of Taxes to calculate the net income by using the Calculation Norms, shall be considered choosing to keep an accounting, and shall therefore not be allowed anymore to calculate the net income with the Calculation Norms, without the increase as referred to in paragraph (7).

(5) A Tax Payer as referred to in paragraph (2) calculating his net income by applying the Calculation Norms, shall be obligated to make records on his gross turn over and income.

(6) A Tax Payer obligated to keep an accounting or records on the turn over or gross income, but not or not fully executing it as stipulated by this Law, or not showing the accounts and records as well as other evidences required by the Director General of Taxes in respect to the obligation to keep said accounting or records, his net income shall be calculated by applying the Calsulation Norms.

(7) The tax yielded from the calculation as referred to in paragraph (6) shall be added by the increase as regulated in Law No. 6 Year 1983 re General Provisions and Procedure on Taxes.

Article 15

The Minister of Finance can issue a decree to stipulate Special

Calculation Norms for calculating the net income of a certain Tax Payer, which can not be calculated on the basis of Article 16 hereof.

CHARTER IV

METHOD OF TAX CALCULATION

Article 16

(1) The taxable income, as the basis of tariff application for domestic Tax Payers in a fiscal year, shall be calculated by deducting the income as referred to in Article 4 paragraph (1), with the reductions as referred to in Article 6 paragraph (1), Article 7 paragraph (1) and Article 9 letters b, c and d.

(2) The taxable income for a certain domestic tax Payer as referred to in Article 14 paragraph (2) shall be calculated by applying the Calculation Norms as referred to in Article 14 paragraph (1).

(3) The taxable income for a foreign Tax Payer shall be the amount of the gross income received or obtained.

Article 17

(1) The tax tariff applied on the taxable income as referred to in Article 26 herein, shall be as follows :

Taxable income	Tax Tariff
up to Rp. 10,000,000.00 (ten million rupiahs)	15% (fifteen percent)
exceeding Rp. 10,000,000.00 (ten million rupiahs) through Rp. 50,000,000.00 (fifty million rupiahs)	25% (twenty five percent)
exceeding Rp. 50,000,000.00 (fifty million rupiahs)	35% (thirty five percent).

(2) The amount of the taxable income as referred to in paragraph (1) shall be adjusted with an adjusting factor as stipulated by a Decree of the Minister of Finance.

(3) For the purpose of applying the tariff as referred to in paragraph (1), the taxable income shall be rounded down to full thousands of rupiah.

(4) For an individual Tax Payer whose subjective obligation as a domestic Tax Subject starts after the begining of the fiscal year or ends in the fiscal year, the indebted tax shall amount to the number of days of the part of the fiscal year divided by three hundred sixty, multiplied by the indebted tax for one fiscal year yielded, due to the application of paragraphs (1) and (2).
The net income obtained during the part of the fiscal year shall first be calculated into the amount of one year.

(5) For the purpose of calculating the tax as referred to in paragraph (4), each full month shall be calculated at 30 (thirty) days.

Article 18

(1) The Minister of Finance shall be competent to determine the ratio, of the debts/liabilities to capital, of the company to for the purpose of the tax collection on the basis of this Law.

(2) The Director General of Taxes shall be competent to re determine the amount of the income and/or reduction and the debts/liabilities as capital to calculate the amount of the taxable income for a Tax Payer having a special relationship.

(3) The special relationship as referred to in Article 5 paragraphs (1) and (2), Article 9 paragraph (1) letter e and paragraph (2) of this Article shall be :

a. in case the tax payer is a body/entity :

1. relationship between two or more Tax Payers under the same ownership or control, both directly and indirectly;
2. relationship between Tax Payers having a participation of 25% (twenty five percent) or more in two or more parties, likewise the latter mentioned relationship between two or more parties.

b. in case the Tax Payer is an individual person: blood relation family and by marriage in straight horizontal lines of one grade.

(4) Two or more parties respectively constituting a Limited Liability Company, association or other association having a special relation-

ship with a participation of 50% (fifty percent) or more, the tax imposition calculated by applying the lowest tariff level as referred to in Article 17, shall only be applied once.

Article 19

With a Government Regulation, the adjustment factor can be stipulated in case of disharmony between the cost elements and income, due to price development.

CHAPTER V

TAX SETTLEMENT IN THE CURRENT YEAR

Article 20

(1) The tax estimated to be indebted in a fiscal year shall be fully settled by the Tax Payer in the current year via the deduction and collection of tax by other parties as well as tax payment by the Tax Payer himself.

(2) The settlement of tax through the deduction and collection of tax by another party as well as the payment thereof by the Tax Payer himself, shall constitute a tax installment to be credited against the indebted Income Tax for the whole fiscal year concerned.

(3) The tax period shall be used as the period to determine the amount of the Tax Object and the indebted tax which should be settled as the installement in the current year.

(4) The tax period as referred to in paragraph (3) shall be 1 (one) month or of other period as stipulated by the Minister of Finance.

Article 21

(1) The tax deduction on income in relation to a work and the deposit thereof to the State Treasury, shall be conducted by :

a. the employer paying the salary, wage and honorarium under any name whatsoever, as the remuneration for the work performed by an employee or another person in Indonesia;

b. the Government Treasurer paying the salary, wage, honorarium, permanent alowance and other payments under any name whatsoever in respect to a work of position, charged to the State Finance.

c. Pension fund body/entity, paying the pension;

d. the company and bodies/entities paying the honorarium or other payments as the remuneration of a service rendered in Indonesia by an expert and/or association of experts as the domestic Tax Payer conducting free, employment.

(2) The part of the income ded''cted by tax for each tax period, shall be that exceeding one twelveth of the non taxable income as reffered to in Article 17.

(3) At the time a person starts working or is pensioned in order to obtain the deduction as referred to in Article 7, he shall submit`a statement to the employer, State Treasurer or pension fund entity, stating the number of the dependants in his family.

(4) The statement as referred to in paragraph (3) shall be used by the employer, State Treasurer or pension fund entity to determine the amount of the taxable income, except if the relative Tax Payer submits a new statement on an amendment.

(5) The tariff of the tax deduction on salary, wage and honorarium shall be equal to the taxable income tariff as referred to in Article 17.

(6) The amount of tax deducted from the wage part of each tax period, shall be included in to a Manual issued by the Director General of Taxes as referred to in paragraph (9).

(7) Any person having no other income than that in respect to work already actually and accurated deducted by his tax, the already deducted tax amount as referred to in paragraphs (2) and (5) shall constitute the settlement of the indebted tax of the relative year on the basis of this Law.

(8) Any person having an income other than that in relation to work, and any person obtaining an income in respect to work of more than one employer, shall submit the Anuual Tax Return as referred to in Article 30 of this Law and Article 3 of Law No. 6 Year 1983 re General Provision & Procedure on Taxes. The total indebted tax shall be deducted by the already deducted tax as the credit as referred to in article 28 herein.

(9) The Director General of Taxes shall issue the Manual on Tax Deduction on payment of salary wage, honorarium and others in relation to work or other services rendered.

Article 22

(1) The Minister of Finance can determine certain bodies/entities to collect tax from the Tax Payers, conducting activities in the import sector or other activities in other sectors receiving payment for goods and services from the State Expenditures Budget.

(2) The basis and amount of collection shall be stipulated by a Decree of the Minister of Finance, based on the consideration that the amount of the collection shall be estimated to approach the amount of the indebted tax on income from the relative business activities.

Article 23

(1) On the income as mentioned hereunder, under any name and in any form whatsoever, paid or indebted by a Government Agency, State owned Undertaking Body and Regional State Owned Undertaking Body under any name and in any form whatsoever, or by another domestic Tax Payer body/entity to domestic Tax Payer, other than banks or financial institutions, shall be deducted by a 15% (fifteen percent) tax from the gross amount, by the party obligated to pay :

a. dividend, of a domestic corporation;

b. interest, including remuneration due to a debt payment guarantee,

c. rent, royalty and other income in respect to the utulization of assets/property;

d. remuneration paid for technical and managerial services conducted in Indonesia.

(2) An individual person as a domestic Tax Payer can be appointed by the Director General of Taxes to deduct the tax as referred to in paragraph (1).

(3) A certain interest and dividend not exceeding an amount to be further regulated by the Government Regulation shall be excepted from the tax deduction as referred to in paragraph (1).

Article 24

(1) The tax imposed in a fiscal year calculated on the basis of the provisions of this Law shall be credited with the tax paid or indebted abroad by the Tax Payer in the same fiscal year on the income received.

(2) The credit allowed in respect to the income received or obtained abroad for the relative fiscal year, shall be limited to the amount of the tax calculated on the income abroad, on the basis of this Law.

(3) In calculating the limit of the creditable tax amount, the income as referred to in Article 26 paragraph of this Law, shall be considered originating from Indonesia, and in determining the other sources of income, the same principle shall be applied.

(4) If the tax on income abroad, requested to be credited is apparently reduced or re-imbursed, then the tax indebted on the basis of this Law shall be added by said amount in the year when the reduction or re-imbursement is conducted.

Article 25

(1) The amount of tax installments in the current year to be paid by the Tax Payer himself for each tax period, shall amount to the difference of the indebted tax of the previous year substracted by the deduction and collection of tax as well as the tax paid or indebted abroad as referred to respectively in Article 21, 22, 23 and 24, divided by the number of tax periods.

(2) The meaning of indebted tax in paragraph (1), shall be the tax according to the latest Annual Tax Return, except if the tax as lastly stipulated by the Director General of Taxes is larger in amount.

(3) The amount of the tax instalments in the current year to be paid by a certain Tax Payer himself for every tax period shall further be regulated by the Government regulation.

Article 26

On the income as mentioned hereunder, under any name and in any form whatsoever, paid or indebted by a Government Agency, state owned undertaking body and regional state owned undertaking body and under any name and any form whatsoever, or by another domestic tax payer to a foreign tax payer, shall be deducted by a final tax of 20% (twenty percent) of the gross amount by parties obligated to pay :

a. dividend of a domestic corporation;

b. interest, including remuneration due to debt repayment guarantee;

c. rent, royalty and other income due to the utilization of assets/properties;

d. remuneration paid for technical and managerial services conducted in Indonesia;

e. profit after tax deduction of a certain permanent undertaking form in Indonesia.

Article 27

The further arrangements of the tax obligation, fuldilment as referred to in Articles 21, 23 and 25, shall be stipulated by the Government regulation.

CHAPTER VI

TAX CREDIT, SETTLEMENT OF TAX PAYMENT SHORTAGE, ANNUAL TAX RETURNS AND REIMBURSEMENT OF EXCESS TAX PAYMENT

Article 28

For a domestic tax payer, the indebted tax for the whole year according to this Law, shall be deducted by the tax credit, in the form of :

a. tax deduction on income from work as referred to in Article 21;

b. collection of tax on income from an undertaking as referred to in Article 22;

c. tax deduction on income in the form of interest, dividend, royalty, rent and other remunerations as referred to in Article 23;

d. tax paid or indebted abroad as referred to in Article 24;

e. payment conducted by the Tax Payer himself from the relative fiscal year as referred to in Article 25.

Article 29

If the indebted tax of a fiscal year is apparently bigger than the tax credit amount as referred to in Article 28, then the indebted tax shortage shall be settled at the latest at the end of the third month after the expiry of the relative fiscal year, prior to the submission of the Annual Tax Return.

Article 30

(1) A Tax Payer shall be obligated to submit an Annual Tax Return Attached with financial statements, such as the balance sheet and profit/loss statement, in compliance with the provisions as contained in Article 4 of Law No. 6 year 1983 re General Provisions and Procedure on Taxes.

(2) The Annual Tax Return as referred to in paragraph (1) shall at least contain the amounts of turn over, income, taxable income, indebted tax, the tax already settled in the current year, and the shortage or excess of tax.

(3) Excepted from the obligation as referred to in paragraph (1), shall be individual persons :

a. having no other income than that in respect to work of function of an employer as referred to in Article 21;

b. obtaining a net income not exceeding the amount of the non taxable income as referred to in Article 7.

(4) The amount of the indebted tax according to the Annual Tax Return submitted by the Tax Payer, shall be the tax amount indebted according to this Law.

(5) If the Director General of Taxes obtains proof, that the indebted tax according to the Annual Tax Return is not correct, then the Director General of Taxes shall stipulate the proper amount of the indebted tax.

Article 31

(1) If the indebted tax of a fiscal year is apparently smaller than the tax credit amount as referred to in Article 28, then the excess thereof shall be re-imbursed or calculated with the other tax liabilities.

(2) Prior to making the reimbursement or calculation of the excess payment tax as referred to in paragraph (1) the Director General of Taxes is authorized to audit the financial statements, accounts and other records, as well as other matters as considered necessary to assess the amount of the indebted tax in compliance with the provisions in this Law.

CHAPTER VII
OTHER PROVISIONS

Article 32

The procedure of collection and sanctions in respect to the implementation of this Law shall be regulated in Law No. 6 Year 1983 re General Provisions and Procedures on Taxes, except if otherwise stipulated in this Law.

CHAPTER VIII
TRANSITIONAL PROVISIONS

Article 33

(1) A Tax Payer using a fiscal year ended on June 30, 1984, and between June 30, 1984 and December 31, 1984 may opt/choose to calculate his tax on this basis of the Corporate Tax Ordinance 1925 or the Income Tax Ordinance 1944, or based on the provisions in this Law.

(2) The tax facilities already granted through December 31, 1983, of which :

a. the period is limited, can be enjoyed by the relative tax payer until the expiry thereof;

b. the period is not limited, can be enjoyed by the Tax Payer through the fiscal year preceeding the 1984 fiscal year.

(3) The taxable income received or obtained in oil operations, in the framework of a Contract of Work and Production Sharing Contract which is still valid at the time this Law comes into force, shall be

imposed with tax on the basis of the provisions of the Corporate Tax Ordinance 1925 and Law of Tax on Interest, Dividend and Royalty 1970 as well as all implementing regulations thereof.

Article 34

By the coming into force of this Law, the implementing regulations on the imposition of corporate Tax 1925, Income Tax 1944 and Tax on Interest, Dividend and Royalty 1970 shall remain applicable as long as they are not yet replaced by new implementing regulations.

CHAPTER IX

CONCLUDING PROVISIONS

Article 35

Any matters not yet sufficiently regulated herein shall further be regulated by the Government Régulation.

Article 36

(1) This Law shall come into force as from January 1, 1984, for the imposition of the 1984 Fiscal Year Income Tax.

(2) This Law shall be called the Income Tax Law 1984.

For the public knowledge, this Law shall be promulgated in the State Gazette of the Republic of Indonesia.

Enacted in Jakarta

on : December 31, 1983

THE PRESIDENT OF THE REPUBLIC OF INDONESIA

SOEHARTO

Promulgated in Jakarta

on : December 31, 1983

THE STATE MINISTER/STATE SECRETARY OF THE REPUBLIC OF INDONESIA

SUDHARMONO, SH

STATE GAZETTE OF THE REPUBLIC OF INDONESIA YEAR 1983 NO. 50

Appendix 24

ELUCIDATION
ON
THE LAW OF THE REPUBLIC OF INDONESIA
RE
INCOME TAX

A. GENERAL

1. Based on the Pancasila and 1945 Constitution, Article 23 paragraph (2) the tax system and legislation function as the base for collecting state taxes, including Income Tax, have to be stipulated by law.

2. The development implementation as the application of the Pancasila is aimed at enabling this country to finance the National Development with domestic sources by dividing the development load among groups with both high and low income respectively to bolster the National Development spread in order to streng then the National Resilience.

3. Income Tax as one of the state revenues originating from the People's income needs to be regulated with the Law able to give legal certainty in accordance with life in the Pancasila Democratic State.

4. This Income Tax regulates the tax imposition material which basically concerns the Tax Subject (who is imposed with) Tax Object and Tax Tariff (how to calculate tax) with equal imposition and just burdering. Whereas the collecting procedure shall be regulated in a separate law for creating the uniformity so that it will facilatate the people to learn, to understand and to observe it.

5. In the previous legislative regulations on taxes, the income tax imposition is regulated in various laws, namely :

   (a) The 1925 Corporate Tax Ordinance Regulating the imposition material and procedure of income taxes for bodies.

(b) The 1944 Income Tax Ordinance, regulating the imposition material and procedure of income tax to individual.
This also regulates is the tax deduction upon the employees' income by their employer.

(c) Law of Tax on Interest, Dividend and Royalty 1970 regulating the imposition material & procedure of tax upon interests, Dividend and Royalty, which should be deducted by the people and bodies paying the interest, dividend and Royalty.

(d) Law No. 8 Year 1967 of Government Regulation No. 11 Year 1967 regulating income Tax imposition procedures, particularly in the form of business profit, as long as the collecting procedure by another party (MPO) and the payment by the tax payer himself (Periodical MPS) were in the current year and the calculation in the end of the year (Final MPS).

6. The new tax legislative regulations regulate as follows :

(a) all provisions concerning the application of taxes upon incomes obtained by individuals and bodies are regulated in this law.

(b) provisions regarding the imposition procedure for both the income tax and other taxes the imposition of which is conducted by the Directorate General of Taxes are regulated in Law No. 6 Year 1983 Re General Provisions and Procedure on Taxes.

The objective of this simplification as aforementioned is to facilitate the community to learn, understand and observe it. This law simplifies the tax structure such as the kinds of taxes, tariff and ways of fulfilling the tax obligation. The Tax tariffs are stipulated properly based on the principles of equitability in collecting and justice in burdening the tax. The tariff structure is simplified and progressive, which means that the higher the income, the bigger the percentage of the tax tariff. The tariff for individuals is the same as that of a body, with the highest tariff level lower than that of the former one; therefore the following advantages can be obtained :

(a) simple, means easy for the Tax Subject to calculate for the tax administration to test the tax calculation by the Tax Payer; there are no longer different tariff for body Tax Payer, so this support the aforemartioned simplicity and facility more.

(b) Justice and equitable burden, the application of the same tariff to the same income level disregarding the origin thereof.

(c) improving the observance of the Tax Payer; because the highest marginal tariff is only 35% (thirty five percent), the willingness to pay the income tax increases; the increasing willingness to pay and the getting easier for the tax administration to test will improve the observance of the Tax Payer.

(d) reducing the transfer of income from a body to an individual or vice versa, because it will not bring any benefit to the Tax Payer.

B. ARTICLE BY ARTICLE

Article 1

This law regulates the imposition of tax on income, both received or obtained by an individual and body which is indebted for one fiscal year.

Article 2

Paragraph (1)

The meaning of Tax Subject shall both an individual and undivided inheritance or body.

Letter a.1.

An individual here shall be a Tax Subject both living in Indonesia and abroad. The one residing in Indonesia will become a Tax Subject since their birth in Indonesia or if an individual has been in Indonesia for more than 183 (one hundred and eighty three) days within a period of 12 (twelve) months, therefore he will become a Tax Subject since he arrives in Indonesia. Said 183 (one hundred eighty three) days is unnecessarily consecutive.
An individual residing or staying in Indonesia is no longer a Tax Subject at the time he dies or leaves Indonesia for good. For those residing outside Indonesia will become The Tax Subject in Indonesia if they can receive or obtain income from Indonesia.
The are no longer Tax Subject in Indonesia since they no longer receive or obtain income from Indonesia, that is the income as referred to in article 26.

Letter a.2.

The undivided inheritance constitutes the Substituting Tax Subject, that is the entitled one.

The undivided inheritance starts becoming Tax Subject since said inheritance exists (the death of the deceased) and it comes to an end when it is divided to those entitled to it. The new inheritance become a Tax Subject if it yields income.

Letter b

The bodies such as limited liability companies, limited partnership, state-owned undertaking bodies and regional state-owned undertaking bodies under any name and form whatsoever, associations, corporations or other associations, firms, partnerships, cooperatives, foundations or institutions become Tax Subjects since they are founded or since they begin to receive income as refered to in article 26 for bodies founded or domeciled outside Indonesia.
Bodies founded or domiciled in Indonesia are no longer the Tax Subjects after the liguidation settled, and the bodies founded or domiciled outside Indonesia are no longer to become the Indonesian Tax Subjects after the 'termination of the economic relation to Indonesia, that is since they can no longer receive or obtain income from Indonesia.
It should be noted that every certain unit of state-owned body which carries out a socioeconomic operation regularly becomes a Tax Subject as a state-owned companies.
A body outside Indonesia which has a permanent undertaking form in Indonesia starts to become an Indonesian Tax Subject since the existence thereof.

Paragraph (2)

Self explanatory

Paragraph (3)

Letters a and b

Self explanatory

Letter c

A permanent business form in Indonesia from a foreign company or body is categorized as a domestic Tax Subject.
Basically a domestic Tax Subject shall be imposed with the tax upon its total income from wheresoever it is obtained, both from or outside Indonesia. The income from a permanent business form

as a domestic Tax Subject is separately formulated in Article 5. Not only can any body possess a permanent business in Indonesia, but also any Company including private one outside Indonesia. By the permanent business form we mean a certain form or something having permanent nature as a partial or total operation of business in Indonesia from a body or company founded domiciled or available outside Indonesia.

By carrying out business regularly we mean carrying out business operation which shows the intention to run it continuosly.

For example, in case of furnishing of services, which include consultancy services, if once rendered by a foreigner coming to Indonesia as a tourist because of the request from his friend in Indonesia, such a consultancy services is not categorized as a regular business operation and therefore it is not regarded as a permanent business form in Indonesia.

However, if the tourist comes back to Indonesia to provide consultancy services, on behalf of a foreign company, to a company in Indonesia because he is recommended by the aforementioned friend, this can be regarded as a permanent business form in Indonesia because there has been an indication of the intention to continuously provide consultancy services in Indonesia.

A foreign insurance company possesses a permanent business form in Indonesia if the company receives insurance premium in Indonesia or bears the risk in Indonesia through its employees or other representatives but not an independent agent.

A foreign company is regarded as not having a permanent business form in Indonesia if in its operation in Indonesia the company uses a broker or an independent agent provided that the broker or agent acts on behalf of its own company. Therefore, if the agent acts fully or almost fully on behalf of the foreign company, the agent does not meet the requirement as an independent agent, in other words, the broker or agent still performs the operation of the foreign company.

Paragraph (4)

Foreign Tax Subject shall be that residing or domiciling outside Indonesia, but receiving or obtaining income from Indonesia. The Tax Subject who really obtains income and because of this reason is obligated to pay taxes, herein called a Tax Payer. In the other words, a Tax Payer is a person or a body who has met, the subjective and objective obligations.

The major difference between the domestic Tax Payer and foreign one is that the domestic Tax Payer after the expiry of the fiscal year has to submit an annual Tax Return. The Tax Payer shall report the income received or obtained, the calculation of taxable income and the indebted tax therein The Tax Payer also reports all payment of the indebted taxes. If the annual Tax Return has been correctly completed and the indebted tax has been properly paid, therefore it is no necessary to issue the Tax Assessment Letter for him. This Tax Assessment Letter is issued if only the Tax Payer does not submit the annual Tax Return or if the Annual Tax Return is not correct or incomplete, so that the payment deficiency should be collected by a Tax Assessment Letter plus the relative administrative sanction.
Whereas the foreign Tax Payer is not obligated to submit the Annual Tax Return.

Paragraph (5)

To stipulate whether or not a person or a body resides or domiciles in Indonesia shall be according to the actual condition or reality, not according to formal cases.

Paragraph (6)

In certain cases, the Director General of Taxes is competent to stipulate where a person or body is staying, residing or domiciling. This is based on practical consideration in order to give the legal certainty.

Article 3

Letter a and b

According to the international custom, a member of a diplomatic representative, councellor and other officials are excepted from being the Tax Subjects in the countries for which they represent. Likewise the Armed Forces members of foreign countries and international organization representatives like the World Health Organization (WHO), International Monetary Fund (IMF) and the others. The reciprocal condition is an international custom.
If they have another job, or business, this exception is invalid and they will be subject to taxes upon the income they receive or obtain from the job or business.

Letter c

Based on the objective and nature of the State Agency Company, it can be excepted from the Tax Subject on the basis of the Decree of the Minister of Finance.

Article 4

This Law follows an idea of a wide income namely any additional economic benefit.

The addition of economic capability received or obtained by person or body is the best measurement for a person or body to take part in bearing the expenses required by the government in financing its routine activities and the development. This is one of the characteristics of this Income Tax system to equalize the development burden. Any addition of economic benefit wheresoever it comes from means an additional capacity in helping the government finance its activities. The definition of income in this law is no longer bound to whether or not there is a certain income source like in the former low.

An income can be seen from the flow of the additional of the economic benefit to the Tax Payer, and this can be grouped into :

- Income from the job, that is the job in an employment relation and free employment like income from general practitioners, notary, public acountant, actuary (life insurance mathematician), lawyer etc.;
- income from business activities, that is activities by means of companies;
- income from a capital, either from moveable goods capital such as interest, dividend, royalty, or from a immovable goods capital such as house rent and others; also included in this capital income is that from the self operated property, such as that obtained from cultivating a piece of land, the profit of the sales of the properties or right not used in carrying out business activities.
- other incomes, such as lottery prize, the debt exemption and other income which are not included in other groups.

Viewed from the point of usage, an income can be used for consumption and saving further used to obtain property which is not

finished for one-year consumption. Although income can be grouped the definition of income is limited to that obtained from certain sources.
Examples mentioned herein are simply to clarify the definition of the extensive income and not limited to what has been stated herein.

Paragraph (10)

Letter a

All remuneration or payment upon work within an employment relation which can be in the form of wage, salary and other, included therein non life and life insurance premium paid by the employer.
Remuneration in nature is not included in the income of the recipient, for instance, housing (except in remote places where there is no house to rent), motorvehicles and others. For the employer, said expenses cannot be deducted as the cost as referred to in Article 9 Paragraph (1) Letter d.

Letter b

Honorarium paid to artists, sportsmen, speakers like in international seminar.
Lottery prize also includes the rewards given without lottery.

Letter c

Undertaking gross profit means gross income obtained from an undertaking/business. Undertaking gross profit plus other gross incomes makes total gross income.
The Annual Tax Return shall also contain the gross profit of the undertaking and the deduction allowed by this law. So it does not mean that the Annual Tax Return only contains the taxable incomes. The addition of other income and cost deduction upon the undertaking net profit reflect the tax world as the horizontal compensation. Both undertaking nett profit and other income after being deducted by their respective costs can be negative. Such a horizontal compensation is permitted in the calculation of taxable income.

Letter d

If a Tax Payer sells property at more than the balance book price or the aguisition price/value at the time of sales, the price difference is an income. If the sold property does not belong a company and has become the possession by the Tax Payer before this law is effective, the obtained income is the difference between the selling price and the selling value at the time this law is effective.
Similarly, if a company sells its property to a shareholder, for instance, a car with a book price of Rp. 1,000,000.00 (one million rupiahs) and the market price is Rp. 5,000,000.00 (five million rupiahs), therefore the difference of Rp. 4,000,000.00 (four million rupiahs) is an income for the company and for the shareholder the amount Rp. 4,000,000.00 (four million rupiahs) is an income.

Letter e

The return of tax calculated as the cost when calculating the taxable income, for example, value added tax on goods and services and sales tax on luxury goods, which after being restipulated turns out to be over-paid, the surplus becomes an income.

Letter f

The interest includes other rewards in connection with debt returning guarantees, either promised or not.

Letter g

This stipulation regulates the income in the form of dividend, that is part of the profit received by a shareholder or an insurance policy. Whatever name is given to or in whatever form the part of the profit is received, this is not subject to consideration.
Included in the definition of dividend shall be :

1. Profit distribution both directly and indirectly, under any name or form whatsoever;
2. Repayment due to the liquidation exceeding the paid up capital;
3. The gift of a bonus share conducted without any deposit not originating from the company property revaluation;
4. The recording of capital addition conducted without any deposit not originating from the company property revaluation;
5. Anything received or obtained due to rebuying of the shares by

the relative company, exceeding the investment;

6. The total or partial repayment of the paid up capital if in the previous years profits have been obtained, except if the repayment is due to the statutory decrease of the authorized capital;
7. Payment upon profit indications, including those reveived as the redemption of said indications;
8. Profit from the bonds participated in the profit distribution;
9. The company expense for personal needs of the shareholder, which is burdened to the company cost.

It should be emphasized that from items 1 through 9 it can be concluded that the dividend or company profit distribution cover an extensive meaning, that is every distribution of the company's profit under any name or form whatsoever. In practice, the distribution/payment of dividend is frequently disguised, for example, by transfer of the company's property to a shareholder or participant by changing the price below the market price.
The difference between the market price and the paid price by the shareholder is a disguised payment of dividend (See elucidation on paragraph (1) letter d).

Example : A car belongs to PT (Company) A. The balance book is Rp. 1,000,000.00 the market price is Rp. 5,000,000.00. The car is tranferred to a shareholder B at the balance book price, of Rp. 1,000,000.00. Thus there is a disguised payment of dividend amounting to Rp. 4,000,000.00. Based on this stipulation, PT A shall deduct an income tax of 15% x Rp. 4,000,000.00 = Rp. 600,000.00.

The difinition of dividend also covers part of the profit received by the management and members of a cooperatives. At the cooperatives level, the balance of the cooperatives profit merely originating from the operation performed by and for the members' benefit is not included in the definition of the taxable income. Therefore, for the management and members of the cooperatives, the amount of the distribution or payment of the cooperatives operation profit is a taxable income.
If the amount received by each staff of the management and member of the cooperatives does not exceed the amount of the non taxable income, the distribution and repayment of the cooperatives operation profit is not taxable.

Letter h

The payment of royalty herein under any name whatsoever in connection with the use of rights such as patent, license, trade mark, pattern or model, plan, company secret, method of work, copy right of an art or scientific work, including cinemographic film work.

Basically royalty payment comprises three groups, namely upon the use of :

i. right upon intangible property copy right, patent, trademark, company secret or formula;

ii. right upon tangible property: right upon industrial equipment, commerce and science;

iii. services: providing information needed on business and investment in general, experience in the field of industry, trading and science in particular; the information herein means that which is not yet disclosed.

Letter i

This provision regulates the rental received or obtained upon the leased property, both movable like a car or a immovable like a house.

Letter j

Example : Periodically paid life long allowance.

Letter k

The debt examption by the creditor constitutes an income to the debtor.

Paragraph (2)

In line with the provision in Paragraph (1) Letter f of this Chapter, an interest constitutes a tax object.

The community's saving is also a fund source for the development. With the Government Regulation, interests for the time deposit and other savings are exempted from taxes by due observance of the monetary development and development implementation.

Paragraph (3)

Letter a

Granted property or aid received which has no relation to business or work between the relative parties is excluded from an income. This is to balance Article 9 letter f which regulates that a granted property or an aid shall not be deducted from the income by the giver.

Letter b

Inheritance as an additional economic capability received by that entitled is not a tax object even though the amount is big. Inheritance as a tax subject is taxable if it can bring in income, such as the rent received from an inherited house.

Letter c

Payment by an insurance company to policy holder due to an accident, loss or death of the person, and also the receipt of a scholarship from the insurance company is not an income.

Article 9 Paragraph (1) Letter c regulates that the premium of the insurance of life, health, double function (dwiguna) insurance, and scholarship insurance are not to be deducted from the income unless it is guaranteed by the employer.

Letter d

If an employer as a Tax Subject in compliance with this law gives a convenience in nature to an employee or another person having relation to the work, it is not considered as an income to the recipient. By a reward in nature we mean an additional economic capability received or obtained not in the form of money, for instance, the use of a car from the company free of charge, occupying a company owned or rented house, the gift of rice free of charge and others.

The employer is not permitted to deduct said amount as a cost from the income. The convenience of occupying a state owned houses by civil sevants, state official functionaries and functionaries of non ministerial institutions is not part of the income of the relative people. This also applies to state owned companies. If the convenience provider is not a Tax Subject according to this law, it is a part of an income for the recipient.

Example : An employee working for a diplomatic representative receives convenience to occupy a house rented by the deplomatic representative which is not a Tax Subject in this country, it shall be included in the income of the recipient. This also applies to other kinds of convenience. This is intended to motivate the employer to give allowance in the form money to the employee so that the tax can be easily paid.

Letter e

Transfering property by somebody or a member of a firm, association, limited partnership, or partnership transfering the association property to found a limited liability company with the payment in the form of shares, the profit in the form of the discrepancy between the book balance price an the sales price of the property does not constitute an income if after it the transfering party or collectively transfering parties owns at least 90% (ninety percent) of the total invested share value of the limited liability company receiving the transfer. The 90% requirements should be fulfilled at the time of the transfer.

Letter f

The property transfered to a limited liability company, association or other bodies as the substitue of a share or capital participation is not taxable on the transfer, but in the future if said property gets another transfer or is sold; therefore the valuation of said proterty should be the same as the book balance price on the transfer.

Letter g

A dividend received or obtained by a domestic limited liability company from another limited liability company is not considered an income if the receiving company is not only taking insterest the unused money, but basically permanent and the two companies are actually of one unit of business line. Dividend from the interest of the money, as long as the money is not used, is subject to tax.

Example : PT A, is a textile company, PT B is a weaving yarn company. There is an economic relation in their business line. PT A possesses 25% (twenty five percent) of the equity of PT B, so the dividend received by PT A from PT B is not included in the definition of income.

If the body receiving or obtaining a dividend possessed 25% (twenty five percent) or more of the authorized shares, whereas the two companies have no economic relation in their business line, the dividend received of obtained is excluded from the exception as a Tax Object as referred to in this provision.

Example : PT X is a textile company. PT Y is a beverages company. PT X possesses 25% (twenty five percent) of the authorized shares of by PT Y. Between PT X and PT Y there is no economic relation in their business line. Therefore, the dividend received of obtained

by PT X from PT Y is not excluded as a Tax Object. In other words, the dividend received or obtained by PT X from PT Y is a Tax Object.

Letter h

Contributions received by pension funds the foundation of which has been approved by the Minister of Finance, paid periodically or in cash by both the employer and the tax payer are not included in the taxable income.

Letter i

The definition of the operation exclusively intended for public interest is that meeting the following requirements :

a. the operation shall be social in characteristic such as in field of religion, education, health and culture;

b. the operation shall be exclusively intended to help promote public welfare;

c. the operation is not for making profit.

Profit of the foundation excluded from the difinition of income is not other than the excess of the financial operation proceeds from the income realization exceeding the realization of cost incurred within the fiscal year. This profit excludes the definition of Tax Object according to this law as long as the profit is merely an excess from the operational proceeds as explained above, which has been calculated to perform social activities of the foundation or association. If the profit is big enough and so that the excess is then distributed to the members of the foundation executibes, the operation is no longer merely for public interest and excess becomes the part of taxable income.

Letter j

The foundation's income from the capital received outside the operation which is merely for public interest, which is used to finance the foundation social activities is not a tax object. For instance, a foundation or edification in financing its activities receives a contribution. The excess of thereof to finance the activities is invested outside its social activities. The income received or obtained from this investment as long as it is used to finance its social activities is not a tax object.

Letter k

The distribution of profit received or obtained by members of limited partnership the capital of which is comprising from shares, firms, union, and association is not a tax object.
But, this law gives competent to the Minister of Finance to apply income tax upon this profit distribution above if this provision is misused so that it inflict loss to the State Finance.

Article 5

Paragraph (1)

The income constituting tax objects of a permanent undertaking form shall be as follows :

Letter a

That imposed with income tax is the income of the operation of a permanent undertaking form or assets controlled or possessed by the permanent undertaking form. Any income both from operation and assets, either obtained in Indonesia or outside Indonesia, is taxable according to this law, for instance income from the possession of shares outside Indonesia by the permanent undertaking form in Indonesia is that which should be taxed in Indonesia.

Letter b

If the parent company or other body a abroad which has special relation carries out the same activities as that by its permanent undertaking form in Indonesia, the Indonesia income tax should be applied to the income from the operation.
This is intended to apply tax to the permanent undertaking form upon its incomes from its particular activities which are basically

the operation of the permanent undertaking form, to prevent the a reason that particular activities of a permanent undertaking form, whereas the income tax of the activities should be the reponsibility of the permanent undertaking form.

Paragraph (2)

This law is not intended to impose tax to the permanent undertaking form, if it receives an income from a parent company which has no connection with the permanent undertaking form whereas upon this income the tax has been deducted in accordance with article 26. The costs for obtaining, maintaining and collecting the parent company's income is not taxable to the permanent undertaking form in Indonesia.

Article 6

Included in the routine business cost (costs for obtaining, collecting and maintaining the income) are those spent for basic material, auxiliary materials and packing, rent and royalty, travel fare for performing the work, the indirect taxes for example Value-Added Tax upon goods and services and sales tax for luxury goods. Costs spent to obtain goods having usage period of more than one year can only reduce the taxable income through depreciation or amortalization. If pension funds founded by a company or other pension funds approved by the Minister of Finance, the contribution paid to the pension funds can be deducted from the income.

Paragraph (1)

Letter a

The taxable income is calculated by totalling all income in one fiscal year deducted by the total of cost incurred within the fiscal year in accordance with this Article.

The cost spent for obtaining, collecting and maintaining the income is the cost or expenditure which has a direct connection with the income received by the tax payer. Cost to obtain, to collect and maintain the income an undertaking (which can be called overhead) includes the payment of the salary to the employees of the relative company, except that in nature or convenience (convenience of occupying a house free of charge). The payment of premium by the employer to the employee can be deducted as the company cost whereas for the employee it constitutes an income. The salary to an employee who is also a shareholder if the amount extravagant, exceeding other's who are not shareholders performing the work, tasks or occupation more or less the same as the shareholder, the excess cannot reduce the income. This cost also includes the interest paid in connection with the company debt, except if the amount exceeds that stipulated by the Minister of Finance as referred to in Article 18 Paragraph (1).

The interest paid in connection with that of a personal debt cannot reduce the income because such an interest is the use of an income. The payment of interest for embezzlement which may occur in a special relation cannot reduce the taxable income either.

Letter b

The terms of depreciation for tangible assets and amortization of the intangible properties or right have usually been used in the field of accountancy.

Letter c

Self explanatory

Letter d

The usage of income cannot be used as a deducting factor in calculating the taxable income. The purchase of goods for perpersonal purposes which is not to be used to obtain an income cannot be depreciated. If the goods for own use is then sold with a loss, the loss cannot reduce the taxable income. It should be confirmed that goods the sales loss of which can reduce the taxable income is that which is used to perform an undertaking (which is also used to obtain income), therefore the loss of selling the company's land included in the company's assets can reduce the taxable income. This should be clarified because of to Article 11, Paragraph (1), land is an underpreciatable property.

Letter e

The balance of the cooperatives operation in connection with the activities merely from and for its members is not taxable at the cooperatives lebel.

Paragraph (2)

To an individual as a domestic Tax Payer for calculating his taxable income there still be given a reduction in the formof non taxable income as referred to in Article 7. (See further elucidation on Article 7).

Paragraph (3)

If after the reduction of gross income by the allowable burdens in accordance with paragraph (1) yields a loss, the loss can be compensated within 5 (five) year as from the following year of the loss. In line with a Decree of the Minister of Finance, for certain undertakings, which according to the objective consideration does not bring any profit within 5 years, it can be compensated within 8 (eight) years at the most.

Article 7

Paragraph (1)

To an individual as a domestic tax payer to reach the taxable income shall be granted a reduction in the form of a non taxable income. For the Tax Payer himself the non taxable income is Rp. 960,000.00 (nine hundred and sixty housand rupiahs). For a married one, it is added by Rp. 480,000.00 (four hundred and eighty thousand rupiahs). In case a wife receives an income from a job which has been taxed on the basis of Article 21, her non-taxable income is Rp. 960,000.00 (nine hundred and sixty thousand rupiahs) while in calculating the tax upon the husband's income, a reduction of Rp. 960,000.00 (nine hundred and sixty thousand rupiahs) plus Rp. 480,000.00 (four hundred eighty thousand rupiahs) is granted. In such a case, if the employer is calculating the taxable income of the wife, it is reduced by Rp. 960,000.00 (nine hundred and sixty thousand rupiahs) but not added by the reduction of Rp. 480,000.00 (four hundred and eighty thousand rupiahs). In case the wife has an income, the amount of non taxable income is added by Rp. 960,000.00 (nine hundred and sixty thousand rupiahs).
The addition of non-taxable income of Rp. 960,000.00 (nine hundred and sixty thousand rupiahs) mentioned above is not granted anymore in case the wife has an income from a job which

has received reduction of a non taxable income amounting to Rp. 960,000.00 (nine hundred and sixty thousand rupiahs).

An additional reduction of Rp. 480,000.00 (four hundred and eighty thousand rupiahs) is granted to a wife if she receives only from the job, whereas the husband does not receive any income. In such a case, the additional reduction for the family is given to the wife.

By such a reduction the employer obtains the facility in collecting from the income of his employees, because the employer is not burdened by too much obligations to further verify whether the wife works or not, the wife's income has been taxed or not, etcetera.

For every person of the blood relation family and by marriage in vertical line, for example, parents, parents in law, children, step-children grandchildren and others who are the full dependants of the tax payer, he is granted a reduction amounting to Rp. 480,000.00 (four hundred eitghy thousand rupiahs) with a limit to 3 (three) persons.

To an individual as a foreign tax payer that is the one staying in Indonesia for loss than 183 (one hundred eighty three) days within 12 consecutive months of a fiscal year will not be granted reduction in the form of non taxable income as referred to in Paragraph (1). For an individual of a foreign tax payer, the taxable income shall be the gross income as referred to in Article 16, Paragraph (3).

Paragraph (2)

To calculate the amount of the reduction in the form of non taxable income, is determined according to the situation of the begining of fiscal year and on becoming the domestic tax subject.

For instance, a tax payer on Jan. 1 gets married and has 1 (one) dependant. If in the middle of the year the second baby is born, for the fiscal year when the second child is born the marriage is considered to have only one child.

Paragraph (3)

The Minister of Finance is competent to adjust the amount of non taxable income by considering the changes in field of economy and monetary.

Article 8

Paragraph (1)

Based on this paragraph, the income as well as the loss of a woman, who has got married in the beginning of the fiscal year is regarded as the income or loss of her husband.

This provision emphasizes on the economic capability, that is, the husband and wife are of one unit, and with provision, the tax imposition does not lose the progressive elements in the tariff imposition.

The combination of incomes is not conducted in the case that the wife receives her income by working as an employee or the husband receives merely from working as an employee and upon said incomes, tax have been collected according to Article 21, except if the wife's income is obtained from the work which has connections with the husband's business or other family member's.

By other family member we mean one which is the full dependant of the husband as referred to in Article 7, Paragraph (1) Letter d. This means that to them (who receives income from working as employees) in the tax imposition, an income reduction is granted in the form of non-taxable income as refered to in Article 7 for each person amounting to Rp. 960,000.00 (nine hundred sixty thousand rupiahs).

To give clearer elucidation, some examples are given here under.

1. Determinant time :

   a. A women who gets married after Jan. 1 (in this case the fiscal year is the same as the calendar year) fiscally she is considered unmarried, so that the tax is imposed to her.
      The income or loss of the women is considered the income or loss of the husband as from the commencement of the next fiscal Year.

   b. For the husband and wife having got married since they stay in Indonesia, the income and loss of the wife is considered as the income and loss of the husband.

2. Income of a wife as an employee :

   a. Both the husband and wife get income from working as employees and to each of them the tax has been collected in compliance with Article 21. In this case no wife's income

is regarded as the husband's.
Their tax as employees which have been collected in accordance with Article 21 is final. They do not need to submit their Annual Tax Return as referred to in Article 30.

b. A wife receives an income as an employee, which has been taxed in accordance with Article 21.
Besides that, she also receives another income outside working as an employee, for instance the income from her business of running a beauty salon. Her husband receives an income merely from working as an employee the tax of which has been collected according to Article 21.
In this case, the income of the wife regarded as that of the husband is only that gained from running the beauty salon. The wife's income from working as an employee which has been taxed according to Article 21 is final. This is also applicable in the case where the husband and/or wife are not clearly taxed by the employer, because the amount of their income is below the non taxable incomes. Therefore, the indebted income tax which should be accounted through the submission of the Annual Tax Return is only based on the husband's income plus the wife's from running the beauty salon. In calculating the taxable income, they may reduce the amount by Rp. 480,000.00 (four hundred eighty thousand rupiahs) in compliance with Article 7 Paragraph (1) Letter b, besides Rp. 960,000.00 (nine hundred sixty thousand rupiahs).
The tax which has been collected upon the husband's income from his job is calculated as a credit.

c. The wife receives an income merely from working as an employee the tax of which has been collected according to Article 21. The husband besides receiving an income from working as an employee the tax of which has been collected according to Article 21 also receives another, for instance from/taxi business. In this case, the income of the wife which has been taxed according to Article 21 is not considered the husband's and is final. Therefore, the indebted income tax is based on the husband's income from working as an employee and from his taxi business. In the calculation of the taxable income under the name of the husband, a reduction as a non-taxable income as referred to in Article 7 is granted to the husband amounting to Rp. 960,000.00 (nine hundred sixty thousand rupiahs) plus Rp. 460,000.00 (four hundred sixty thousand rupiahs) because he is married. The tax collected upon the husband's income from working as an employee is calculated as a credit of the indebted tax.

d. The wife's income besides as an employee which has been taxed according to Article 21 is also from her beauty salon. Likewise the husband besides that from working as an employee which has been taxed according to Article 21 he also receives another income from his taxi business. In this case the income of the wife regarded as the income of the husband is, that coming from running the beauty salon only; The income of the wife received by working as an employee which has been taxed according to Article 21 is final. Therefore, the indebted income tax which should be reported in the Annual Tax Return is the amount of the indebted tax upon the income of the husband from working as an employee from the taxi business and from his wife's beauty salon business.

   In calculating the tax, outside that which has been deducted and paid by the wife's employer, the reduction in the form of non taxable income as referred to in Article 7 of is Rp. 960,000.00 (nine hundred sixty thousand rupiahs) plus Rp. 480,000.00 (four hundred eighty thousand rupiahs) because he is married. (The addition of non taxable income of Rp. 960,000.00 (nine hundred sixty thousand rupiahs) is no longer granted because it has been calculated when deducting the wife's income tax.

Paragraph (2)

The income of a child, including the adopted one, not yet of age is combined with that of the parent's.

In line with the objective of the imposition of tax to the Tax Payer not yet adult, the definition of adult in tax provisions should pay attention to definition of the samething in another law, including the that in labour, that an adult is a man or woman of 18 (eighteen) years who has got married is regarded an adult. Men or women of 18 (eighteen) years up and those who are under 18 years old but they have been married, in the community are stated as people who are capable to perform legal acts and regarded as able to and obligated to earn their living themselves. Based on this consideration, the definition of adult is a man or woman who is of 18 (eighteen) years up or one who has got married though he/she is below 18 (eighteen) years old.

Article 9

Paragraph (1)

Letter a

Dividend shall not be deducted from the income of the distributing company, because it is the part of the company's income included as taxable according to this law, therefore if dividend is allowed to be reduced, the taxable income of the company will decrease. Upon said distributed devidend an income tax is imposed according to Article 23 or Article 26.

Letter b

The establishment or accumulation of a reserve fund is generally intended to extend the company and to guarantee the company operation. Such establishment or accumulation cannot be burdened as reduction in calculating the taxable income.

In this case there should be differentiation between reserve and separation. Separation is intended for the definite or compulsory burden, eventhough the exact amount is not yet known, for instance the separation for the Regional Development Contribution (Ipeda), additional tax and others.

For particular undertakings, it requires the reserve to cover the possible burden or loss, for instance banking and insurance. In this case, this regulation refers to a Government Regulation to regulate its further implementation.

Letter c

The insurance premium paid by the Tax Payer himself cannot be deducted from the income. When the policy holder receives the payment, it is not an income as referred to in Article 4 paragraph (3) Letter c.

Letter d

All convenience granted to the employee cannot be deducted from the income of the employer because it is not an income for the recipient (employees) according to Article 4 paragraph (3) Letter d. Concerning the isolated regions, the Minister of Finance is competent to issue a decree on the definition of isolated that is a region where there is no home to rent available, so that the company has to provide homes for the employees. Therefore, only this expenditure can be deducted.

Letter e

As an example is an expert who happens to be a shareholder of a body provides some services to said body. For his services he receives a payment of Rp. 500,000.00 (five hundred thousand rupiahs), whereas for the same job performed by another expert the payment is only Rp. 100,000.00 (one hundred thousand rupiahs). As there is a special connection, the amount Rp. 400,000.00 (four hundred thousand rupiahs) shall not be deducted because it exceeds the reasonableness. For him said payment is also taxable as dividend.

Letter f

Granted property, inheritance and aid payment shall not be deducted because to the recipient it does not constitute an income as referred to in Article 4 Paragraph (30) Letter a and b.

Letter g

An income tax shall not be deducted because it is not a cost for obtaining or collecting an income, and the indebted tax is calculated upon the taxable income as a result of the calculation after undergoing the allowable deduction.

Letter h

Cost spent for personal needs of the Tax Payer or his dependant are not company costs, but the use of income, therefore such an expenditure cannot deduct the taxable income.

Letter i

Donations in any form whatsoever cannot be deducted from income.

Paragraph (2)

This cost is for example the cost for a big advertisement regarding the introduction of a new product which will not occur again in the next few years, therefore this cost cannot be directly deducted from the income, but through amortization.

Article 10

Paragraph (1)

In general purchase, the evaluation basis is the acquisition price. In the case of exchanging or being bought by from another Tax Payer which has special connection, the acquisition value is used, that is the price which should be paid according to the normal market price. The following is an exchange.

	PT A Property X	PT B Property Y
Book balance Price	Rp. 10,000,000.00	Rp. 12,000,000.00
Market price	Rp. 20,000,000.00	Rp. 20,000,000.00

Between PT A and PT B there is a property exchange. Eventhough there is no payment realization between the two parties, because the market price of the property exchanged is Rp. 20,000,000.00 (twenty million rupiahs), therefore the sum of Rp. 20,000,000.00 (twenty million rupiahs) constitutes an acquisition value which should have been incurred. This acquisition value also becomes the net income for the application of Article 11 Paragraph (7) Letter b. While the difference between the market price and the book balance price of the property exchanged is a taxable profit.
To PT A there is a profit amounting to Rp. 20,000,000.00 minus Rp. 10,000,000.00 = Rp. 10,000,000.00 while to PT B the profit is Rp. 20,000,000.00 minus Rp. 12,000,000.00 = Rp. 8,000,000.00. The exceptions from the provisions of said application of the acquisition value or price shall be in :

Letter a

The exchange of shares of a body with an individual's property as referred to in Article 4 Paragraph (3) Letter e, therefore the basis for share valuation or other participation is the same as the transfered property value (deformation from an individual to a body does not result in tax debt, and if the shares are transfered with profits, the profits are taxable).

Letter b

For the body or corporation receiving the property in exchange to the shares, the property valuation basis is the property value or book balance price of the property exchanged.

Letter c

Example :
Someone receiving inheritance, the acquisition value is that for the heir/heiress in case of undepreciable property or the book balance price of the said property at the time of transfer in case of depreciable property. The provisions in Letter a and Letter b are also applicable to this case, that is if the inherited property is sold, the profit thereof is taxable.
The same thing applies to the case of the granted property or an aid which is non taxable.

Paragraph (2)

In case there is an addition, repair and other expenditure which are normally spent to increase the capacity of the said property, the acquisition price should be adjusted to said expenditure. An addition can mean an expenditure to obtain an additional assets and can also be as referred to in this paragraph that is an expense to add the capacity of particular assets.
By adjustment upon acquisition price or property use mean :

- the decrease of value due to depreciation;
- the addition of value due to the additional expense to add, repair or change in increasing the capacity of said property.

For instance, a property has an initial amount of Rp.100,000,000.00 (one hundred million rupiahs). In the current year, an addition or repair has been conducted at the cost of Rp. 25,000,000.00 (twenty five million rupiahs), therefore, the initial value thereof next year is Rp. 100,000,000.00 plus Rp. 25,000,000.00 minus depreciation.
The expense burdening in connection with property extimate is basically of 2 (two) groups, namely :

a. Expenditure which can be regarded as overhead for instance the costs for maintenance and repair which are usually conducted periodically, to main tain the technical benefit of the property;

b. Expenditure not regarded as overhead, for instance the cost for rehabilitition, big repair, which are usually conducted to increase the capacity of said property.

Expenditure belenging to group b, the benefitial period of which is not only in the same fiscal year but for a definite longer time, therefore it is reasonable if the expenditure is burdened to the property estimate (decapitalization) and the reduced by the depreciation in accordance with the beneficial period of the relative property.

Paragraph (3)

In general there are 3 (three) groups of goods stocks, namely :

a. finished goods;

b. goods in production process;

c. Raw and auxiliary materials.

The provision in this paragraph regulates that the valuation of goods stock is only allowed to use the acquisition price. While the valuation of stock use to calculate the basic price can be conducted only with pro rata method or by giving precedence to the stock firstly obtained (by using "first in first out" method abbriviated into FIFO).

Example :

1.	Initial stock	100 ea	@ Rp. 9.00
2.	purchase/obtained	100 ea	@ Rp. 12.00
3.	purchase/obtained	100 ea	@ Rp. 11.25
4.	sales/used	100 ea	
5.	sales/used	100 ea	
6.	last stock	100 ea	

Evaluation of stock used for basic price calculation with pro rata method

No	Obtained	Used	Balance/stock
1.			100 s @ Rp. 9.00 = Rp. 900.00

No	Obtained	Used	Balance/stock
2.	100 s @ Rp. 12.00 = Rp. 1,200.00		200 s @ Rp. 10.50 = Rp. 2,100.00
3.	100 s @ Rp. 11.25 = Rp. 1,125.00		300 s @ Rp. 10.75 = Rp. 3,225.00
4.		100 s @ Rp. 10.75 = Rp. 1,075.00	200 s @ Rp. 10.75 = Rp. 2,150.00
5.		100 s @ Rp. 10.75 = Rp. 1,075.00	100 s @ Rp. 10.75 = Rp. 1,075.00

Evaluation of stock used for basic price calculation by giving precedance to the stock received first.

No	Obtained	Used	Balance/stock
1.			100 s @ Rp. 9.00 = Rp. 900.00
2.	100 s @ Rp. 12.00 = Rp. 1,200.00		100 s @ Rp. 9.00 = Rp. 900.00 100 s @ Rp. 12.00 = Rp. 1,200.00
3.	100 s @ Rp. 11.25 = Rp. 1,125.00		100 s @ Rp. 9.00 = Rp. 900.00 100 s @ Rp. 12.00 = Rp. 1,200.00 100 s @ Rp. 11.25 = Rp. 1,125.00
4.		100 s @ Rp. 9.00 = Rp. 900.00	100 s @ Rp. 12.00 = Rp. 1,200.00
5.		100 s @ Rp. 12.00 = Rp. 1,200.00	100 s @ Rp. 11.25 = Rp. 1,125.00

Once a Tax Payer opt, a method of stock valuation used for basic price calculation, the same method shall be used in the following years.

Article 11

The burdening of cost to obtain, to collect and to maintain an income which has a beneficial period of more than one year, according to this law is conducted through depreciation (for tangible property) and amortization (for intangible property), and for both of them the same principles are applied.

In the depreciation system according to this provision, all assets are grouped into four groups of property, depending on its beneficial period. To each of the groups, depreciation percentage is determined and said percentage is applied upon an amount as the basis of depreciation. If within one fiscal year there is no assets addition and withdrawal from usage, the amount of the book balance price of the previons year, having the initial price for the current year can be directly multiplied by the percentage of depriciation tariff.

Paragraph (1)

What is depreciat able is all tangible property owned and used in the company or which is owned to obtain income. Land cannot be depreciated except if the land is used in the company or owned to obtain income on condition that the value of the land decreases because it is used to obtain income, for instance land which is used by rooftile manufacturers. So what can be depreciated is not only company property but also the property used for production, for instance the cost to build a house which can be used to obtain rents.

Paragraph (2)

Every kind of property is grouped according to its economic life. For each group of property the tariff or depreciation percentage is determined. Property grouping is regulated in Paragraph (3), for instance a machine which belongs to Group 2, the tariff or depreciation percentage is 25% (twenty five percent), which is applied to the initial amount of the property group in the beginning of the fiscal year plus the purchase or addition minus the net income of the sold property.

Paragraph (3)

This paragraph divides properties into 4 (four) groups. Each group of property may consist of many kinds of properties which have

almost the same economic life. To facilitate the Tax Payer in following the development of the property, either in the form of decrease or increase, a list of properties should be made for each group, including among other things the year of acquisition/purchase, acquisition price, property group, and depreciation tariff so that at any time the depreciation amount to each of the properties can be known. This is important for the Tax Payer, especially when there is a withdrawal due to an extra ordinary cause, see elucidation on Paragraph (7) of this Article.
A separate estimate shall be made for each buildings and other immovable property.

Paragraph (4)

The depreciation basic calculation is the amount in the beginning of the fiscal year, plus the additions, either in the form of the new properties or addition upon the property conducted to increase the capacity of said property, repairs or changes and minus the reduction as stipulated in Paragraph (7) of this Article.

Paragraph (5)

For non building group that is Groups 1, 2 and 3 the initial amount of the groups is the book balance price of the previous fiscal year which remains upon for the addition of new property and reduction by net income of the sold property, then the depreciation tariff is applied. If within the current fiscal year there is an additional expenditure to obtain the company property depreciable according to this law, the initial amount is added by the expenditure to obtain the new property. If one of the kinds of property is no longer used and is sold (due the general cause), the net income from the sales is deducted from the initial amount of the relative.

Paragraph (6)

For the Category of Buildings, the deprediation shall be calculated from the acquisition price.

Paragraph (7)

Letter a

For several types of assets, there is the possibility that they can not be used anymore, for example struck by a dissaster. It can also happen due to the fact that the company has ceased a major portion of its production, by reasons beyond the Company's Control.
The withdrawal of said assets is called withdrawal from usage/ operations due to extra-ordinary reasons. The value to the amount of the book value balance of said assets shall be deducted from the initial amount of the relative assets category, and said amount shall be charged to the profit and loss account in the fiscal year concerned. If said asset is sold, or obtains an insurance indemnification, then said, sales price or insurance indemnification shall constitute an income/revenue in the fiscal year concerned.

1984 EXAMPLE OF DEPRECIATION OF CATEGORY

Initial amount per Jan 1, 1984	= Rp.	0.00
Addition : Car "A" = Rp. 1,500.–		
Car "B" = Rp. 2,500.–		
Car "C" = Rp. 1,200.–		
	= Rp.	5,200.00
Deduction	= Rp.	0.00

Depreciation Calculation

Initial amount (Jan 1, 1984)	= Rp.	0.00
Additions ("A", "B", "C")	= Rp.	5,200.00
Deduction	=(Rp.	0.00)
Depreciation basis	= Rp.	5,200.00
Depreciation (5%)	=(Rp.	2,600.00)
Initial amount per Jan 1, 1985	= Rp.	2,600.00

1985

Addition : Car "D" .... = Rp. 3,000.00

Deduction : Car "C", burnt.
(due to extra-ordinary reasons)
acquisition price (1984) Rp. 1,200.00

depreciated (1984) Rp. 600.00
book value balance (1985) Rp. 600.00
insurance indemnification Rp. 800.00

Calculation of depreciation

Initial amount (Jan 1, 1985)	= Rp. 2,600.00
Addition ("D")	= Rp. 3,000;00
(Loss) Deduction ("C" book value balance)	= Rp. 600.00
Depreciation basis	= Rp. 5,000.00
Depreciation (50%)	= Rp. 2,500.00
Initial amount per Jan 1, 1986	= Rp. 2,500.00
(Profit) Income/revenue (insurance indemnification on Car "C")	= Rp. 800.00

Letter b

A withdrawal other than mentioned above, is called withdrawal from usage due to normal reasons, for example said asset is sold. The net proceeds from the sale of said asset, namely the difference between the sale price with appropriate expenses and actually in curred related to said sale, shall be deducted from the begin amount of the asset category concerned.

Example (continuance of the calculation at Letter a).

Begin amount per Jan 1, 1986 .... = Rp. 2,500.00

1986 Addition .... = Rp. 0.00

Deduction : Car "B" is sold
(due to normal season)
acquisition price (1984) Rp. 2,500.00
depreciated ('84 & '85) Rp. 1,875.00
book value balance
(1986) Rp. 625.00
sale price Rp. 1,000.00

Calculation of Depreciation

Initial amount (Jan 1, 1986)	= Rp. 2,500.00
Addition /	= Rp. 0.00
Deduction ("B" sale price)	=(Rp. 1,000.00)

Depreciation basis .... = Rp. 1,500.00
Depreciation (50%) .... =(Rp. 750.00)

Initial amount .... = Rp. 750.00

Note : the book value balance amounting to Rp. 625.00 is ignored.

Paragraph (8)

The depreciation basis shall be negative, if negative, the a. .ount causing this negative value, shall be added as income/revenue.
If the amount serving as depreciation basis is negative, then this means that the not proceeds of the assets not used anymore in the operation activity exceeds the year initial amount serving as depreciation basis. In other words, the sales proceeds exceed the book value balance of the asset category concerned; accordingly, said difference constitutes a profit of the sale of an asset, which, based on this law, shall be imposed with tax at the moment said profit is received or obtained.

Example :
The book value balance of Category I asset per
Jan 1, 1984 .... = Rp. 1,000,000.00

Withdrawal from usage in 1984

Sale price	Rp. 1,500,000.00
Sale cost	Rp. 200,000.00

Net proceeds of assets sale .... = Rp. 1,300,000.00

Negative difference .... = Rp. 300,000.00

accordingly the depreciation basis for 1984
is : N I L.
The difference amounting to Rp. 300,000.– constitutes income for fiscal year 1984.

Paragraph (9)

The depreciation tariff shall be determined by the benefit period of defreciable assets.

Paragraph (10)

In Article 9 paragraph (2), it is stated that the cost for obtaining taxable income having a benefit period of more than one year may not be deducted in one lumpsum from the income. The acquisition price of an intangible asset and other expenses having a benefit period more than one year, shall be amortised by the tariff applicable for Category 1 or Category 2 or Category 3, or amortised by applying the production unit method as mentioned in paragraph (12) and paragraph 13 of this Article.

Paragraph (11)

Establishment expenses and capital expension can be amortised as Category 1, or charged as expenses according to Article 6 Paragraph (1) letter a.
The tax payer can choose to amortise or charge as an expense.
If the tax payer chooses charging in one lumpsum, this must be consistent with its bookkeeping, meaning, that it will be charged in the fiscal year chosen by him.

Paragraph (12)

Expenses for acquiring a mining right, besides oil and natural gas and forest exploitation right, can be deducted as amortisation by applying the production unit method. It means, that the amortisation percentage of said expenses shall eash be equal to the percentage of mining or filling each year of the estimate of the overall production volume as example in the case of a mining concession estimated having a deposit of 100,000 tons, and in one year is producet 10,000 ton.
Accordingly, said mining concession in the relative fiscal Year is amortised by 10% (ten percent). Nevertheless, it is not allowed to conduct an amortisation of more than 20% (twenty percent) in one fiscal year.

Paragraph (13)

Particularly in respect to the oil and natural gas mining sector, the expenses for acquiring a right/concession and/or other expenses having a benefit period of more than one year, shall be amortised by the production unit method without certain percentage limitation.

Paragraph (14)

The Minister of Finance has the authority to issue a decision on the classification of depreciable assets. In said decision, the classification of the asset type into the asset category, shall be based on the benefit period of said asset type as well as the relative activity type.

Article 12

Paragraph (1)

Basically the fiscal year is the calendar year.
The tax payer can apply a fiscal year different from the calendar year namely covering the period for 12 (twelve) months. If the bookkeeping of the Tax Payer covers a period of less or more than 12 (twelve) months, then the tax computation shall be based on the relative fiscal year, by observing the calendar months of said year.
If the Tax Payer applies a fiscal year, then this matter shall be declared when submitting the Annual Return to the Director General of Taxes.
Mentioning the fiscal year. For the fiscal year equal to the calendar year, the mentioning of said fiscal year shall be said calendar year. If the fiscal year is not the same as the calendar year, their the mentioning of the fiscal year concerned shall use the year, in which are included the first six months or more of the six months of said fiscal year.

Example :

a. The fiscal year is the same as the calendar year.
   The bookkeeping is January 1 thorough December 31, 1985.
   The fiscal year is year 1985.

b. The fiscal is not the same as the fiscal year:
   1) Bookkeeping is July 1, 1985 through June 30, 1986
      the fiscal year is 1985, as the year 1985 has the First six months of the fiscal year.
   2) Bookkeeping April 1, 1985 through March 31, 1986
      The fiscal year shall be 1985, as year 1985 has more than 6 of said fiscal year.
   3) Bookkeeping October, 1985 through September 30, 1986.
      The fiscal year shall be year 1986, as the year 1986, has more than six months of said fiscal year.

Paragraph (2)

The application of the fiscal year, both based on a calendar year or fiscal year, shall be consequent consistent. This is particularly to prevent the possibility of shifting profits or losses, if the Tax Payer is provided the liberty to change his fiscal year at any time.
Accordingly, if the Tax Payer is desireous of introducing a change of the fiscal year, he shall be obligated to apply for a prior approval from the Director General of Taxes.

Article 13

Paragraph (1)

Each Tax Payer obtaining an income from an undertaking and/or free occupation, shall be under obligation to keep books in Indonesia. Said bookkeeping shall be available and conducted in Indonesia, because said bookkeeping is the basis for calculating the amount of taxable income as inserted in the Annual Tax Return, so that it can be verified in Indonesia, in order to know that said bookkeeping has been conducted correctly, confirm to the provision of this law. From the bookkeeping, it should be able to know the net profit of the undertaking or the nett revenue/income.
From the net profit or from said nett revenue, shall subsequently be calculated the taxable income of said Tax Payer as the bookkeeping conducted by the Tax Payer serves as the starting point for calculating the taxable income, the bookkeeping shall be based on a method or system namelly applied in Indonesia, for example based on the Indonesia Accountancy Principles Composed by the Indonesian Accountants Association.
The bookkeeping can be conducted by the Cash System as well as the Accrual System. The Cash System is a calculation without which is based on the income received, and the expenses an paid in cash. According to this method, an income shall be considered only as an income, it actually received in cash in a certain period, and costs shall be considered as costs, if actually paid in cash in a certain period.
Mainly the Accrual System is the method of calculating income and expenses, namely said income is determined at the time of acquisition, and the costs determined at the time it is indebted. So it does not depend on when said revenue is received, and when said cost is paid in cash.

Example :

a. **Sale**

The amount of the delivery = Rp 10,500,–

Consisting of – delivery already received the payment thereof = Rp 10,000.–
– delivery the payment of which is not yet received = Rp 500,–

Accrual System : Revenue (sale) Rp 10,500.–

Cash System : Revenue (sale) Rp 10,500.–
The Rp 500 is determined as revenue of the following period, if received in cash

b. **Income in the form of interest**

Loan for 6 month (September 1, 1984 through February 28, 1985).

A loan amounting to 12% per annum and to be paid at the expiration of the loan period.

Interest calculation: September 1, 1984 through December 31, 1984 = 4 months = Rp 400.–
Jan 1, 1985 through February 2, 1985 = 2 months = Rp 200.–

Accrual System : Interest revenue of 1984 = Rp 400.–
1985 = Rp 200.–

Cash System : Interest revenue of 1984 = Rp 0.–
(not yet received in cash)
1985 = Rp 600.–
(the moment received in cash).

2. **Expenses costs (in this case a lease example is given).**

A motor car rental during 4 months (October 1, 1984 through January 31, 1985).

The rental amounting to Rp 4,000 is paid at the beginning of the lease period.

Rental calculation : October 1, 1984 through December 31, 1985 = 3 months = Rp 3,000.–
Jan 1, 1985 through Jan 31, 1985 = 1 month : Rp 1,000.–

Accrual System : rental year 1984 = Rp 3,000.–
Rental year 1985 = Rp 1,000.–

Cash System	:	rental year 1984	=	Rp 4,000.–
		(When paid in cash)		
		1985	=	Rp 0.00

The Cash System is normally applied by small individual companies on service companies, for example transportation, entertainment, restaurant, of which the time lapse between the delivery of the service and the receipt of its payment does not last long. In a pure cash system, the income/revenue of the delivery of the goods/ services are determined at the moment the payment is received from the customer, and the expenses are determined upon payment of the goods, services and other operational expenses.
By this method, the application of the cash system can cause an observed calculation on revenues, namely the amount of the revenues from year to year can be adjusted by regulating the cash receipts and the cash disbursements.
Accordingly, for the purpose of Income Tax compertation, in case of cash system application, attention shall be paid, among other things, to the following matters;

1) The calculation of the sales amount in a certain period shall cover the entire sales, both cash and non cash. In calculating the sales cost price, also shall be the entire purchases and stock thereof.
2) In acquiring a depreciable asset and amortizable Concessions/ rights, the expenses deducted from the revenue can be conducted only through depreciation and amortization.
3) The cash system application shall be conducted consistently.

Paragraph (2)

The provision in this paragraph is to provide a confirmation on the bookkeeping system and principles to be conducted consistently.

Article 14.

Paragraph (1) and paragraph (2)

In principle, in order to be able to fulfil the tax obligation on the revenue of an undertaking and free accupation as best as possible a bookkeeping is essential. The law intends to stimulate all Tax Payer to keep books, although it is also realized, that not all Tax Payer are capable of conducting said bookkeeping. The Tax Payers who are allowed not to conduct a complete bookkeeping cover Tax Payers whose business/undertaking turn-over on their gross revenues are less than Rp 60,000,000 = per year.

For these persons, an open and just method is required, besides the necessity of guidance, in order that they are later on able and capable at conducting a bookkeeping.

The Calculation Norm is a guideline which can be used as a means for determining the gross turn-over or gross revenue, and finally to determine the nett revenue.

Basically, the Calculation Norm is only appliced for calculating or determining the nett revenue in case of :

– the non-Existent of other letter calculation basis, namely bookkeeping;

– a Tax Payer's bookkeeping, which is apparently conducted incorrectly.

  The Calculation Norm is in the form of a percentage or other comparative/ratio figures composed in such a way, based on the result of meticulous research, so that it is.

– simple

– specified by undertaking type group

– differentiated in several classifications of towns/places.

– differentiated for Tax Payers whose undertaking turn-over amount to on the gross revenues are less than Rp 60.000,00 from those with more than Rp 60,000,000.–

– the percentage level or comparative/ratio figure is not for from the reasonableness, but can stimulate the Tax Payer to conduct a bookkeeping.

Accordingly, the Calculation Norm constitutes a means to be applied in emergency, due to lach of another basis, but still accountable in respect to its implicity, openness and reasonableness. The Calculation Norm is very helpful to the Tax Payers who are still unable to conduct a bookkeeping, for calculating the nett revenue to be inserted in the Annual Tax Return. As the Tax Payer himself will determine his tax, the existence of a Norm for calculating several revenues declare previously, will be very helpful. Only if it is proved that the Annual Tax Return is incorrect, them the Director General of Taxes shall have the authority ro assess the tax based on correct data, by applying the Calculation Norm added by an administrative sanction in the form of an increase.

Said Calculation Norm being open of nature, besides for facilitating the implementation obligation fulfilment for the Tax Payer, is simultaneously also for preventing the occurence of arbitrary actions of the Tax administration by estimating an unreasonable revenue amount. The Calculation Norm concerned shall be prepared and introved continuously as well as issued by the Director General of Taxes, guided by a guideline stipulat ed by the Minister of Finance.

The guideline stipulated by the Minister of Finance shall Contain:

a. interlinking factors to be applied for determining the amount of :

- turn-over (the number of employees, the number of tables for a restaurant undertaking, the number of machines for an industrial enterprise, the number of rooms for a hotel enterprise, etcetera).
- the gross revenue (the amount of material purchased, the amount of employees' salaries, etcetera).
- the nett revenue (the amount of concrete disbursements or the cost of living standard, etcetera).

b. method items to be observed in Composing the Calculation Norm;

c. the ways of improving the Calculation Norm.

Paragraph (3)

Self explanatory

Paragraph (4)

A Tax Payer as referred to in paragraph (2), who fails to in form as having chosen the nett revenue calculation by applying the Calculation Norm, shall be considered as conducting a bookkeeping. In case said Tax Payer is evidently not conducting a bookkeeping then the nett revenue shall be calculated by the Calculation Norm, and

the tax resulting from said calculation shall be added with an administrative sanction in the form of an increase, as provised from in paragraph (7) of this Article.
With this provision, the Tax Payer is stimulated to conduct his bookkeeping properly, correctly and completely.
Accordingly, the Calculation Norm shall be composed as best as possible, by observing a good and efficient undertaking or free occupation. For an honest Tax Payer who in his undertaking does not succeed in obtaining an revenue as a good and efficient undertaking the application of the Calculation Norm can be disadvantageous.
For preventing the application of said disadvatageous Calculation Norm, the Tax Payer can choose to conduct a proper correct, complete bookkeeping, so that the computation of his tax shall be based on the actual condition in accordance with his bookkeeping.

Paragraph (5)

A Tax Payer choosing to calculate his net income by applying the Calculation Norm, shall automatically be able to show, that the turn-over amount of his undertaking or the gross revenue of his free occupation in one year is less than Rp 60,000,000 = (sixty million rupiah), which can be proved from the turn-over or gross revenue records conducted by him.

Paragraph (6)

According to this provision, the net revenue shall be calculated based on the Calculation Norm in respect to Tax Payers who:

a. have the obligation to conduct a bookkeeping, but do not conduct a bookkeeping as stipulated by the law;

b. have the obligation to conduct records on the gross turn-over or his gross revenue, but fail to conduct the records as obligated.

c. are not willing to show their books, records as well as other proofs demanded by the Director General of Taxes.

It should be emphasized, that those having the obligation to conduct a bookkeeping shall be the Tax Payers, whose undertaking turn-over or gross revenues amount to Rp 60,000,000.– (sixty million Rupiahs) per year, and Tax Payers whose undertaking turn-over or gross revenues are less than Rp 60,000,000.—(sixty million rupiah) per year, but choose or are considered having chosen to conduct a bookkeeping.

Paragraph (7)

The Income Tax resulting from the net income calculated by applying the Calculation Norm as referred to in paragraph (1), shall be added by an administrative sanction constituting an increase as provided for in Article 13 paragraph (3) of Law Number 6 Year 1983 on General Provisions and Procedures on Taxes.

Article 15.

The provisions in this Article provide for a Special Calculating Norm for certain Tax Payer Categories, based on a Decree of the Minister of Finance.
In practice, difficulties are often faced in calculating the revenue amount and taxable income for certain Tax Payer Categories, so that based on practical considerations, by this law, the Minister of Finance is authorized to issue a Decree on the determination of a Special Calculation Norm for calculating the net revenue, which shall automatically serve as the calculation basis of the taxable revenue amount for said certain Tax Payer Category.

Article 16.

The taxable revenue shall constitute the calculation basis for determining the Income Tax amount indebted.
As inserted in Article 2 paragraph (2), 2 (two) categories of Tax Payers are identified.

Domestic Tax Payers and
Foreign Tax Payers.

For domestic Tax Payers, there are 2 (two) methods for determining the taxable income amount :

- the ordinary calculation method
- the calculation method by applying the Calculation Norm.

Paragraph (1)

The Ordinary calculation method

Example :

–	Income obtained in a certain fiscal year according to Article 4 paragraph (1)		Rp 50,000,000.–
–	Expenses according to Article 6 paragraph (1) :		
	expenses for obtaining, collecting and maintaining the income	Rp 30,000,000	
	depreciation and amortisation	Rp 6,000,000	
	contribution to Pension on fund	Rp 1,000,000	
			Rp 37,000,000.–
–	**Net Income**		Rp 13,000,000.–
–	Compensation of previous years' losses		Rp 2,000,000.–
	Taxable Income (for entities, besides cooperati ves)		Rp 11,000,000.–
–	For a cooperative entity it is allowed to deduct the re-imbursement the Operation Result Balance obtained from activities of and for the members.		
–	Deduction for the individual Tax Payer Article 7 Paragraph (1), for example a Tax Payer is married, with 2 (two) children		Rp 2,400,000.–
–	Taxable Income		Rp 8,600,000.–

Paragraph (2)

The application of the Calculation Norm shall be Conducted on certain Tax Payers, namely Tax Payers whose undertaking turn-over on gross revenues of their free occupation in a year are less than Rp 60,000,000.– (sixty million rupiah).
For Tax Payers, whose undertaking turn-over or the gross revenues

of their free occupation in one year are less than Rp 60,000,000.— (sixty million rupiah), according to the provisions, of this law, shall not be obliged to keep books.
Towards them, the calculation of the taxable income shall be conducted by applying the Calculation Norm.
However, if desired by the Tax Payer, the calculation of the taxable income can be conducted by the ordinary calculation method as referred to in paragraph (1) with the provision that they conduct a bookkeeping is provided for in this law.
(Vide elucidation on Article 14).

Paragraph (3)

Self explanatory

Article 17.

Paragraph (1)

For domestic Tax Payers the Income Tax tariff shall be applied to the entire income received or obtained in one fiscal year, by a very simple system.

Example :

Taxable Income amount Rp 80,000,000.—

The Income Tax indebted :

15% x Rp 10,000,000 = Rp 1,500,000.—
25% x Rp 40,000,000 = Rp 10,000,000.—
35% x Rp 30,000,000 = Rp 10,500,000.—

Taxable Income amount Rp 80,000,000 Tax Rp 22,000,000.—

Paragraph (2)

The taxable income strata limit is referred to in said paragraph (1) shall be adjusted to an adjustment factor, among other things the inflation rate.

The Minister of Finance is authorized to issue a decree regulating said adjustment factor.

Paragraph (3)

For example, the taxable income amounts to Rp 1,050,650.– (one million fifty thousand six hundred fifty rupiahs), so, far applying the tariff, the taxable income is rounded-off to Rp 1,050,000.– (one million fifty thousand rupiahs).

Paragraph (4)

For example an unmarried individual whose subjective tax obligation as domestic Tax Subject is 3 (three) months, and within said period has obtained an income amounting to Rp 1,000,000.– (one million rupiah), then the calculation of the Income Tax shall be as follows :

The income during 3 (three) months	Rp 1,000,000.–
The income in one year amounts to $\frac{360}{3 \times 30}$ x Rp 1,000,000.–	Rp 4,000,000.–
Non taxable income	Rp 960,000.–
Taxable income	Rp 3,040.000.–
The Income Tax indebted (one year) 15% x Rp 3,040,000.–	Rp 456.000.–
So the Income Tax indebted during a part of the fiscal year, namely during 3 (three) months, shall be : $\frac{3 \times 30}{360}$ x Rp 456,000.–	Rp 114,000.–

Paragraph (5)

Self explanatory.

Article 18.

Paragraph (1)

This Law authorises the Minister of Finance to issue a Decree on the ratio amount between the liability and the capital of the Company, Justifiable for tax calculation purposes.

In business circles, there is a certain reasonable ratio level in respect to the extent of liability and capital (debt equity ratio). If the ratio between debt/liability and capital is very substantial (above the limit of reasonability), then actually said company is in unsound condition.

In such a case, the law assumes the existence of disguised capital.

Paragraph (2)

The aim of the insertion of this provision is to prevent the occurrence of tax avoidance, which can occur due to the existence of a special relationship.

In case a special relationship exists, the possibility may occur that a revenue is reported below the appropriateness, or expenses are overcharged than appropriate, if a transaction is effected among the parties concerned. Likewise, the possibility may occur of a disguised capital participation, by declaring said capital participation is a liability/debt.

In such a case, the Director General of Taxes is authorized to redetermine the revenue amount and/or expenses which should appropriately occur, if no special relationship exists between said parties.

Likewise, if based on the examination conducted, apparently a disguised participation or capital, as if debts, are existing, then the Director General of Taxes shall be authrorized to determine said debt (s) as the company's capital.

Accordingly, the interest paid in connection with the debt which assets constitutes a capital participation, shall not be allowed to be deducted, whereas for the interest receiving-or obtaining shareholder, it shall constitute a taxable income. In Article 6 paragraph (1) letter a, interest constitutes an expense allowed to be deducted from the income, however, on the other hand, dividends paid-out to the shareholder may not be deducted.

Paragraph (3)

Letter a.

A special relationship is considered as existing if there are two or more Tax Payers under the same ownership or control. Meant by this ownership or control, is if the person owning said undertakings is holding the majority of shares, which can affect the undertaking's operations.

A special relationship can also be formulated as follows :

- Entity AA has a participation in the undertaking BB amonting to 25% (twenty-five per cent), so AA and BB have a special relationship.
- An individyal YY has 25% (twenty–five per cent) participation in undertaking AA and also 25% (twenty-five per cent) participation in undertaking BB, so that between YY, AA and BB a special relationship exists.

Letter b

Meant by one degree straight blood line family relationship shall be father, the mother and child (ren), whereas one degree horizontal bload relationship shall be brothers/sisters.
Meant by straight line family relationship by marriage, shall be parents in law and step child, whereas one degree horizontal family relationship by marriage, shall be brother/sister in law.

Paragraph (4)

In case there are several parties having special relationship with 50% (fifty percent), participation or more, their the lowest 15% (fifteen per cent) tariff can be applied only once.
In case one of the parties suffers a loss, said loss can not be compensated against the income of the other party (ies), but the vertical compensation shall apply as refered to in Article 6 paragraph (3).

Article 19.

In case of disharmony/inconsistency between cost elements with the income due to conspicuous price development, their the Goverment can make adjustments, for example by applying an endoxation.

Article 20.

Paragraph (1)

Tax payments in the current year, in order that at the end of the year it approaches the indebted tax amount, shall be effected by:

a. deduction and collection of tax by other parties in the event a revenue is obtained by the Tax Payer from (work in employment relationship and free occupation) as referred to in Article 21 of this Law, and the deduction of tax on the revenue of capital and certain services as referred to in Article 23 of this law.

b. besides tax settlement through deduction or collection of tax by other parties, the Tax Payer himself shall also be obliged to effect payment in the current year as referred to in Article 25 of this law.

Paragraph (2)

The settlement of tax in the current year shall constitutes installments of tax payment, which in due course can be calculated by means of crediting against the Income Tax indebted in respect to the entire fiscal year concerned.

Paragraph (3)

Self-explanatory

Paragraph (4)

Self-explanatory

Article 21
Paragraph (1)

The party obliged to deduct Income according this provision Tax, or called the tax deduction, shall be :

a. the company of an individual or the entity constituting a parent company or company's branch, which pays salary, wages, honorarium and other remuneration to employee (s) or other person(s), with the provision that the work is performed in Indonesia. In the concept of work providers/they are error necessarily Tax Subjects according to this law but can alsobe any person or entity, in an employment relationship, paying a salary wages, etcetera;

b. for example, the salary paid to an employee of an Embassy of the Republic of Indonesia abroad, as it is changed to the State

Treasury, the Income Tax shall be deducted. In the concept of State Treasury, is included the Regional Administration Treasury.

c. A pension fund entity paying pension money paid to civil servants or pensioned employees as well as to their heirs. In the concept of pension, are included allowances, both paid-out periodically and not

d. Companies or entities, in case there is a payment to an expert personnel or expert personnel association as domestic Tax Payer for services, performed in Indonesia. In the concept of company, including Government agency, and in the concept of entity, are included foreign state representative bodies and internasional bodies.

Paragraph (2)

The amount from which tax is deducted, shall the part of the monthly revenue exceeding one twelfth of the non taxable income as referred to in article 7, for example in the case of or married employee with 3 (three) dependants, the non-taxable income is Rp 2,880,000.– (two million eight hundred eighty thousand rupiahs) or each month Rp 240,00.– (two hundred forty thousand rupiahs) If the revenue of said employees amounts to Rp 250,000.– (two hundred fifty thousand rupiahs) per month, their the revenue from which tax is deducted, shall amount to Rp. 10,000.– (ten thousand rupiahs)

Paragraph (3)

Consistent with the nature of the Income Tax as a personal tax and not a material tax, meaning that Tax Payer, family who are fully dependent shall also determine the amount of the Income Tax indebted, so the correctness of the Tax Payer, Statement Letter in respect to the composition of Payer, Statement Letter in respect to the composition of his family is absolutely necessary. As a comparative means the Tax Payer's Family Card can also be used issued by the local Regional Administration.

Paragraph (4)

Self-explanatory

Paragraph (5)

Self-explanatory

Paragraph (6)

In the Manual of the Director General of Taxes a table is inserted which can be used by the work providers/employers to deduct the Income Tax amount to be deposited to the State Treasury.

Paragraph (7)

If the employer has conducted the deduction and deposit of the Income tax correctly, then at the end of the fiscal year, said employees or the persons whose Income Tax has been deducted, shall not be imposed with the obligation to submit an Annual Tax Return.

In other words, the Income Tax correctly deducted shall be declared as final pursuant to the provisions of this law.

Paragraph (8)

Employees having other income besides their wages/salary are obligated to fill out and submit an annual Tax Return. The obligation on submitting the annual Tax Return shall also be applied to those persons who receive or obtain income from work from more then one employer.

Paragraph (9)

In order to facilitate the implementation of Income Tax deduction by the paying party, the Director General of Taxes shall publish an Income Tax Deduction manual.

Article 22.

Paragraph (1)

This provision regulates the authority of the Minister of Finance to appoint certain entities, both private as well as Governmental, as collectors of Income Tax, which has been greatly limited for reducing excessive advance collections. The Income Tax is levied on Tax Payers performing undertaking activities with or through said collectors.

This law firmly stipulates, that only from undertaking/business activities in the import sector and undertaking activities in other sectors obtaining payments of goods and services from the State Revenues and Expenditure Regional Revenues and Expenditures Budget, conducted with or through the designated collectors Income can be collected.

Meant by the payment of goods and services from the state budget shall be the payments of goods purchases and payments of services conpensation, by using State Finances, both the Central Government as well as the Regional Administration.

Paragraph (2)

The amount of said Income Tax collected shall automatically be determined in such a way, that it approches the Income Tax amount indebted by the relative Tax Payer.

For that purpose the Minister of Finance is authorized to stipulate the basis and amount of the collection, which is adjusted to the amount of Income Tax which will be indebted for the whole fiscal year pursuant to this law.

Article 23.

Paragraph (1)

The payment of dividend, interest, rental, royalty, remuneration of technical services and management services, constituting an income, shall be settled in the current year, through deduction by the domestic Tax Payer entity in Indonesia or the Goverment entity effecting said payment. The payment of interest and other remunerationes related to the borrowing of money from Banks or other financial institutions, non Income Tax shall be deducted by the paying party.

The tariff applied here is the lowest tariff, namely 15% (fifteen per cent) the Tax Payer whose Income Tax is deducted, still has to submit the annual Tax Return for calculating the tax indebted for his entire income in one fiscal year.

Paragraph (2)

Besides entities, both private as well as governmental, individuals

as domestic taxpayers can also be designated by the Director General of taxes for deducting the Income Tax, from the payments mentioned above.
The authority to designate an individual to serve as tax deductor on the income of this capital shall rest with the Director General of Taxes.
Individual persons shall be under obligation to deduct the tax since the time they are designated by the Director General of Taxes.

Paragraph (3)

Meant by certain interests and dividends in this paragraph shall be:

a. Interest paid by a bank or Post Office on the savings of small savers,

b. Dividend received or obtained by the holders of PT. Danareksa Share Certificates, of which the amount does not exceed an amount stipulated in a Government Regulation.
This provision is intended for small savers or holders of the PT. Danareksa Share Certificates of which generally the income received or obtained in one year does not exceed the non taxable tax amount.
If towards said small savers or share certificate holders a tax deduction is conducted their said matter shall become a burden for them to handle there imbursement thereof..
The exemption of Tax deduction on said interest and dividend does not mean that the interest and dividend are excepted as Tax Object, but they will be imposed with tax, if the interest or dividend amount excees the non taxable income.

Article 24.

Paragraph (1)

Foreign Income Tax is the tax collected abroad on income received or obtained there, constituting a part of the whole income on which Income Tax is imposed in Indonesia.
The foreign Income Tax which can be credited is the Income Tax improved on foreign income of a domestic Tax Payer.
Accordingly, the foreign Income Tax imposed on a foreign entity

paying dividend, can not be credited on the tax of an Indonesia Tax Payer receiving said dividend.

In other woods, the Income Tax credited from the tax indebted in Indonesia, shall only be the Income Tax directly imposed on the income received or obtained by the domestic Tax Payer concerned.

A domestic Tax Payer shall be imposed with tax on all income firm wherever obtained firm an income source abroad.

On said income obtained from abroad, has automatically already been imposed with tax by the country of origen of said income. The Income Tax paid in said foreign country can be creditted against the whole Income Tax indebted, as longes it is respect to the same fiscal year.

In other words, the Income obtained, the Income Tax indebted can be deducted, for the same fiscal year.

Example

1. An Indonesian Consultant A has worked for one year in the Philippines and has obtained a remuneration (fee) of the services performed there, amounting to X.

   The Tax imposed in the Philippines on said fee, is for example 15% X.

   So said amount of 50% x X. can be credited against the whole Income Tax in debted by A.

2. An individend B deposits his money in one the banks in England.

   The interest of the deposit received, amounts to Y.

   The tax tariff on deposit interest there, is for example 30%. So said amount of 30% x Y can be credited against the whole Income Tax indebted by B.

3. PT. AB in Indonesia is the sole shareholder of Z Incorporated in the USA. For example Z Incorporated gains a profit amounting to .... US$. 100,000.–

   Income Tax on Z Incorporated (corporate Income Tax) 48% .... US$. 48,000.–

   ==========

   US$. 52,000.–

The tax on dividend is for example 38%:	US$. 19,760.–
Dividend remitted to Indonesia	=============
	US$. 32,240.–

The Income Tax which can be credited against the whole Income Tax indebted by PT. AB is the tax directly imposed on the income received or obtained abroad, in the above example, namely to the amount of US$. 19,760.– The Income Tax (Corporate Income Tax) on Z, Incorporated amounting to US$. 48,000.– cannot be credited against the Income Tax indebted by PT. AB, as said tax amounting to US$. 48,000.– is not improved on the income received or obtained by PT. AB from abroad but the tax imposed on the profit of Z. Incorrporated in the U.S.A.

Paragraph (2)

Foreign Income Tax which can be credited against the Income Tax indebted, shall be to the amount of the Income Tax actually indebted (for a Tax Payer applying the accrual system) and already paid (for a Tax Payer applying the Cash System) abroad, but maximally to the amount of the result of the Indonesian tax tariff application, against said foreign income, calculated according to this law.

Paragraph (3)

This constitutes a confirmation, that the income as referred to in Article 26 of this law, orginates from an income source in Indonesia (provisions on income source). This provision on income source shall also apply to several other types of income having a relationship with the income as referred to in Article 26 for example in case of income related to an asset (in the form of rental), according to the provision on the source adopted by Article 26 of this law it shall be the income obtained in the country where said asset is used. Other types of income related to said asset, for example in case said asset is sold, the profit from the sale of said asset, constitutes an income obtained in the country where said asset is located or utilized, because in said country the rental is improved with Income Tax, so its source is located in the country where the relative rental is yielded.

Paragraph (4)

For example, if in 1985 a reduction or refund apparently occurs of the foreign. Income Tax in respect to foreign Income Tax year 1984 amounting to Rp. 2,000,000.– (two million rupiah), then said deduction or refund of tax amounting to Rp. 2,000,000.– (two million rupiahs), shall be added to the Income Tax indebted in years 1985.

Article 25.

The provisions in this article provide for tax instalment payments by the Tax Payer himself in the current year, which contains the concepts :

a. the amount of the instalment,
b. the calculation basis of the instalment amount.

Paragraph (1)

For facilitating the interpretation an example is given of the tax payment instalment calculation for year 1985, as follows:

The Income Tax indebted in fiscal year 1984 : Rp. 10,000,000
Deducted by :

a.	Income Tax deducted by the employer Rp. :	Rp. 3,000,000.–	
b.	Income Tax collected by other parties from undertaking activities	Rp. 2,000,000.–	
c.	Income Tax deducted by other parties on income of capital (rental, interest etc) :	Rp. 500,000.–	
d.	Credit of foreign Income Tax	Rp. 1,000,000.–	Rp. 7,000.000.–
		============	============
	Substraction result		Rp. 3,000.000.–

This substraction result amounting to Rp. 3,000,000.– shall be distributed over the number of tax periods in year 1985.

If the tax period applied for settling the tax in the current year is one month, then in one fiscal year there will be 12 tax periods, and so the instalment amount for each tax period, is :

$$\text{Rp. } \frac{3{,}000{,}000}{12} = \text{Rp. } 250{,}000.–$$

Paragraph (2)

By the introduction of the renewal of this tax law, if the Taxpayer's annual Tax Return has been filled - out appropriately, and the calculation of the tax has been conducted correctly, and the indebted tax has been settled, then no tax asessment will be issued anymore by the Director General of Taxes.

If a tax assessment is still issued by the Director General of Taxes, then this means, that the tax indebted according to the annual Tax Return and what has been paid or settled by the Tax Payer, is apparently less, than it should be according to the law.

Accordingly, if there is a tax assessment, then the concept Income Tax indebted shall basically be based on said tax assessment.

Except if in the next year, the Tax Payer's income increases and the tax is calculation correctly, then the Income Tax indebted according to the annual Tax Return of the next year will be larger.

The tax instalment amount in the current year, after it has been settled by the Tax Payer himself, shall be the tax according to the annual Tax Return of the following year divided by twelve. Therefore, in principle the Income Tax indebted shall be the Income Tax amount known form the last fiscal year.

If the Income tax indebted according to the annual Tax Return submitted, is smaller than the tax already deposited during the relative fiscal year, and accordingly the Tax Payer submits a request for refund of the excessive tax payment or a request for calculating it against other tax liabilities, before being decided by the Director General of Taxes in respect to the refund or setting-off said excess, the monthly instalment amount shall be the same as in the months before said annual Tax Return is submitted.

After a decision of the Director General of Tax has been issued, the instalment of the following month, offer the date of said decision, shall be based on the tax amount indebted according to said decision. If the tax indebted according to the assessment on the last Annual Tax Return Contains a compensation of the loss of previous years, their the tax serving as the basis for determining the instalment amount in the current year, shall be re-calculated based on the tax indebted before the loss compensation is conducted. In case the assessment or the annual Tax Return is not availabe, because the Tax Payer is a new Tax Payer, then the arrangement of the instalment amount as an estimate of the tax amount to be indebted, shall be regultated in a Government Regulation pursuant to Article 27 of this law.

Paragraph (3)

The amount of the tax instalment in the current year, which shall be paid by the Tax Payer himself for each tax period, shall as best as possible be endeavoured to be consistent with the amount of tax indebted for the relative tax period. For a financial institution as Tax Payer, for example, the amount of this instalment word be more consistent, if based on the latest Financial Statement, whereas for a State Owned Corporate Body/BUMN. and Regional state Owned Corporate Body, it shall be based on the Company's Revenues and Expenditures Budget Bill of the relative fiscal year. The kinds of undertakings/enterprises can calculate the amount of tax instalments for each tax period by applying basis other than the annual Tax Return or the latest Tax assessment, will be stipulated by a Government Regulation.

Article 26.

This article provides for the tax deduction for a foreign Tax Payer, obtaining the following matters :

a. the tax deduction basis shall be the gross amount of said payments to the foreign Tax Payer;

b. the tax tariff, shall be 20% (twenty per cent);

c. the nature of the deduction, namely that said Income Tax deducted, shall be final in nature.

Obliged by this law to deduct tax, shall also be individual Tax Payers paying or owing interest, dividend, etcetera. Final shall mean, that the Tax Payer is not obligated any longer to submit an annual.
Tax Return, which is different from the term "settled" in the new system, meaning that the Tax Payer is still obligated to submit an annual Tax Return.

Article 27.

By Government Regulation is further regulated the fulfilment of the tax obligation as referred to in Article 21, Article 23 and Article 25, including the application of the prorata tariff on income in the form of severance pay and pension redemption money received or obtained in one lumpsum.

Article 28.

In respect to income Tax which is settled in full in the Current year, both which is paid by the Tax Payer himself as well as that collected or deducted by other parties, the total amount there-of will be credited against the Income Tex indebted.

Example :

The Income tax indebted : Rp 10,000,000.–

Tax credits :

- Tax deducted from work based on Article 21 : Rp 1,000,000.–
- Tax collected by other parties on income from undertakings based on Article 22 : Rp 2,000,000.–
- Tax deducted by other parties on income from capital based on Article 23 · Rp 1,000,000.–

– Tax credit on foreign income tax Article 24 :	Rp 3,000,000.–	
– Payment by the Tax Payer himslef year based on Article 25	Rp 2,000,000.–	
	=============	
The total income tax amount which can be credited :	Rp 9,000,000.–	
	=============	
Income Tax still to be paid		Rp. 1,000.000,–

Article 29.

In the example as presented in the elucidation on Article 28 the shortage or the Income Tax indebted, amounting to Rp 1,000.000.– (one million rupiah) shall be fully settled before submitting an annual Tax Return, namely at the latest as the end of the third month after the relative fiscal year has expired.

Article 30.

Paragraph (1)

Each annual Tax Return submitted by a Tax Payer conducting an undertaking activity or free occupation or with a gross revenue of Rp. 60,000,000.– (sixty million rupiahs) or more, shall be accompanied by a Financial Statement.

Paragraph (2)

The obligation to submit an annual Tax Return, constitutes an obligation to implement the provisions on the tax imposition to be transformed into tax payments to the State Treasury Office. Accordingly, this law stipulates that the annual Tax Returns shall contain data which can be used as basis for determining the amount of Income Tax indebted, as well as the shortage or excess of tax payment.

Paragraph (3)

In principle, each Tax Payer shall be under obligation to submit an annual Tax Return.

This obligation shall not apply to individual Tax Payers :

a. who do not have other income from work as referred to in Article 21, except individual Tax Payers who obtain income from work from more than one employer.

b. who receive or obtain a net income not exceeding the non-taxable income amount, for example :
a married Tax Payer with 3 family dependants whereas his wife does not earn an income from work or an undertaking, then the non-taxable income shall amount to Rp. 2,880.000.– (two million eight hundred eighty thousand rupiahs) or less then he shall not be obligated to submit an annual tax Return.

Paragraph (4)

By this provision it is intended, that tax Payers who have calculated and paid the tax amount indebted correctly pursuant to the provisions of this law, and have declared it in the annual Tax Return, no Tax assesment Letter not a decision letter from the tax administration, need to be issued to him.

Paragraph (5)

If later on it is learnt, based on an audit result, or based on information obtained otherwise than audit, that the tax calculated and reported in the annual Tax Return concerned is incorrect, for example the cost charge apparently exceeds the actual amount then the Director General of Taxes shall determine the appropriate amount of the indebted tax, according to the law.

Article 31.

Excessive tax payment can be refunded or calculated against other tax liabilities;

Example

The Income Tax indebted : Rp 10,000,000.–

Tax credits :

– Tax deduction from work based on Article 21	Rp 1.000.000,–
– Tax collection by other parties on income from an undertaking based on Article 22 :	Rp 4,000,000.–
– Tax deduction by other parties on income from capital based on article 23	Rp 1,000,000.–
– Payment by the Tax Payer himself in the current year based on Article 25	Rp 6,000,000.–
	==============

Total amount of Income Tax which can be credited :	Rp. 12,000,000.–
	==============
Excessive tax payment	Rp. 2,000,000.–
	==============

This excessive tax payment amounting to Rp. 2,000,000.– can be refunded or calculated against other tax liabilities.

Paragraph (2)

The Director General of Taxes or a designated functionary shall be authorized to conduct an audit on the Financial Statements, etcetera, of the Tax Payers, before effecting a refund or setting off the excessive tax.

The matters which shall serve as consideration material before effecting a refund of or setting off the excessive tax, shall be :

a. the material correctness of the Income Tax indebted;

b. the authenticity of the collection proofs, and the deduction of tax by the Tax Payer himself during and for the relative fiscal year.

Accordingly, for the purpose of examination and audit, the Director General of Taxes or other designated functionaries, shall be authorized to conduct an audit on the Financial Statements, books and other records, as well as other audits relating to the determinati on of the indebted Income Tax, the correctness of the tax payment amount to be refunded. The objective of this audit is to ensure, that the amounts refunded to the tax Payers as restitution actually constitute the right of the Tax Payers.

Meant by other audits are those covering local inspection, conducting verification towards other parties having a relationship with the Tax Payer, etcetera.

Article 32.

As set forth in the General section of this elucidation, the provisions pertaining to the tax imposition procedure, are provided for in Law Number 6 Year 1983 on General Tax Provisions and Procedures regulating the procedures on collections relating to errors, non adherence, violations and crimenal acts, except if the tax imposition procedure is determined otherwise in this law.

Article 33.

Paragraph (1)

For a Tax Payer whose fiscal year is the book year, there is possibility that a part of that fiscal year is covered in the calendar year 1984.

According to the provision of this paragraph, if 6 (six) months of said fiscal year an included in the 1984 calendar year, then the Tax Payer is allowed to choose, wheter he desires to apply the Income Tax Ordinance 1944 or the Corporate Tax Ordinance 1925, or to choose the application of the provisions contained in this Law, The opportunity for such a chois shall also apply apply to a Tax Payer, for 6 (six) months or more whose fiscal year are included in the Calendar year 1984.

Paragraph (2)

Letter a.

A tax facility of which the period is limited for example the tax facility pursuant to Law Number 1 year 1967 on Foreign Investment, and Law Number 6 Year 1968 on Domestic Investment, granted up to and including December 31, 1983, can still be enjoyed until the expiration of said tax facility.

Letter b.

A tax facility of which the period is not deferred, can not be enjoyed anymore as from the date this Law comes into force, such as for example :

– the tax facility granted to PT. Danareksa, constituting Corporate Tax exemption on the business activities, and exemption of Capital Stamp Duty or the subscription and deposit of share capital pursuant to the Decree of the Finance Minister No. KEP–1680/MK/II/2/1076 dated December 28, 1976;
– Tax facilities granted to Limited Liability Companies selling shares through the Capital Market, constituting a tariff reduction/relief of Corporate Tax pursuant to the Decree of the Minister of Finance No. 112/KMK/04/1979 dated March 27, 1979.

Paragraph (3)

The Corporate Tax Ordinance 1925, and the Tax Law on Interest, Dividend and Royalty 1970, as well as implementation regulations thereof shall remain effective on the taxable income received or obtained in the field of oil and natural gas mining, conducted within the frame of a Work Contract and Production Sharing Contract, as loing as said Work Contract and Production Sharing Contract agreements are still effective at the moment this law comes into force.

The provisions of this law shall only apply to taxable income received or obtained in the field of oil and natural gas mining conducted in the form of a Work Contract and Product Sharing Contract agreements, if said work Contract and Product Sharing Contract agreements, are drawn up after this law come into force.

Article 34.

Self - explanatory.

Article 35.

With a Government Regulation matters still insufficiently provided for in this law, regulated.

The Government Regulation in question shall concern, among other things:

a. The application of the adjustment factor to calculate the income originating from profit due to the sale of an asset as referred to in article 4 paragraph (1) letter d, and the application of the prorata effective tariff to said profit;

b. Depreciation and amortization guidelines;

c. All regulations regulated in order that this law can be implemented as best as possible, also including the transition regulations.

Article 36.

Paragraph (1)

This paragraph (1) confirms, that the Income Tax Law 1984 shall be effective as from January 1, 1984.
For Tax Payers, whose fiscal year is the same as the calendar year, this law shall be effective for them as from fiscal year 1984.

For Tax Payers applying a book other than the calendar year, this law shall be effective for the book year starting after January 1, 1984.

Paragraph (2)

Self-explanatory.

SUPPLEMENT TO THE STATE GAZETTE OF THE REPUBLIC OF INDONESIA NUMBER 3263.

Appendix 25

LAW OF
THE REPUBLIC OF INDONESIA
NO. : 8 YEAR 1983.

R E

VALUE ADDED TAX ON GOODS AND SERVICES
AND SALES TAX ON LUXURY GOODS

BY THE GRACE OF GOD,

THE PRESIDENT OF THE REPUBLIC OF INDONESIA,

Considering : a. that the Republic of Indonesia is a legislative state on the basis of Pancasila and the 1945 Constitution highly appreciating the rights and obligations of the rights and obligations of the citizens, she therefore positions tax as one of the manifestations of the obligation of every citizen constituting the participation in financing the state and national development;

b. that the system constituting the basis of the state taxes collection implementation so far applicable is not in accordance anymore with the socio-economic living standard of the people of Indonesia, both in the aspect of the national mutual aid principle and the already achieved national development growth rate;

c. that the tax system, particulary that manifested in the indirect tax provisions so far applicable has not motivated the participation of all taxable entrepeneur increase the state revenue urgently required to manifest the continuity of state financing and development on the basis of the national development principles;

d. that the currently prevailing sales tax does not comply anymore as the means to support the aforementioned needs;

e. it is therefore deemed necessary to rearrange the sales.tax system by the value added tax on goods and services and sales tax on luxury goods with a law;

In view of : 1. Article 5 paragraph (1) jo Article 20 paragraph (1) and Article 23 paragraph (2) of the 1945 Constitution;

2. Act of the People's Deliberative Assembly of the Republic of Indonesia No. II/MPR/1983 re Outline of State Policy of the Republic of Indonesia;

3. Law No. 6. Year 1983 Re General Provisions and Procedure on Taxes : (State Gazette Year 1983 No. 49, Supplement to State Gazette No. 3263);

4. Law No. 7 Year 1983 re Income Tax Year 1984 (State Gazette Year 1983 No. 50, Supplement to State Gazette No. 3263).

With the approval of the
PEOPLE'S HOUSE OF REPRESENTATIVES
OF THE REPUBLIC OF INDONESIA
HAS DECIDED:

By revoking : Law No. 35 Year 1953 re Stipulation of Emergency Law No. 19 Year 1951 re Collection of Sales Tax (State Gazette Year 1951 No. 94) as a Law (State Gazette Year 1953 No. 85, Supplement to State Gazette No. 489) as several times amended lastly by Law No. 2 Year 1968 re Amendment on and Addition to the 1951. Sales Tax Law (State Gazette Year 1968 No. 14, Supplement to State Gazette No. 2847).

To stipulate : LAW RE VALUE ADDED TAX ON GOODS AND SERVICES AND SALES TAX ON LUXURY GOCDS.

CHAPTER I
GENERAL PROVISIONS

Article 1.

In this Law, the meaning of :

a. Customs Area shall be the territory of the Republic of Indonesia;

b. Goods shall be tangible goods which by their nature can be movable and immovable;

c. Taxable Goods shall be goods as referred to in letter b, as a processing result (fabrication) of goods taxable on the basis of this law;

d. Taxable Goods Delivery :

   1. a) delivery of rights on Taxable Goods due to an agreement;

      b) Transfer of Taxable Goods due to a hire purchase agreement and leasing agreement;

      c) Transfer of products in movable condition;

      d) delivery of goods to a broker or via an auctioneer;

      e) own use and free gifts;

      f) Taxable Goods stock balance on the liquidation of a company.

   2. Those excluded from the definition of the Taxable Goods Delivery, shall be :

      a) delivery of Taxable Goods to a broker as regulated in the Commercial Code:

      b) delivery of Taxable Goods for debt secu eity/collateral;

      c) partial or total transfer of a company;

e. Services shall be any business activity and services rendering on the basis of a commitment or legal act causing a goods, facility or right is ready for use;

f. Taxable Services shall be the service as referred to in letter e taxable on the basis of this Law;

g. Taxable Services Rendering shall be any activity to render the Taxable Services conducted within a company or the work thereof including the Taxable Services for own interest;

h. Import shall be any activity to put goods into the Customs Area;

i. Export shall be any activity to dis, atch goods out side the Customs Area;

j. Trade shall be any activity to buy and sell goods without changing its form or nature;

k. Entrepreneur shall be a person or body in whatever form within a company, and of which its operation is to produce goods, import goods, export goods, conduct trade and render services;

l. Taxable Entrepreneur shall be that as referred to in letter k taxable on the basis of this law. Excluding from this definition shall be the small scale entrepreneur the definition and scale of which shall further be stipulated by the Minister of Finance;

m. Producing, shall be any activity to process by changing the form or nature of a goods from its original form to a new one or have a new efficiency including to manufacture, cook/boil, assemble, mix, pack, bottle and to mine or to have some one or another body conduct the activity.

Excluding from this definition shall be :

1) planting or harvesting agricultural produce or breeding cattle;

2) catching or breeding fish;

3) drying or salting food;

4) wrapping or packing commonly occurring in wholesale or retail trade;

5) **serving food and drinks at restaurant, inn/hotel, or catering.**

n. Basis of Tax Imposition shall be the amount of Sales Price, Compensation demanded or should be demanded by a seller or Services provider or Import value used as the basis for calculating the indebted tax;

o. Sales Price shall be the value in term of money, including all costs demanded or should be demaned by the seller due to Goods delivery, excluding tax collected by this law, price reduction included in the Tax Invoice and reimbursed Goods price;

p. Compensation shall be the value in term of money, including all costs demanded or should be demanded by the service provider due to Services rendering, excluding the tax collected by this law and price reduction included in the Tax Invoice;

q. Import value shall be the value in terms of money constituting the basis for calculating the import duty plus other levies imposed on the basis of the provisions int he customs Law for the importation of Taxable Goods, but excluding the tax collected on the basis of this Law;

r. Buyer shall be a person or body receiving the Taxable Goods Delivery;

s. Services recipient shall be a person on body receiving the rendering of services;

t. Tax Invoice shall be the evidence of the tax collection made by a Taxable Entrepreneur or the Directorate General of Customs and Excises on the delivery of Taxable Goods or Services or on the importation of Taxable Goods;

u. Input Tax shall be the Added Value paid by the entrepreneur on the purchase of Taxable Goods, receipt of Taxable Services or import;

v. Output tax shall be the Added Value Tax Collected by the entrepreneur on the delivery of Taxable Goods or Services.

Article 2.

(1) In case the Sales Price or Compensation is influenced by a special relation, the Sales Price or Compensation shall be calculated on the basis of the reasonable market price on the delivery of Taxable Goods or Services.

(2) The special relation as referred to in paragraph (1) shall be considered existing if :

a. two or more entrepreneurs, directly or indirectly, are under the ownership or control of the same entrepreneur, or

b. one Entrepreneur has a capital participation of 25% (twenty five percent) or more of the total capital in the other Entrepreneur, or the relation between the Entrepreneur participating his capital of 25% (twenty five percent) or more in two or more parties, likewiss the relation between two latter two or more parties.

CHAPTER II.
CONFIRMATION OF TAXABLE ENTREPRENEUR

Article 3.

(1) An entrepreneur who, on the basis of the provisions under Article 4 paragraph (1) letters a and d is imposed with tax, shall be obligated to report his business to the Directorate General of Taxes at his domicile or residence, to be confirmed as as Taxable Entrepreneur within the period stipulated by the Government Regulation.

(2) A person or body exporting goods and/or delivering Taxable Goods in the customs area to a Taxable Entrepreneurs, can choose to be confirmed as Taxable Entrepreneur at the residence or domicils of that person or body.

(3) The Director General of Taxes shall issue the confirmation Decree.

(4) A Taxable Entrepreneur who does not report his business as referred to in paragraph (1), shall be sanctioned by an administrative fine of 2% (two percent) of the Tax Imposition Basis.

CHAPTER III.

TAX OBJECT AND OBLIGATION TO MAKE RECORDS.

Article 4.

(1) The Value Added Tax shall be imposed on :

a. delivery of Taxable Goods conducted in the Customs Area within his company or work by an Entrepreneur who :

1) produces said goods;

2) imports said Taxable Goods;

3) has a special relationship with the other Entrepreneur as referred to in letter a numbers 1) and 2);

4) acts as the main distributor or sole agent of the Entrepreneur as referred to in latter a number 1;

5) acts as the right or patent or trademark holder of said Taxable Goods;

b. delivery of Taxable Goods to a Taxable Entrepreneur in the Customs Area within his company or work by the Entrepreneur opting/choosing to be confirmed as Taxable Entreneur;

c. importation of Taxable Goods;

d. Taxable Services Rendering.

(2) With a Government Regulation :

a. The Value Added Tax can be applied to any delivery of Taxable Goods conducted in the Customs Area within his company or work by a wholesaler or distributor or agent or retailer;

b. shall be regulated the rendering of types of services imposed with Value Added Tax.

Article 5.

(1) In addition to the tax imposition as referred to in Article 4, Sales Tax on Luxury Goods shall also be imposed in respect to :

a. delivery of Luxury Goods by an Entrepreneur producing the Luxury Goods in the Customs Area within his company or work;

b. importation luxury Goods.

(2) Sales Tax on Luxury Goods shall only be imposed once at the time of delivery by the producing entrepreneur, or at the time of importation.

Article 6.

(1) Each Taxable Entrepreneur shall be obligated to record the total acquisition price and Taxable Goods delivery or rendering of Taxable Services in the company's accounts.

(2) In the accounting records shall be included separately and clearly, the amount of the total acquisition price and goods delivery or rendering of services on which tax is indebted, and not tax indebted, imposed with tariff of 0% (zero percent), and those imposed with Sales Tax on Luxury Goods.

(3) An Entrepreneur, when on the basis of the 1984 Income Tax, opts/chooses to be taxable according to the calculation norm,, as far as Added Value Tax on Goods & Services is indebted, shall be obligated to make records of the gross circulation value regularly, constituting the basis for the Value Added Tax imposition.

CHAPTER IV.
TAX TARIFF, AND METHOD OF TAX CALCULATION

Article 7.

(1) The tax tariff of the Value Added Tax shall amount to 10% (ten percent).

(2) The export of goods shall be imposed with tax at a tariff of 0% (zero percent).

3) With a Government Regulation, the tax tariff as referred to in paragraph (1), can be amended to a minimum of 5% (five percent), and a maximum of 15% (fifteen percent).

Article 8.

(1) The tariff of Sales Tax Luxury Goods shall be 10% (ten percent) and 20% (twenty percent).

(2) The export of Luxury Goods shall be imposed with tax at a tariff of 0% (zero percent).

(3) With a Government Regulation, the tax tariff as referred to in Article (1) can be amended to a maximum of 35% (thirty five percent).

(4) With a Government Regulation shall be stipulated the group of Goods imposed with Sales Tax on Luxury Goods as referred to in paragraph (1).

(5) The kinds and types of Goods imposed with Sales Tax on Luxury Goods according to paragraph (4) shall be stipulated by the Minister of Finance.

Article 9.

(1) The indebted Value Added Tax in a Tax Period, shall be calculated by multiplying the tariff as regulated in Article 7 on the basis of Tax Imposition.

(2) The Input Tax in a Tax Period can be credited the Output Tax for the same period.

(3) If in a Tax Period, the Output Tax is bigger than

the Input Tax, then, the difference thereof shall Constitute the tax to be paid by the Taxable Entrepreneur.

(4) If in a Tax Period the Input Tax is bigger than the Output Tax, then, the difference thereof shall be the tax which can be compensated with the indebted tax in the following Tax Period or can be re-imbursed.

(5) If in a Tax Period, a Taxable Entrepreneur, in addition to conducting a taxable delivery, also conducts a non-taxable delivery, as far as the parts of said taxable delivery can be properly know from the accounting records, then the amount of Input Tax which can be credited, shall be only to the amount of the Input Tax already paid at the time of acquisition or importation of Taxable Goods delivered by the Taxable Entrepreneur, or used to produce the Taxable Goods.

(6) In case partial taxable delivery as well as partial non-taxable delivery as referred to in paragraph (5) can not be known exactly, the Minister of Finance shall stipulate a guideline for calculating the Input Tax which can be credited for the parts of taxable delivery.

(7) An Entrepreneur who an the basis of the 1984 Income Tax Law opts/chooses to be imposed with tax on the basis of the calculation norm as far as Value Added Tax is indebted, can credit the Input Tax already paid against the Output Tax to be collected, by using the guidelines for calculating the Input Tax credit as stipulated by the Decree of the Minister of Finance.

(8) The Input Tax can not be credited according to the method as regulated in paragraph (2) for the expenditures of :

a. purchase of Goods or Services prior to the confirmation as Taxable Entrepreneur;

b. purchase of Goods having to direct linkage with the process to produce the Taxable Goods or Services;

c. The purchase and maintenance of sedan, jeep, station wagon, van or combi.

Article 10.

(1) The Sales Tax on Luxury Goods indebted in a Tax Period shall be calculated by multiplying the tariff as regulated in Article 8 on the basis of the Tax Imposition.

(2) The Sales Tax on Luxury Goods already paid at the time of acquisition or importation of Luxury Goods, can not be credited with the Added Value Tax collected according to the provisions as regulated in Article 7.

(3) An Taxable Entrepreneur exporting Luxury Goods may request the re-imbursement of the tax already paid at the time of acquisition of the exported Luxury Goods.

CHAPTER V

TIME AND PLACE OF INDEBTED TAX AND TAX CALCULATION REPORT

Article 11.

(1) The indebted tax in the Tax Period will occur at the time of the delivery of Taxable Goods or Services or at the time of Importation of Taxable Goods.

(2) In case the payment is conducted prior the delivery of Taxable Goods or Services then the indebted tax in the Tax Period will occur at the tima of payment.

Article 12.

(1) A Taxable Entrepreneur delivering the Taxable Goods or rendering the Taxable Services, shall be tax indebted at the residence, domicile and/or at the place where his business in conducted.

(2) On the written request of a Taxable Entrepreneur having more than one place of business, the Director General of Taxes can stipulate one of them as the place of indebted tax.

(3) In the case of import, the indebted tax at the place of the Taxable Goods shall be included, and collected via the Directorate General of Customs and Excises.

Article 13.

(1) Each Taxable Entrepreneur shall be obligated to prepare a Tax Invoice, at the time of delivery of Taxable Goods or services.

(2) If the payment is conducted prior to the delivery of the Taxable Goods or Services then the Tax Invoice shall be prepared at the time of payment.

(3) Deviating from paragraphs (1) and (2), a Taxable Entrepreneur can be permitted by the Director General of Taxes to prepare a Tax Invoice covering all deliveries made to the Buyer or Recipient of the Taxable Goods or Services for one calendar month after the and of the relative calender month.

(4) An entrepreneur, who on the basis of Article 4 paragraph (1) letter b is imposed with tax, shall only prepare the Tax Invoice exclusively for the delivery of Taxable Goods to a Taxable Entrepreneur.

(5) The Directorate General of Customs and Excises shall prepare a Tax Invoice for such tax collection as referred to in Article 12 paragraph (3).

(6) In the Tax Invoice shall be stated the records on deliveries imposed with tax on the basis of this Law, covering.

a. Name, address and Tax Payer Registration Number of the Entrepreneur delivering the Taxable Goods or Services;

b. Name, address and Tax Payer Registration Number of the Buyer of the Taxable Goods or Recipient of the Taxable Services;

c. Kinds, types, quantity, unit price and amount of Sales Price or Compensation;

d. Amount of the collected Value Added Tax;

e. Amount of the collected Sales Tax on Luxury Goods;

f. Date of delivery.

(7) The form, size and provision/supply as well as the submission procedure of the Tax Invoice, shall further be regulated by the Minister of Finance.

(8) A Taxable Entrepreneur not producing or not completing the Tax Invoice according to the provisions as regulated in paragraphs (1), (2) and (6), shall be sanctioned with an administrative fine of 2% (two percent) of the Basis of the Tax Imposition.

Article 14.

(1) A person or body not confirmed as a Taxable Entrepreneur shall be prohibited to prepare a Tax Invoice.

(2) In case a Tax Invoice has already been prepared, then the person or body as referred to in paragraph (1) shall deposit the tax amount as stated in the Tax Invoice, to the State Treasury, and shall be sanctioned by an administrative fine of 2% (two percent) of the Basis of the Tax Imposition.

Article 15.

(1) A Taxable Entrepreneur shall be obligated to report the calculation as referred to in Article 11 and 12 to the Directorate General of Taxes within twenty days after the expiry of the Tax Period, by using a Periodical Tax Return.

(2) The particulars and documents to be stated in and/or attached to the Periodical Tax Return shall be stipulated by the Minister of Finance.

(3) A Periodical Tax Return shall be considered as not having been submitted, if the Taxable Entrepreneur does not or does not fully execute the provisions as regulated in paragraphs (1) and (2).

Article 16.

(1) On the written request of the Taxable Entrepreneur, the tax payment excess not yet compensated as referred to in Article 9 paragraph (4) shall be reimbursed within the time as regulated In Law re General Provisions and Procedure on Taxes or within the other period stipulated by the Minister of Finance.

(2) An excess of tax payment on exported Goods will be reimbursed within one month.

CHAPTER VI.

OTHER PROVISION

Article 17.

Anything concerning the definition, the procedure of collection and administrative & Criminal sanctions in respect to the implementation of this Law, not yet specially regulated herein shall apply the provisions of Law re General Provisions & Procedure on Taxes and other Legislative Regulations.

CHAPTER VII
TRANSITIONAL PROVISIONS

Article 18.

(1) By the coming into force of this Law :

a. any delivery of Taxable Goods or Services and importation of Taxable Goods already conducted prior to the effectiveness hereof, shall remain tax indebted, according to the Sales Tax Law 1951.

b. as long as the implementing regulations hereof has not been issued the implementing regulations not in contravention with this Law nor have been revoked and substituted shall remain valid.

(2) The implementing regulations as referred to in paragraph (1), shall further be regulated by the Minister of Finance.

CHAPTER VIII
CONCLUDING PROVISIONS

Article 19.

Any matter not yet sufficiently regulated herein, shall further be stipulated by a Government Regulation.

Article 20.

This Law can be called the 1984 Added Value Tax Law.

Article 21.

This Law shall come into force as from July 1, 1984. For the public knowledge, this Law shall be promul-

gated in the State Gazette of the Republic of Indonesia.

Enacted in Jakarta
on : December 31, 1983
THE PRESIDENT OF THE REPUBLIC
OF INDONESIA

S O E H A R T O

Promulgated in Jakarta
On : December 31, 1983
THE STATE MINISTER/STATE
SECRETARY OF THE REPUBLIC
OF INDONESIA

SUDHARMONO, S.H.

STATE GAZETTE OF THE REPUBLIC OF INDONESIA YEAR 1983
NO. 51.

Appendix 26

ELUCIDATION
ON
LAW OF THE REPUBLIC OF INDONESIA
RE
VALUE–ADDED TAX ON GOODS AND SERVICES AND SALES TAX ON LUXURY GOODS.

GENERAL.

The national development which is based on the Outlines of the State Policy, which has been and will be continuously implemented to realize the just and prosperous society based on the Pancasila and the 1945 Constitution has not only resulted the improvement of the socio-economic life of the entire Indonesian people, but has also created the drive and demand to modernize all fields of the social life.

To achieve the goal of the national development, substantial amount of investment is required, of which the implementation must be based on self capability. It is the moment therefore, to lay down a basic principle which enable to give more assurance to the availability of that fund from domestic sources as the reflection of the national mutual aid principle in its efforts to detach its dependence on offshore sources, so that foreign aid will solely constitute as a complement of which the role becomes smaller in the future.

Apart from the above, serious efforts are needed to mobilize investment fund originated from the public and Government savings, foreign exchange earnings from export, so that in eventually we are able to finance the entire national development on our own.

The currently prevailing systems, especially the Sales Tax 1951, is not adequate anymore to accommodate the social activities and has not yet achieved the targets of the development needs, among others to increase the State's revenue, to drive export and for the equity of the tax burdening.

In this context, basing seriously on the capability of the people, the justice feeling and the development needs as well as to drive to improve the competitive ness of non oil export commodity in the international market, supported by the condition and the capability of the apparatus which expanded continuously, this sales tax with value added tax system and sales tax on luxury goods shall be validated to substitute the currently prevailing sales tax.

In view of the system, this law can be mentioned as the Law re Value Added Tax on Goods and Services and Sales Tax on Luxury Goods to indicate that the two kinds of taxes provided in it constitute a unit of tax on domestic consumption.

Sales Tax on Luxury Goods is collected once at its source i.e.at the producer level, or at the time of import. Value Added Tax can be collected several times at the various links of business. Although it is collected several times, since its imposition is only on the Value added resulted on each delivery of goods or services rendered at the next link of business, eventually this tax burden does not become heavier.

That value added itself arises due to the application of the production factors on each business link in preparing, producing, dealing and trading goods or in rendering services to the consumers. All costs to gain and to maintain profit including capital interest, land rent, wage, and enterpreneur's profit constitute value added elements which become the basic principle for the imposition of Value Added Tax.

The valid tariff on Taxable Goods Delivery and Services are more simplified by implementing a uniform tariff, it means, that one tariff is valid for all kinds of Taxable Goods, So that its implementation becomes easier, not requiring a list of goods grouping with different tariffs.

Apart from being imposed with Value Added Tax, luxury goods is also imposed with Sales Tax as a concrete effort to uphold the justice in tax burdening which also simultaneously constitutes as an effort to diminish the high consumption scheme which is not productive in the society. On the contrary all agricultural plantation, forestry, fishery, cattle breeding and other unprocessed agrarian products are not the target of tax imposition.

Further, the tariff on export of goods is 0% (zero percent) which means, tax exempted, even the Value Added Tax which was included in the exported goods could be reimbursed. The exemption and the reimbursement of taxes paid on the exported goods is are in conformity with the principle of tax imposition on domestic consumption (general use) of goods and services or within the Customs Area. On unconsumed domestic goods (to be exported) therefore, are not taxable. Another basic considerations is in order that in the price of the exported goods will not be included the tax burden so as to assist their basic prices and increase their competitiveness in the international markets. On the contrary, the imported goods are taxable similar to the domestic products.

All producing, importing, goods trading or services rendering persons or bodies are subject to taxes nevertheless. The law, provides regulation to impose tax on the delivery of goods by the enterpreneur who acts as agent or dealer and/or retailer as well as certain services when based on the consideration of the national development, its readiness to its implementation has been achieved.

The Small Scale enterpreneur who produces and sells goods or renders services is exempted from tax. Thus only enterpreneur producing (manufacturer) and trading goods is subject to tax. So this law has clearly regulated the taxable Entrepreneur, Goods, Services and Delivery of Goods or Services.

Tax Invoice shall be prepared on Delivery of Goods or Services as proff of indebted tax on Goods Delivery transaction. This tax invoice constitutes the typical character of the Value Added Tax, since it functions as an evidence for the Enterpreneur whose collection could be credited to the indebted tax.

Special policy on creditable tax is applied to Enterpreneur who apart from delivering Goods to a Taxable Enterpreneur also delivers Goods to a person or body who is not a confirmed Taxable Enterpreneur, as well as to a Taxable Enterpreneur whose tax calculation is based on Input Tax on Delivery of Goods. Thus the multiple effect of tax collection could be eliminated, since an Enterpreneur is obliged to pay only the difference between the to be collected and the payable taxes. The Multiple effect occurs only on Sales Tax on Luxury Goods and this is consciously imposed to uphold the principle of justice in tax imposition.

Apart from the educational element, this law also contains the promotion cultivation of awareness as well as the responsibility of the entrepreneur by giving confidence in collecting and paying his own indebted tax to the State.

In this context should also be considered the provisions concerning the implementation procedures such as inspection, tax assessment, additional tax assessment, administrative and penal sanctions as well as protection on enterpreneur's rights by giving the opportunity to submit its objection and appeal to the Tax Appeal Council currently called the Tax Advisory Council which is regulated by the Law on the General provisions and Procedure on Taxes.

In this context, the Law on the General provisions and Procedure on Taxes must be seen as an integral part of the Value Added Tax on Goods and Services and Sales Tax on Luxury Goods, since the provisions and the procedures or rules of its implementation and the tax sanctions as the complementary provisions included in Law of Value Added Tax on Goods and Services and Sales Tax on Luxury goods.

ARTICLE BY ARTICLE.

Article 1.

a. The territories of the Republic of Indonesia not included within the Customs Area are the free harbours bonded areas and other stipulated by the other legislative regulations.

b. Goods herein is the tangible goods, movable as well as immovable as stipulated by the Civil Code.

c. Taxable Goods are that as product of fabrication. Goods not originating from fabrication, such as agricultural, plantation, forestry, cattle breeding, fishery and other agrarian products not to be further processed, are not included in the definition of Taxable Goods.

d.1 Included in the definition of Taxable Goods Delivery shall be :

a) the agreement mentioned in this provision covers buying and selling by installment or other agreement resulting the transfer of rights on Goods;

b) apart from the system as mentioned in letter a) above, Delivery of Goods may also occur through hire purchase and leasing agreements. Delivery of Goods is considered materialized at the moment the transfer of right from the seller or lessor to the buyer or lessee takes place, although the payment in hire purchase agreement is on installments;

c) transfer of Goods in movable condition i.e. the transfer of Goods made due to order or to produce Goods from the material as instructed by the customer.

d) by a broker we mean a person or body whose profession in the business circle is to close agreement or binding agreement on behalf and upon the responsibility of another person, for example a commissioner by an auctioneer we mean a Government auctioneer or anyone designated by the Government;

e) own use means for the interest of the Entrepreneur, the Directors, or his employees. While complimentary/free gifts is that given not against any payment, among others, samples of goods for promotion given to relation or buyers;

f) the remaining Taxable stock at the liquidation of a company is considered similar to the own use Goods, therefore considered a Delivery of Taxable Goods.

2. Excluded from the definition of Delivery of Taxable Goods as mentioned in no. 2 shall be as follows :

a) self explanatory.

b) self explanatory.

c) by a company or its parts we mean the assets which as according to the initial purpose is not for sales.

e. All service performances and activities, inter alia/transportation, contract, movable goods leasing, immovable goods leasing, entertainment, travel agency, hotel, notary public, lawyer, accountant consultant, administrative bureau and commissioner, are included in the definition of Service.

f. Taxable Service is a Service imposed with tax based on Article 4 paragraph (1) letter d and paragraph (2) letter b.

g. See the elucidation on Article 4 paragraph (1) letter d and paragraph (2) letter b.

h. Activities to import Goods from a free harbour or bonded area into a Customs Area are also included in the definition of Import.

i. Activities to export Goods from a Customs Area to a free harbour or to a bonded area are also included in the definition of Export.

j. Included in the definition of Trade is the exchange of Goods.

k. Enterpreneur can be in the form of a personal undertaking or body which consists of limited liability company, limited partnership, State owned and Regional state owned companies under any name or in any form whatsoever association, corporation or other association, firm, partnership, coperatives, foundation or institution and a permanent undertaking. The aforementioned person or body shall engage in the following activities.

   1. producing Goods as mentioned in letter m. The enterpreneur is called the Manufacturer or Producer.
   2. Service activity. The Enterpreneur is called Service Provider.
   3. trade activity. The Enterpreneur is called Trader.
   4. Import. The Enterpreneur is called Importer.

   To prevent the possibility of a very wide interpretation, the definition of an Enterpreneur is limited to a person or body that performs the aforementioned activities within their company or work. If this element is not met the person or body mentioned above is not an Enterpreneur.

l. The definition "taxable based on this law" is taxable based on Article 4 and Article 5. Principally any Enterpreneurs are taxable, but this law gives exception to Taxable Enterpreneurs who belong to the small scale category although engages in the Delivery of Taxable Goods. This exemption is meant to drive the growth of the small scale Enterpreneur.

m. The deformation or change of character of Goods occured due to to processing by applying one or more producing factors, shall include the following activities.

   – assembling : to join loose parts of Goods into half processed or processed Goods such as car assembling, electronic goods, household appliances, etc;

   – cooking : to process Goods by heating. It includes boiling, burning, smoking, roasting, frying, mixed or unmixed by other ingredients;

   – mixing : to mix one or more elements to produce one or more other things.

   – packing : to place Goods under protective thing to prevent damage and/or to increase its marketing strength.

— **bottling** : **to put drinks or other liquids into sealed bottles by certain methods;**

— **mining** : **to extract natural sources from the surface or underground, on land or in sea;**

and other activities which can be similarized, or to order another person or body to perform such activities. This stipulation also regulates certain activities of which the results are not taxable according to no. 1) to no. 5) which can be elucidated as follows :

- no. 1) and no. 2) are activities in the agrarian business (agriculture, plantation and forestry, cattle breeding and fishery) of which the products are obtained through cultivation and population (not fabrication) process and substantially influenced by natural factors.
- no. 3) are activities through drying and salting process of food produced by business activities mentioned in no. 1) and no. 2) in a simple way such as drying and salting fish to become salted fish;
- no. 4) are activities to wrap or pack Goods as further service performance as a part of selling activities performed by the wholesaler or retailer, which is different with the definition of packing;

n. Self explanatory.

o. All Costs such as for installation, insurance, technical aid, maintenance, despatching, commission, guarantee, interest and others as long as related to Delivery of Goods are elements of Sales Price imposed with tax. Deductable from Sales Price shall be :

1) Discounts such as on cash payment or on rabate as long as those are within the good tradesman's usages, are deductable from the Sales price , Provided they are included in the Tax Invoice. Excluded from the definition of discounts are bonus, commission, premium, or other remunerations in the framework of selling Goods;

2) Rejected Goods due to damage, quality, kinds or type differences and missing Goods on journey.

p. Self explanatory.

q. The Import Value becoming the Basis for Tax Imposition is the Check Price for Import (HPI) or Cost Insurance and Freight (CIF) as the basis for import duty calculation plus all cost and other levies according to the Customs Regislative regulations.

r. The definition of Buyer herein is more extensive than that in general, since it includes a person or body that receives or is considered receiving Delivery of Taxable Goods as meant by letter d.

s. Self explanatory.

t. Self explanatory.

u. Buyer, Service Receipient or Importer are obliged to pay Value Added Tax and receive the evidence of tax collection at the time of Delivery on Taxable Goods or Taxable Service or Import Taxable of Goods. Those paid taxes are called the Input Tax.

v. a Taxable Enterpreneur who delivers Taxable Goods or Taxable Services is obliged to collect Value Added Tax. This collected tax is called the Output Tax.

w. This provision is meant to give assurance to Taxable Enterpreneur that the indebted tax on the entire Taxable Goods or Taxable Services delivery are made during one calendar month. The Minister of Finance, Nevertheless, is competent to stipulate another Tax Period other than one calendar month, to facilitate other Government Agency assisting the tax collection, for example in the case of import.

Article 2.

Paragraph (1)

The in effect of a special relation as meant herein is the possibility of the suppressed price lower than the market price, in this case the Director General of Taxes is competent to adjust the Sales Price or give Reimbursement becoming the Basis of the Tax Imposition at the price prevailing in the free market.

Paragraph (2)

a. The ownership in this paragraph, relates to capitalization, while authorization relates to management, including family relationship between the parties concerned.

The word direct in this Article means that the total or part of the capital or management of two or more companies involved in Delivery of Goods (seller and buyer) is owned and managed by or under the control of the same Entrepreneur. The word indirect means when the ownership and control are obtained due to the existing family relationship between the Entrepreneur and the capital owner or the executive management of said companies, for example when the total or part of the capital is in the hand of the wife, children or other relatives of the Entrepreneur;

b. Capital participation of 25% (twenty five per cent) of the company's equity or placed or paid up capitals. If one of the calculations show a capital participation of 25% (twenty five per cent) or more, it is considered that there is a special relation.

Article 3.

Paragraph (1)

Self explanatory.

Paragraph (2)

A person or body that exports Goods and/or that delivers Goods in the Customs Area to a Taxable Enterpreneur is not obliged to report its activity. But if based on several considerations for example to obtain credit or to request reimbursement of the Input Tax, that person or body can opt or to request to be confirmed as a Taxable Enterpreneur.

Paragraph (3)

A Decree on Confirmation issues by the Director General of Taxes does not constitute a basis to fix the starting period of the indebted tax, but only serves as an administrative means of control form the taxation apparatus, since the starting period of the indebted tax is determined by the presence of a taxable object.

Paragraph (4).

If a Taxable Enterpreneur does not report his business activity it is considered violating his obligation by ill will and neglecting the confidence entrusted. It is natural, therefore, that upon that violation, besides the obligation to pay the indebted tax, the Taxable Enterpreneur is also subject to sanction in the form of administrative fine of 2% (two percent) of the entire Basis of Tax Imposition arising before the Enterpreneur is confirmed as a Taxable Enterpreneur.

Article 4.

Paragraph (1)

a. The Indebted Tax Goods Delivery must meet the following conditions :

- the delivered Goods is the Taxable Goods;
- the delivery action is taxable delivery;
- the delivery is conducted by Taxable Enterpreneur or Entrepreneur who opts to be confirmed as Taxable Enterpreneur;
- delivery is conducted within the Customs Area of the Republic of Indonesia, including delivery on Export, although it is subject to 0% (zero percent) tariff;
- delivery is conducted within the company or work as Taxable Enterpreneur, of meaning that in the framework of his routine activities, as a taxable enterpreneur. The goods delivery not conducted in the framework of running the company or work, for instance transferring assets not for sales shall not be tax indebted.

  The Groups of Taxable Enterpreneur who are tax indebted shall be as follows :

  1) Taxable Enterpreneur who produces Taxable Goods. This Group of Enterpreneur is called the Manufacturer or Producer. The Delivery of Taxable Goods produced by Manufacturer to any party shall be tax indebted;
  2) Enterpreneur who imports Taxable Goods. The Delivery of Taxable Goods by this Importer to any party shall be tax indebted;
  3) Enterpreneur who has special relationship with Manufacturer and/or Importer. Delivery of Taxable Goods by an Enterpreneur who has special relationship with Manufacturer or Importer to any party shall be tax indebted;
  4) Agent and main dealer of Manufacturer and Importer. The confirmation of agent and main dealer of Manufacturer and Importer as Taxable Enterpreneurs is based on the consideration of the existing special

relationship among them which is influential to the trade and marketing system of Goods. The Manufacturer and Importer are the ordering, or requesting or giving right parties to the dealer or main agent to market their products or their Imported Goods according to the sort and or certain marketing territory on the basis of the mutually approved aggreement;

5) The Enterpreneur, holder of right to use patent and trade mark of Taxable Goods.
Confirmed as Taxable Enterpreneur, since that Enterpreneur has had the right and competence to produce, market or order other person to perform activities according to the mutually approved agreement.
The Delivery of Taxable Goods by that Enterpreneur to any party shall be tax indebted;

b. Enterpreneur who opts to be confirmed as Taxable Enterpreneur is only tax indebted upon Delivery of Taxable Goods executed to Manufacturer or other Taxable Enterpreneur.

c. Tax is also collected at the time of Importation of Goods. Collection is conducted by the Director General of Customs and Excise. Different from the Delivery of Taxable Goods as mentioned in letters a and b, whoever imports Taxable Goods into the Customs Area, disregarding whether it is performed within anyone's company or work or not shall always be subject to tax imposition;

d. In principle, all Services may be taxable. However, Services in the field of education, religion, and health for the public interest and not for making profit, are not intended to be taxable in the context of public protection.

Paragraph (2)

a. Bassed on the consideration of the economic development and the rising demand for development fund, the Government is competent to expand the Imposition of Value Added Tax on Delivery of Taxable Goods, performed by wholesaler agent or distributor, and retailer, for example by supermarket;

b. Self explanatory.

Article 5.

Paragraph (1)

The Sales Tax on Luxury Goods is imposed besides the Value Added Tax, which means that delivery or Importation of Luxury Goods is subject to Value Added Tax and on moreover it is also subject to Sales Tax on Luxury Goods. Sales Tax on Luxury Goods is not imposed on all deliveries of Luxury Goods, but only on the delivery performed by :

a. Manufacturer or Producer of Luxury Goods;

b. Anyone who imports Luxury Goods disregarding whether it is done continuously or at occassionally only.

Paragraph (2)

The general definition of Input Tax shall only valid for Value Added Tax, and not for to Sales Tax on Luxury Goods. It is therefore, the Sales Tax on Luxury Goods which has been paid is not creditable to that indebted Sales Tax.
So the principle is that it is imposed only once i.e. on :

a. delivery by the Manufacturer or Producer of Luxury Goods or

b. Importation of Luxury Goods.

Further phase of delivery is not more subject to tax.

Article 6.

Paragraph (1)

The recording of the entire acquisition prices and Delivery of Taxable Goods and Services and all related matters thereto constitute the reflection of the orderly accounting so that the Basis for Tax Imposition could be determined easily and correctly.

Paragraph (2)

The matters obliged to be recorded are stipulated in this Pargraph, inter alia :

- the total acquisition price or Import Value;
- the total Sales Price or Reimbursement;
- the total Sales Price of Non Taxable Goods (agrarian, fishery, forestry products etc.);

- total Export Value;
- total Sales Price on which Sales Tax on Luxury Goods is imposed.

Paragraph (3)

Only the monthly gross circulation value on which the Tax Imposition is Based, is to be recorded by the Enterpreneur who according to the Income Tax Law is taxable with the Calculation Norm.

Article 7.

Paragraph (1)

In general the prevailing tariff of the Value Added Tax is 10% (ten per cent). At the moment of the enforcement of this law the tax imposition is still at the phase of Goods Delivery by Manufacturer or Importer, so that the effective tariff on the consumer's burden will not reach 10% (ten per cent) of the retail price since the prevailing Value Added in the trade sector is not yet imposed by this tax.

Paragraph (2)

The Value Added Tax is a Tax imposed on the domestic consumed Goods, not to the exported or foreign consumed one therefore the exported goods' tariff is 0% (zero per cent).

By imposing 0% (zero per cent) tariff, the Input Tax paid by the Exporter, at the time of acquisition of the Exported Goods can be reimbursed. So there is no more element of the Value Added Tax in the price of the Exported Goods.

Paragraph (3)

Based on the economic development consideration and the rising demand for the development fund, the Government is competent to amend tax tariff to a minimum of 5% (five per cent) and to a maximum of 15% (fifteen per cent). This tariff amendment does not leave the principle of one single tariff, which means that a similar tariff must be enforced on all Delivery on Taxable Goods and Services.

Article 8.

Paragraph (1)

The tariff on Sales Tax on Luxury Goods consists of two kinds i.e. 10% (ten per cent) and 20% (twenty per cent). Said Sales Taxes are imposed as an addition to the Value Added Tax and not as a substitute to it.
Therefore Sales Tax on Luxury Goods is collected together with the Value Added Tax.
The difference of 10% (ten per cent) and 20% (twenty per cent) tariff is applied due to the fact of the existing different grade of luxury of the relative Goods.

Paragraph (2)

See the elucidation on Article 7 paragraph (2).

Paragraph (3)

Based on the economic development consideration and the rising demand for the development fund, equitable tax imposition and control of the luxury comsumption scheme, the Government is competent to amend the tax tariff to a maximum of 35% (thirty Five per cent).

Paragraph (4)

The Government is competent to determine certain group of Goods imposed with the Sales Tax on Luxury Goods at the tariff of 10% (ten per cent) or 20% (twenty per cent).

Paragraph (5)

The kind and sort of Goods imposed with the Sales Tax on Luxury the grouping of which is determined by the Government Regulation according to the provisions contained in paragraph (4) will further be regulated by the Minister of Finance.

Article 9.

Paragraph (1)

The method to calculate the indebted tax is by multiplying the Sales Price, Reimbursement or Import Value by the tax tariff as stipulated in Article 7 Paragraph (1). This indebted tax constitutes the Output Tax collected by a Taxable Enterpreneur.

Paragraph (2)

The Input Tax already paid by a Taxable Enterpreneur at the time of acquisition or importation of Taxable Goods or receipt of Taxable Services can be credited by the Output Tax collected by Taxable Enterpreneur on the Delivery of Taxable Goods and Services. The crediting of Input Tax against Output Tax is conducted within the same Tax Period.

Paragraph (3)

The difference as referred to in this paragraph must be deposited to the State Treasury according to the provisions as regulated in the Law of General Provisions and Procedure of Taxes.

Paragraph (4)

The difference as referred to in this paragraph is the right of the Taxable Enterpreneur which can be compensated or be reimbursed.

Paragraph (5)

A Taxable Enterpreneur in one Tax Period can perform 2 (two) deliveries, i.e. taxable and non taxable deliveries. In this case, the Input Tax which is creditable is only the that relating to taxable delivery, which must be exactly known from the record of the Taxable Enterpreneur.

Paragraph (6)

In the case of the recording of Input Tax the accounting of the Taxable Enterpreneur is not exactly known, the method of crediting the Input Tax is calculated based on the manual stipulated by the Minister of Finance. That manual is meant to facilitate and give certainty to the Taxable Enterpreneur.

Paragraph (7)

For Taxable Enterpreneur as referred to in this paragraph, the method to credit the Input Tax against Output Tax is stipulated by a credit calculation manual of Input Tax determined by the Minister of Finance. This manual, apart from being needed by Taxable Enterpreneur since it is only obliged to make records on the gross circulation as referred to in Article 6 paragraph (3) of this law, it also meant to assist the Taxable Enterpreneur to be able to credit his Input Tax although this group of Taxable Enterpreneur does not have evidence of Input Tax Colection.

Paragraph (8)

In principle the Input is creditable against Output Tax, but especially for expenses as referred to in this paragraph, the Input Tax is not creditable.

a. Input Tax can only be credited by Taxable Enterpreneur who has been confirmed according to the provisions under Article 3 of this law.
b. Self explanatory.
c. Self explanatory.

Article 10.

Paragraph (1)

The method to calculate the indebted Sales Tax on Luxury Goods is by multiplying the Sales Price or Import Value by the tariff as stipulated in Article 8.

Paragraph (2)

Differing from the Value Added Tax which is collected several times is the Sales Tax on Luxury Goods imposed only once at the level of Manufacturer or at the moment of Importation. Therefore, Sales Tax on Luxury Goods which has been paid cannot be credited against the Value Added Tax at the following delivery.

Paragraph (3)

The Sales Tax on Luxury Goods which has been paid at the time of acquisition, can be reimbursed when the Luxury Good is exported. See further elucidation under Article 7 Paragraph (2).

Article 11.

Paragraph (1)

The collection of Value Added Tax follows the acrual principle. It means that tax is indebted at the time of Delivery of Taxable Goods and Services or Importation of Taxable Goods, although upon that delivery payment has not yet been or has been partially received.

Article 12.

Paragraph (1)

This provision clarifies the place of the indebted tax which will also determine the territory where tax is collected.

Paragraph (2)

If a Taxable Enterpreneur has indebted tax at more than one place, while its selling and financing administration is centralized at one location, to facilitate the Taxable Enterpreneur to fulfil his obligation, said enterpreneur concerned can submit a written application for opting the place of the indebted tax. The Director General of Taxes after making the necessary verification will decide the application. If the application is rejected, the stipulation as regulated in paragraph (1) shall apply.

Paragraph (3)

Self explanatory.

Article 13.

Paragraph (1)

The preparation the of Tax Invoice is obligatory for every Taxable Enterpreneur, since a Tax Invoice is an evidence becoming the implementation means of the mechanism in crediting the Value Added Tax.

Paragraph (2)

See the elucidation on Article 11 paragraph (2).

Paragraph (3)

For each Delivery of Taxable Goods or Services by Taxable Enterpreneur one Tax Invoice must be prepared. The preparation of one Tax Invoice covering all Delivery of Taxable Goods or.
Services which occures during one calendar month to the same buyer (permanent customer) is meant to relieve the administrative burden of the Enterpreneur concerned. The preparation of one Tax Invoice must be with the consent of the Director General of Taxes.

Paragraph (4)

The Enterpreneur who opts to be confirmed as Taxable Enterpreneur does not prepare Tax Invoice upon Delivery of Taxable Goods to non Taxable Enterpreneur.

Paragraph (5)

Self explanatory.

Paragraph (6)

Self explanatory.

Paragraph (7)

This provision is meant to uniform the form, size, supply and procedure to submit the Tax Invoice.

Paragraph (8)

A Taxable Enterpreneur who is obliged to prepare Tax Invoice, but fail to do so or not properly fill the Tax Invoice is considered to make violation and subject to sanction in the form of administrative fine.

Article 14.

Paragraph (1)

The Tax Invoice can only be prepared by the Taxable Enterpreneur. Prohibition to prepare by non Taxable Enterpreneur is meant to protect the Buyer from improper tax collection.

Paragraph (2)

If an Enterpreneur who has not been confirmed yet as a Taxable Enterpreneur violates the provisions of paragraph (1) is subject to administrative sanction and is also obliged to deposit the tax which has been entered into the tax Invoice to the State Treasury.

Article 15.

Paragraph (1)

The Report on tax calculation must be submitted in 20 (twenty) days at the latest upon the expiry of the Tax Period by using the Periodical Tax Retûrn as regulated in the Law on General Orovisions and Procedure on Taxes. Of the twentieth day is a holiday, the report must be submitted on the next day at the latest.

Parapgraph (2)

The Records and documents pertaining to the Importation, Delivery of Taxable Goods and Services, for example Tax Invoice, list of the Recapitulation of Tax Invoice, Export documents etc. which are to be entered or enclosed to the Periodical Tax Return shall be determined by the Minister of Finance.

Paragraph (3)

This report is obligatory. If the provisions of paragraphs (1) and (2) are violated, the report is not considered submitted and sanction shall be taken as regulated in the Law on General Provisions and Procedure of Taxes.

Article 16.

Paragraph (1)

The Reimbursement of tax payment excess as referred to in Article 9 paragraph (4) is conducted according to the provisions as regulated in the Law on General Provisions and Procedure of Taxes.
Besides the afore mentioned provisions, the Minister of Finance may stipulate another term, for example reimbursement upon acquisition of capital Goods.

Paragraph (2)

The request for tax reimbursement proposed by the Taxable Enterpreneur who exports Taxable Goods (Exporter) must be completed with evidences/the relative Export documents.

Article 17.

The Provisions concerning the provisions on the collection and sanction procedures, for example competence to perform inspection, assessment, collection, payment, objection, appeal, administrative as well as penal sanctions, are regulated in the General Provisions and Procedure on Taxes, as well as in other legislative regulations.
Other provisions concerning sanctions in the Law on Value Added Tax on Goods and Services and Sales on Luxury Goods are regulated in Article 3 paragraph (4), Article 13 paragraph (8) and Article 14 paragraph (2).

Article 18.

Paragraph (1)

a. self explanatory;

b. All existing implementation regulations, issued in the framework of Sales Tax Law 1951, which are not contrary to the contents and purpose of this Law shall remain valid as long as not yet revoked and replaced by an implementation regulation on the basis of this Law.

Paragraph (2)

The stipulation in paragraph (2) is meant to overcome the difficulty which arises within the transitional period as the result of the coming into force the Law on Value Added Tax on Goods and Services and Sales Tax on Luxury Goods and the annulment of Law on Sales Tax 1951,on the similar object of imposition such as :

long term contract or that of which the validity period covers two periods of the abovementioned Laws;

balance of Sales Price or Reimbursement which has not been paid yet;

Stock of which the Import Tax is not yet available.

In this case the Minister of Finance is competent to stipulate an implementation regulation other than the stipulation mentioned in paragraph (1), to reduce the injustice in tax imposition and to smoothen the implementation of this Law.

Article 19.

Self explanatory.

Article 20.

Self explanatory.

Article 21.

Self explanatory.

SUPPLEMENT TO STATE GAZETTE OF REPUBLIC OF INDONESIA
NO. 3264.

Appendix 27

THE PRESIDENT OF THE REPUBLIC OF INDONESIA
GOVERNMENT REGULATION OF THE REPUBLIC OF INDONESIA
NO. 35 YEAR 1983 DATED DECEMBER 31, 1983
R E
REGISTRATION, GRANTING OF TAX PAYER REGISTRATION NUMBER, SUBMISSION OF TAX RETURN, AND REQUIREMENTS OF LODGING OBJECTIONS

THE PRESIDENT OF THE REPUBLIC OF INDONESIA,

Considering : that for the execution of the Registration of Tax Payers, Granting of Tax Payer Registration Number, Submission of Tax Return and Requirements for, Lodging Objections as referred to in Article 2, Article 3 and Article 25 paragraph (2) of Law No. 6 Year 1983 re General Provisions and Procedure on Taxes, it is deemed necessary to stipulate a further arrangement concerning the aforementioned matters with a Government Regulation.

In view of :
1. Article 5 paragraph (2) of 1945 Constitution;
2. Law No. 6 Year 1983 re General Provisions and Procedure on Taxes (State Gazette Year 1983 No. 49; Supplement to State Gazette No. 3262);
3. Law No. 7 Year 1983 re Income Tax (State Gazette Year 1983 No. 50, Supplement to State Gazette No. 3263).
4. Law No. 8 Year 1983 re Value Added Tax on Goods and Services and Sales Tax on Luxury Goods (State Gazette Year 1983 No. 51, Supplement to State Gazette No. 3264).

HAS DECIDED

To stipulate : GOVERNMENT REGULATION RE REGISTRATION, GRANTING OF TAX PAYER REGISTRA-

TION NUMBER, SUBMISSION OF TAX RETURN, AND REQUIREMENTS OF LODGING OBJECTIONS.

Article 1.

(1) The place for a Tax Payer to register himself to obtain a Tax Payer Registration Number shall be the Office of the Directorate General of Taxes, of which the working area covers the residence or domicile of the relative Tax Payer.

(2) In case the residence or domicile of the Tax Payer is situated in two or more working areas of the office of the Directorate General of Taxes, then the Director General of Taxes shall determine the residence or domicile of the Tax Payer as referred to in paragraph (1).

(3) A Tax Payer already registered at the Office of the Directorate General of Taxes and already having obtained a Tax Payer Registration Number prior to the validity of Law No. 6 Year 1983 re General Provisions and Procedure on Taxes, need not register himself anymore.

(4) A Tax Payer who in a Fiscal Year gains an income exceeding the non Taxable income limit shall register himself to obtain a Tax Payer Registration Number at the latest at the end of the relative Fiscal Year, and shall submit the Annual Tax Return.

Article 2.

(1) A Tax Payer who will register himself, shall be obligated to fill out the Registration Form for Tax Payers.

(2) The completion filling out and signing of the form can be conducted the Tax Payer himself, or by another person given a special power of attorney.

(3) The submission of the already completed and signed registration form for Tax Payers can be conducted by the Tax Payer himself or his proxy as referred to in paragraph (2), or by another person given a special power of attorney for that purpose.

Article 3.

(1) Within 3 (three) days after the date of the receipt of the registration form, the Tax Payer shall be granted a Receipt of Registration by sending it to the address of the relative Tax Payer containing the provisional Tax Payer Registration Number, and shall be valid up to the receipt issuance of the Tax Payer Registration Number Card.

(2) At the latest 3 (three) months after the date of the receipt of the registration form, the Office of the Directorate General of Taxes shall grant the Tax Payer Registration Number Card to the Tax Payer, by sending it to the address of the relative Tax Payer.

Article 4.

The obligation to submit a Tax Return for civil servants, members of the Armed Forces of the Republic of Indonesia, other state Officials, employees of State owned Corporation and Regional State owned Corporations under any name and in any form whatsoever whose income is gained merely from work, shall be regulated by a Presidential Decree.

Article 5.

A Tax Payer who lodges an objection as referred to in Article 25 paragraph (1) of Law No. 6 Year 1983 re General Provisions and Procedure on Taxes, in addition to the requirement to meet the conditions as stipulated in Article 25 paragraph (2) of said law, shall also be obligated to state the tax amount which according to his calculation should be indebted.

Article 6.

Anything not yet sufficiently regulated in this Government Regulation, shall further be stipulated by the Minister of Finance.

Article 7.

This Government Regulation shall come into force as from the date of promulgation.

For the public knowledge this Government Regulation shall be promulgated in the State Gazette of the Republic of Indonesia.

Stipulated in : Jakarta
on : December 31, 1983.

THE PRESIDENT OF THE
REPUBLIC OF INDONESIA

signed

SOEHARTO

Promulgated in Jakarta
on December 31, 1983

THE MINISTER/SECRETARY OF
STATE OF THE REPUBLIC OF
INDONESIA

signed

SUDHARMONO, S.H.

STATE GAZETTE OF THE REPUBLIC OF INDONESIA YEAR 1983
NO. 52.

Appendix 28

THE PRESIDENT OF THE REPUBLIC OF INDONESIA

GOVERNMENT REGULATION OF THE REPUBLIC OF INDONESIA NUMBER 36 YEAR 1983 DATED DECEMBER 31, 1983

CONCERNING

IMPLEMENTATION OF THE INCOME TAX LAW 1984.

THE PRESIDENT OF THE REPUBLIC OF INDONESIA,

Considering : that the implementation. of Article 9 paragraph (1) letter b and letter d, Article 21, Article 22, Article 23 paragraph (3), Article 25, Article 27, and Article 35 of the Law on Income Tax should be regulated further with a Government Regulation;

With a view to :
1. Article 5 paragraph (2) of the 1945 Constitution;
2. Law Number 6 Year 1983 concerning General Provisions and Procedure of Taxes (State Gazette Year 1983 Number 49, Gazette Number 3262);
3. Law Number 7 Year 1983 concerning Income Tax (State Gazette Year 1983 Number 50, Supplement to State Gazette Number 3263);
4. Government Regulation Number 35 Year 1983 Concerning Registration, Issuing of Tax–Payer Registration Number, Submission of Tax Returns, and Conditions for the Lodging of Objections (State Gazette Year 1983 Number 52);

HAS DECIDED:

To stipulate : GOVERNMENT REGULATION ON IMPLEMENTATION OF THE INCOME TAX LAW 1984.

CHAPTER I.
SPECIAL RESERVE FUNDS AND ADJUSTMENT FACTOR

Article 1.

(1) To calculate the nett income of banking and insurance enterprises, it is allowed to deduct as expenses, the sums set aside for the formation and fostering of special reserve funds.

(2) The special reserve funds as meant in paragraph (1) consist of :

a. the reserve fund for writing off dubious receivables for banking enterprises;

b. the premium reserve funds for life insurance enterprises;

c. the premium reserve funds and loss reserve funds for loss insurance enterprises.

(3) The amount of special reserve funds and other matters pertaining to the formation and fostering of special reserve funds as meant in paragraph (1) and (2), are further regulated by the Minister of Finance.

Article 2.

(1) The basis for calculation of taxes :

a. for income from the sale or transfer of property not being used in the enterprise and already possessed before January 1, 1984, shall be the difference between the sales prise or value of transfer and the acquisition value of such property on January 1, 1984;

b. for income from the sale or transfer of property not being used in the enterprise, owned after December 31, 1983, the difference between the sales prise or value of transfer at the moment the transaction takes place, and the acquisition price or value of that property.

(2) The acquisition value of the property on January 1, 1984, as meant in paragraph (1) letter a and the acquisition price or value of the property as meant in paragraph (1) letter b, should first be multiplied with an adjustment factor, of which the amount will be determined by the Minister of Finance.

CHAPTER II.
AVERAGE EFFECTIVE RATE

Article 3.

(1) On the income from the sale or transfer of property, which is not used in the enterprise, or on the income of several years, which are received or obtained in one lump sum, Income Tax will be levied, by applying an average effective rate.

(2) The average effective rate as meant in paragraph (1) is obtained by applying Article 17 of the Law on Income Tax 1984, to an income amount consisting of regular income added with the income of several years received or obtained in one lump-sum, the latter divided by the number of tax years concerned.

(3) For private or individual tax payers, the amount of income as meant in paragraph (2) is deducted beforehand with the income not subject to tax.

(4) The average effective rate obtained by the calculation as meant in paragraph (2), is rounded off downwards, if the figure behind the decimal point is 5 or lower, and rounded off upwards if the figure behind the decimal point is higher than 5.

(5) Regular income as meant in paragraph (2) is income which in general is received periodically, or is received in each taxperiod or tax-year.

(6) For pension redemption money received or obtained in one lump sum, the number of tax-years allowed to be calculated, is ten (10) years.

CHAPTER III.
PAYMENT OF TAXES IN THE CURRENT YEAR VIA THIRD PARTIES

Article 4.

(1) Deduction and collection of Income Tax by third parties as mentioned in Article 21 paragraph (1) and Article 22 paragraph (1) of the 1984 Income Tax Law, is indebted at the moment of payment or at another moment as stipulated by the Minister of Financé.

(2) Deduction of Income Tax on income from capital and services by the parties as meant in Article 23 and Article 26 of the Income Tax Law 1984, is indebted at the moment of payment, or at the moment of indebtedness of said income.

Article 5.

Matters partaining to the implementation of deduction of Income Tax by third parties as meant in Article 21 of the 1984 Income Tax Law from the income of daily or weekly paid employess or workers and from the income in the form of honorarium which are not included in regular payments, and the implementation of Income Tax collection by third parties as meant in Article 22 of the 1984 Income Tax Law, will be further regulated by the Minister of Finance.

Article 6.

(1) Dividend from shares traded through the Stock Exchanges and dividend from certificates of which the total amount does not exceed a certain

sum, will not be subject to Income Tax deduction as meant in Article 23 of the 1984 Income Tax Law.

(2) The certain limit amount as meant in paragraph (1), is fixed at Rp. 960,000,— (nine hundred and sixty thousand rupiahs) for each year, or Rp.480,000,– (four hundred and eighty thousand rupiahs) for every 6 (six) months.

(3) The limit amount as meant in paragraph (2) will be adjusted with an adjustment factor to be determined by a Decree of the Minister of Finance.

CHAPTER IV.

PAYMENT OF TAXES IN THE CURRENT YEAR BY THE TAX PAYER HIMSELF

Article 7.

(1) The basis for calculating the Income Tax which has to be paid by the taxpayer himself in the current year as meant in Article 25 of the 1984 Income Tax Law, which will further be abbreviated as PPh Article 25, in case there is a remainder of losses not yet compensated, is the Income Tax calculated on the basis of nett income according to the last Annual Tax Return, Except when the tax which is finally fixed by the Director General of Taxes, is of larger amount, deducted with the total remaining losses not yet compensated.

(2) The basis for calculating PPh Article 25 after the year of implementation of loss compensation has ended, is the Income Tax calculated on the basis of nett income according to the last Annual Tax Return, except when the final tax determined by the Director General of Taxes is of larger amount, in which case the loss compensation is not taken into consideration.

Article 8.

The amount of installments of PPh Article 25 each month for :

a. banking enterprises and other financial institutions as well as other corporations to be appointed by the Director General of Taxes, is the total Income Tax indebted on income subject to tax, on the basis of the financial report of the last quarter, to be made 1 (one) year, divided by 12 (twelve).

b. State and Regional enterprises under whatever name and in whatever form, is the total Income Tax indebted on oncome subject to tax, on the basis of the Revenues and Expenditures Budget Bill (RAPB) already composed at the beginning of the tax year, deducted with tax credit of the previous fiscal year, divided by 12 (twelve).

Article 9.

(1) Regular income as meant in Article 3 paragraph 5, which has been made the basis for calculation of PPh Article 25 on income from the sale or transfer of property or income of several years received in one lumpsum, is the regular income according to the last Anual Tax Return, except if the final tax determined by the Director General of Taxes, is of larger amount.

(2) PPh Article 25 as meant in paragraph (1) is the tax credit for Income Tax indebted of the tax year concerned.

Article 10.

If the basis for calculation of PPh Article 25 includes income as meant in Article 3 paragraph (1), then said income shall first be deducted.

Article 11.

(1) The amount of monthly PPh Article 25 install-

ments for new Taxpayers who are obliged to maintain a bookkeeping, is the amount obtained from the application of the rate according to Article 17 of the 1984 Income Tax Law on nett income on the basis of their bookkeeping to be made 1 (one) year, divided by 12 (twelve).

(2) The amount of monthly PPh Article 25 installments for new taxpayers with a turnover or gross revenues amounting to less than Rp. 60,000,000.- (sixty million rupiahs), who are not obliged to maintain bookkeeping, is the amount obtained from the application of the 15% (fifteen percent) tariff on the percentage of nett income based on the Calculation Norm, multiplied by the turnover or gross revenues divided by 12 (twelve).

CHAPTER V.
OTHER PROVISIONS

Article 12.

(1) A taxpayer who can show, that the Income Tax which will be indebted at the end of the tax year will be less than 3% of the Income Tax Constituting the basis for calculating the amount of installments off PPh Article 25, may submit an application for reduction of the installment amount to the Director General of Taxes.

(2) In submitting his application for reduction of the installments as meant in paragraph (1), the Tax Payer shall state the amount of Taxes and the Tax-installments, which according to his accouning, should be indebted.

(3) If in a period of 3 (three) months since the date of date of receipt of the application for reduction of installments as meant in paragraph (1) the Director General of Taxes has not given his decision, then the application for reduction has been

accepted, and the Taxpayer can carry out installments in accordance with his calculation.

Article 13.

Depreciation and amortization shall start from the year of expenditure, except for property still in the process of being worked, the depreciation and amortization shall start from the year the work on that property has been completed, and for property being leased, the depreciation is started from the year the property concerned was leased.

Article 14.

Expenses constituting costs for obtaining, collecting, and maintaining income in connection with work, may be deducted from the gross income, of which the amount will be determined by the Minister of Finance

Article 15.

Parties obliged to carry out tax deductions as meant in Article 21 paragraph (1) letter d of the 1984 Income Tax Law are among others foundations, state and regional enterprises under whatever name and in whatever form, agencies of the Government of the Republic of Indonesia, agencies of foreign countries' representations, representative agencies of international organizations, and other agencies or organizations of whatever nature and in whatever form.

CHAPTER VI.
TRANSITIONAL PROVISIONS

Article 16.

(1) The basis for calculation of Income Tax which should be paid by the Taxpayer himself for the year 1984 and onward until the indebted Income Tax as meant in

Article 25 on Income Tax Law of 1984, is known, as follows :

a. For a tax-paying corporation, the amount of Corporation Tax according to the last Corporation Tax Assessment Letter subtracted by the tax deductions and tax collections for the year concerned.

b. For private or individual taxpayers, the Income Tax amount according to the last Tax Assessment Letter subtracted by tax deductions and tax collections for the year concerned.

(2) Deduction and collection of taxes by third parties, which may be subtracted as meant in paragraph (1), only concerns the collection of taxes carried out by the Directorate General of Customs & Excises, and the treasurers of the Central and Regional Governments.

Article 17.

Payment in kind and the enjoyment of other benefits by oil and natural gas mining companies and other mining companies is connection with a Work Contract and Production Sharing Contract, which are still valid at the time the 1984 Income Tax Law comes into force, may be deducted as expenses, and for the party receiving or obtaining those benefits, they are calculated as income.

Article 18.

Income subject to tax received or obtained in the field of oil and natural gas mining inconnection with a Technical Assistance Contract, Loan Risk Contract, Joint Venture Contract and other similar contracts, which are still valid at the time the 1984 Income Tax Law comes into force, are equalized to income subject to tax which has been received or obtained in the frame of a Production Sharing Contract, as regulated in Article 33 paragraph (3) of the 1984 Income Tax Law.

CHAPTER VII.
CONCLUDING PROVISIONS

Article 19.

Matters not yet sufficiently regulated in this Government Regulation, will be further regulated by the Minister of Finance.

Article 20.

This Government Regulation comes into force on the date of its promulgation. For the public knowledge this Government Regulation shall be promulgated in the State Gazette of the Republic of Indonesia.

Stipulated in Jakarta
on December 31, 1983,

PRESIDENT OF THE REPUBLIC
OF INDONESIA

Signed,

S O E H A R T O

Promulgated in Jakarta
on December 31, 1983
MINISTER/STATE SECRETARY
OF THE REPUBLIC OF INDONESIA

Signed

SUDHARMONO, S.H.

STATE GAZETTE OF THE REPUBLIC ONF INDONESIA
YEAR 1983
NUMBER 53.

Appendix 29

E L U C I D A T I O N
O N
GOVERNMENT REGULATION OF THE REPUBLIC OF INDONESIA NO. 36 YEAR 1983 DATED DECEMBER 1, 1983 CONCERNING IMPLEMENTATION OF THE INCOME TAX LAW 1984.

G E N E R A L

The 1984 Income Tax Law has been composed in a simple structure. This simplicity comprises regulation, kinds of taxes, rate, and the application method.

This is meant in order that the Taxpayer community can easily fulfill their tax duties, and also to make its control easier. In several matters further provisions and regulations are necesary. Those follow-up provisions and regulations are arranged in this Government Regulation, while the implementation policy will be decided by the Minister of Finance, and its technical implementation will be handled by the Director General of Taxes.

ARTICLE BY ARTICLE

Article 1 :

Paragraph (1)

Actually, the formation and fostering of reserve funds are not allowed to be deducted from the gross income. Especially for banking enterprises, life insurance and loss insurance enterprises, the formation and fostering of reserve funds is a requisite to ensure the continued existence of these enterprises, and which economically are indeed necessary to cover the burdens or losses which will certainly occur. For these kinds of enterprise, the formation and fostering of reserve funds are within certain limits allowed to be deducted from the gross income as expenses for the enterprise.

Paragrap (2)

Self explanatory.

Paragraph (3)

Self explanatory.

Article 2 :

Meant by property not used in the enterprise according to this provision, is property which is not used in the activities of the enterprises. For instance, Limited liability company A operating in the field of cigarette industry, owns as property a rest-house. According to this provision, the resthouse of Company A is included in the definition of property not used in the company.

Paragraph (1)

letter a

This provision is meant to not apply the provisions of the Law on Income Tax 1984 to the income received or obtained by the Taxpayer before the 1984 Income Tax Law was effective.
Therefore, it is necessary to first carry out an evaluation of the price of the property concerned on January 1, 1984. The price evaluation on that property meant in this provision is called the acquisition value of the property.

Example :
Taxpayer A purchased in 1980 a plot of land for the price of Rp. 10,000,000,– (ten million rupiahs).
In the year 1988, that land is sold for Rp. 50,000,000.–– (fifty million rupiahs).
In the first place, it is necessary to determine what the acquisition value of the property is (property in the form of land) on January 1, 1984.

letter b

Self explanatory.

Paragraph (2)

Hereunder, examples are given as follows :

a. Taxpayer A bought in 1980 a plot of land for the price of Rp. 10,000,000,– (ten million rupiahs). In 1988, that land is sold for the price of Rp. 50,000, million (fifty million rupiahs). In the first place, it is necessary to determine the acquisition value of the land on January 1, 1984, for instance Rp. 20,000, 000.– (twenty million rupiahs).
If the adjustment factor for the year 1988 compared to 1984 is a, then the income from the sale of said land is Rp. 50,000,000.-- – Rp. 20,000,000. – x a).

b. Taxpayer B purchases a plot of land in the year 1985 for the price of Rp. 30,000,000,– (thirty million rupiahs). In the year 1989, that land is sold at a price of Rp. 60,000,000.– (sixty million rupiahs). If the adjustment factor for the year 1989 toward the year 1985 is b, then the income from the sale of that plot of lands is Rp. 60,000,000,– – Rp. 30,000,000,– x b).

Article 3 :

Paragrap (1)

Self explanatory.

Paragraph (2), paragraph (3) and Paragraph (4).

To obtain an effective average rate and its application in calculating the indebted Income Tax, the following example is given :

Taxpayer A, married with three (3) children, leases his house by contract for a period of five (5) years (1984 through 1988) for a contract price of Rp. 100,000,000.– (one hundred million rupiahs), which amount is received in May 1984.

A's regular income in 1984 is known to be Rp. 10,000,000.– (ten million rupiahs).

The calculation of Income Tax on income in 1984 is as follows :

Income from the contracted house averagely per year :

1/5 X Rp. 100,000,000.–		= Rp. 20,000,000,–
Regular income in 1984		= Rp. 10,000,000.–
Total	=	= Rp. 30,000,000.–
PTPK (non taxable income)		= Rp. 2,880,000,–
Taxable income		= Rp. 27,120,000.–

Rate : 15% X Rp. 10,000,000,– = Rp. 1,500,000.–
25% X Rp. 17,120,000,– = Rp. 4,280,000,–

Total Income Tax . . . .= Rp. 5,780,000,–

Average effective rate : $\frac{5,78}{27.12}$ X 100% – 21.3% = 21%.
(rounded-off downward).
The calculation of the Income Tax becomes as follows :
21% X Rp. 10,000,000.– + Rp. 100,000,000.–) = Rp. 23.100,000.–

Paragraph (5)

Self explanatory.

Paragraph (6)

Considering that the period of receiving pension money is difficult to know, and to facilitate the calculation of Income Tax on pension redemption money received or obtained in one lumpsum, income is calculated as income of ten (10) years.

Article 4 :

Self explanatory.

Article 5 :

Self explanatory.

Article 6 :

Paragraph (1)

This provision is meant in order that toward certificate and/or shareholders of stock traded via the stock exchange, who in general receive or obtain income in the form of dividend, which in one year does not exceed a certain amount, no deduction of income tax need to be applied, as meant in Article 23 of the 1984 Income Tax Law If toward the certificate and/or share holders concerned, a deduction of tax is applied, then this will become a burden for them, because they would have to arrange its reimbursement/restitution later on.

Exemption from deduction on said dividend does not mean, that said dividend will be exempted from being subject to Income Tax, namely if that dividend, together with other income, exceeds the non-laxable income amount.

Paragraph (2)

Self explanatory.

Paragraph (3)

The Minister of Finance is given the authority to adjust the limit amount exempted from tax deduction, conform to the adjustment as meant in Article 7 paragraph (3) of the 1984 Income Tax Law.

Article 7 :

The Income Tax amount to be paid by the Taxpayer himself in the current year is based on the indebted tax according to the last Annual Tax Return except if the tax, lastly determined by the Director General of Taxes is bigger in amount. In case there is a remainder of losses which have not yet been compensated, then the Income Tax amount to be paid by the Taxpayer himself in the current year, can be explained as follows :

Example :

The Annual Tax Return of an entity Taxpayer shows the following information :

1985 :	The Taxpayer has suffered losses amounting to	Rp. 250,000,000.–
	After an assessment by the Directorate General of Taxes, the loss amounts to	Rp. 200,000,000.–

This loss can be compensated with the nett income in five (5) years, starting with the first year after this loss has been suffered (starting 1968)

Installments of Income Tax in the current year

1986	....	: Zero/Nil
1986 :	Nett income of the Taxpayer .. :	Rp. 50,000,000.–
	Compensation of losses in 1986 . :	Rp. 200,000,000.–
	Remainder of losses not yet compensated. .... :	Rp. 150,000,000.–

Installments of Income Tax in the current year

1987	....	: Zero/Nil
1987 :	Nett income of Taxpayer ...... :	Rp. 80,000,000.–
	Compensation of losses in 1987 . :	Rp. 150,000,000.–
	Remainder of losses not yet compensated. .... :	Rp. 70,000.000,–

Installments of Income Tax for the current year 1988 is based on the Income Tax calculated from the nett income based on the Annual Tax Return of 1987 deducted with the remainder of the losses for the year 1988 = Rp. 80,000,000.– – Rp. 70,000,000.–) = Rp. 10,000,000.–

Installments of Income Tax for each month is the Income Tax calculated on Rp. 10,000,000.– divided by 12 (twelve).

1988 :	Nett income of Taxpayer ...... :	Rp. 100,000,000.–
	Remainder of losses not yet compensated .... :	Rp. 70,000,000.–
	Nett income for 1988 .... :	Rp. 30,000,000.–

The calculation of Income Tax installments for the current year 1989 is as follows :

The nett income for the year 1988 = Rp. 100,000,000.– (three is no more any remainder of losses not yet compensated).

The taxable income in 1988 = Rp. 100,000,000.–
Income Tax indebted for the year 1988 :

15% X Rp. 10,000,000.– . . . . = Rp. 1,500,000.–
25% X Rp. 40,000,000.– . . . . = Rp. 10,000,000.–
35% X Rp. 50,000,000.– . . . . = Rp. 17,500,000.–

Rp. 29,000,000.–

For instance :

Income Tax collected by the Government Treasurer paid in the year 1988 Rp. 4,000,000.–

Income Tax deducted by other parties paid in the year 1988 . . . . Rp. 1,000,000.– 5,000,000.–

Rp. 24,000,000.–

Installments of PPh Article 25 each month for the year 1989 = 1/12 X Rp. 24,000,000.– = Rp. 2,000,000.–

Article 8 :

Letter a

For banking enterprises and other financial institutions as well as other institutions to be appointed/designated by the Director General of Taxes, the quarterly financial reports composed periodically shall show an income which approaches the income received or obtained in the quarter concerned, as it is used as the basis for calculating PPh Article 25. Especially for banking enterprises and other financial institutions, the obligation to submit their quarterly financial reports does not require a prior appointment/designation by the Director General of Taxes.

Example :

The quarterly financial report of Bank A for the months of April through June 1984 shows a nett income of Rp. 60,000,000.–
This financial report shall become the calculation basis of the installments of PPh Article 25 for the following months until the ensuring quarterly financial report is drawn-up.
The amount of PPh Article 25 installments to be paid for those following months is calculated as follows :

Nett quarterly income counted per annum : 4 X Rp. 60,000,000.–
Indebted = Rp. 240,000,000.–
Indebted Income Tax according to Article 17 of the 1984 Income Tax Law :

15% X Rp. 10,000,000.– . . . . = Rp. 1,500,000.–
25% X Rp. 40,000,000.– . . . . = Rp. 10,000,000.–
35% X Rp. 190,000,000.– . . . . = Rp. 66.500.000,–

Rp. 78,000,000.–

Installments of Income Tax for the months of July and further (until there is a new quarterly financial report) = 1/12 X Rp. 78,000,000.– = Rp. 6,500,000.–

Letter b

With the consideration, that the company 15 Bill of state Revenues and Expenditures Budgets composed (RAPB), at the start of each year by state and Regional enterprises, and already legalised by the Minister concerned, can show an income which approaches the income received or obtained in the fiscal year concerned, therefore it is more suitable to be used as basis for the calculation of PPh Article 25.

Example :

A state enterprise has completed at the beginning of 1985 its company RAPB for the year 1985 with Income Tax estimated to be indebted at Rp. 1,800,000,000.–

The tax credit of the preceeding year was Rp. 600,000,000.–
The amount of PPh Article 25 installments for each month in the year 1985 is 1/12 X (Rp. 1,800,000,000.– – Rp. 600,000,000.–) = Rp. 100,000,000.–

Article 9 :

Paragraph (1)

To calculate the amount of PPh Article 25 the following example is given :

Taxpayer A is married and has three (3) children as dependants, and leases his house contractually for a period of five (5) years (1984 through 1988) with a contract price of Rp. 100,000,000.– which is received in the month of May 1984.

A's regular income in the year 1983 is known to be Rp. 10,000,000,-

The calculation of Income Tax on the income from the contract of his house at the moment it is received or obtained in 1984 :

Income from the contract of the house averagely each year :

1/5 X Rp. 100,000,000.–	= Rp. 20,000,000.–
Regular income of 1983 based on the Annual Tax Return (the preceeding year)	Rp. 10,000,000.– +
Total	= Rp. 30,000,000.–
Non-Taxable income	= Rp. 2,880,000.– –
Taxable income	= Rp. 27,120,000,–

Tariff rate : 15% X Rp. 10.000.000,– = Rp. 1.500.000,–
25% X Rp. 17.120.000,– = Rp. 4.280.000,–

Total Income Tax Rp. 5.780.000,–

The everage effective rate : $\frac{5,78}{27,12}$ X 100% = 21,3%

(rounded – off downward).

The Income Tax on the total house contract indebted in the year 1984 which must be settled in the current year = 21% X Rp. 100,000,000.– = Rp. 21,000,000.–

Paragraph (2)

In calculating the Indebted Income Tax on the basis of the Annual Tax Return, the payment of tax of PPh Article 25 on income from the sale or transfer of property or on income of several years received or obtained in one lumpsum, is deductied as tax credit for the fiscal year concerned.

Article 10 :

To calculate the calculation basis of PPh Article 25 installments, the income from the sale or the transfer of property, or the income of several years received or obtained in one lumpsum, is first deducted from the nett income.

Example :

For instance, a Taxpayer is married and has two (2) children as dependants.

Nett income for 1984 is	Rp. 12,000,000.–
In this amount of Rp. 12,000,000.– is included the income from the sale of a house for Rp. 5,000,000.–	Rp. 5,000,000.–
Regular income	Rp. 7,000,000.–
Non-Taxable income	Rp. 2,400,000.–
Taxable income	Rp. 4,600,000.–
Indebted Income Tax 15% X Rp. 4,600,000.–	Rp. 690,000.–
Tax credits	Rp. 210,000.–
	Rp. 480,000.–

The amount of PPh Article 25 installments each month is Rp. $\frac{480,000.–}{12}$ = Rp. 40,000.–

Article 11 :

Meant by new Taxpayer in this Article, is a newly registered taxpayer, who at the time the calculation for PPh Article 25 must be carried out, is not yet obliged to submit his Annual Tax Return and to whom a Tax Assessment Letter has never been issued.

Article 12 :

Paragraph (1)

This provision is made with the aims :

a. not to burden the Taxpayers by having to pay Income Tax, of which the amount far exceeds the amount actually indebted.

b. to relieve the administrative burden, because otherwise it may cause re-imbursements/restitution of excess taxes paid.

Example :

A Taxpayer in accordance with the calculation basis of Income Tax Installments to be paid by himself in the current year, must

pay an amount of Rp. 1,000,000,— each month (= Rp.12,000,000.— a year).
In the month of May an event occurs which causes the tax amount, estimated to be indebted by the Taxpayer in the year concerned, to decrease to Rp. 8,400,000.—
(Rp. 8,400,000.— = 70% X Rp. 12,000,000.—)
Because the tax amount estimated to be indebted is less than 75% of the Income Tax constituting the calculation basis of the Income Tax for the year concerned, the Tax payer concerned my submit an application to the Director General of Taxes for an amendement of the amount of his Income Tax installments.
If the evidences forwarded is accepted, then the calculation basis of Income Tax installments for the following months, starting from the moment the decision letter concerning the relative application is issued, is Rp. 8,400,000.— or $\frac{\text{Rp. } 8{,}400{,}000}{12}$ = Rp. 700,000.— per month.

Paragraph (2)

Self explanatory.

Paragraph (3)

Self explanatory.

Article 13 :

Depreciation and amortization of property of an enterprise is in General started from the year of expenditure. However, for company properties requiring several years for completion, the depreciation and amortization are started in the year the work on the property concerned is completed. For instance, for the construction of a factory, a period of three (3) years is required. The expenses for the construction of that factory during three (3) years, is started to be depreciated and amortized in the year the construction of the factory is completed.
For property in the leasing industry, the depreciation start in the year that property is leased, for instance : a lessor owns property in 1985, which is leased in 1988, so the depreciation is tarted as from 1988.

Article 14 :

For a Taxpayer who receives or obtains income as an employee or a pensioner, it is necessary to consider the expenses paid or indebted for obtaining, collecting, and maintaining said income.

The amount which may be deducted from the gross income of the employee or the pensioner, will be determined by the Minister of Finance.

Article 15 :

Foundation, State or Regional enterprises under whatever name or in whatever form, agencies of the Government of Indonesia, representative agencies of foreign countries, representative agencies of international organisations, and other agencies or organisations of wahatever nature and in whatever form, in their capacity of tax-deductors as meant in Article 21 paragraph (1) letter d of the 1984 Income Tax Law, are also obliged to deduct taxes from payments of honorarium (fees) or other remunerations to experts and/or associations of experts on the services rendered in Indonesia.

Article 16 :

Paragraph (1)

Self explanatory.

Paragraph (2)

Self explanatory.

Article 17 :

According to the provisions of the 1984 Income Tax Law, payment in kind and other benefits for the Taxpayer, except housing in isolated areas, on the basis of the Decree of the Minister of Finance,. are not allowed to be deducted as expenses. On the basis of Article 33 paragraph (3) of the 1984 Income Tax Law, for Taxpayers belonging to the group of il and natural Gas companes as well as other mining companies, in the frame of a Work Contract and Production sharing Contract, are still valid at the moment the 1984 Income Tax Law comes into force, their taxation still applies the mechanism of the old system, namely the provisions of the Corporation Tax Ordonance 1925 (Ordonansi Pajak Perseroan 1925) and the Tax Law on Interest, Dividend, and Royalt of 1970, so that payments as mentioned above are (still) allowed to be deducted as expenses.

As a consequence of the face that payments in kind and other benefits, may be changed as expenses, there for employees or workers receiving those payment and benefits, they constitute income, and are according by subject to Income Tax. Thus, although the mechanism follows the old system, but for the calculation of tax on income of employees or workers, the tariff-rate based on the 1984 Income Tax Law shall be used, inclusive the Non-Taxable Income, which is lower than the tariff-rate based on the Income Tax Ordinance 1944.

Article 18 :

Self explanatory.

Article 19 :

Self explanatory.

Article 20 :

Self explanatory.

SUPPLEMENT TO THE STATE GAZETTE OF THE REPUBLIC OF INDONESIA
NUMBER 3265.

Appendix 30

THE PRESIDENT OF THE REPUBLIC OF INDONESIA

GOVERNMENT REGULATION OF THE REPUBLIC OF INDONESIA NO. 37 YEAR 1983 DATED DECEMBER 31, 1983

R E

TAX ON INTEREST OF TIME DEPOSITS AND OTHER SAVINGS

THE PRESIDENT OF THE REPUBLIC OF INDONESIA,

Considering :

a. that in executing an ever increasing national development, larger financing funds will be required and the efforts to accumulate said funds shall therefore be improved;

b. that the efforts to involve all people of Indonesia in the development, interalia via fund accumulation in the form of the time deposits and other savings, have so far indicated results which should continuously be improved, established and promoted;

c. that to more encourage the community to participate in the fund accumulation via time deposits and other savings, and in compliance with the provisions in Article 4 paragraph (2) of Income Tax Law 1984, it is deemed necessary to postpone the tax imposition on interest of time deposits and other savings;

In view of :

1. Article 5 paragraph (2) of the 1945 Constitution;
2. Law No. 7 Year 1983 re Income Tax (State Gazette Year 1983 No. 50; Supplement to State Gazette No. 3263).

HAS DECIDED :

To stipulate : GOVERNMENT REGULATION RE TAX ON INTEREST OF TIME DEPOSITS AND OTHER SAVINGS.

Article 1.

The income tax imposition on interest of time deposits and other savings belonging to the people of Indonesia shall be postponed until a time to be further stipulated by the Government.

Article 2.

This Government Regulation shall come into force as from the date of promulgation.

For the public knowledge this Government Regulation shall be promulgated in the State Gazette of the Republic of Indonesia.

Stipulated in : Jakarta
on December 31, 1983
THE PRESIDENT OF THE
REPUBLIC OF INDONESIA
Signed.

S O E H A R T O. –

Promulgated in Jakarta
on December 31, 1983
MINISTER/STATE SECRETARY
OF THE REPUBLIC OF INDONESIA
Signed

SUDHARMONO, S.H.

Appendix 31

STATE GAZETTE OF THE REPUBLIC OF INDONESIA YEAR 1983 NO. 54

ELUCIDATION

ON

GOVERNMENT REGULATION OF THE REPUBLIC OF INDONESIA NO. 37 YEAR 1983

RE

TAX ON INTEREST OF TIME DEPOSITS AND OTHER SAVINGS

GENERAL

The execution of the national development is financed by development funds originating from both the Government sector in the form of Government of Government savings and private savings, such as community savings. With the increase of the national development execution and the efforts to maintain the planned national economic growth rate, the amount of the required funds to finance the execution of the development will obviously increase continuously.

For that purpose, the amount of both types of savings must automatically be increased. In this case, the most important community saving sources are the Time Deposit and other savings, such as Tabanas (National Development Saving) and Taska (Time Insurance Saving).

ARTICLE BY ARTICLE

Article 1.

To more encourage the community to continue participating in the community fund accumulation program which is very significant for the continuity of the national development execution, the income tax imposition on the interest received by them from time deposits and other savings, such as Tabanas (National Development Saving) and Taska (Time Insurance Saving), shall be postponed.

This means, that during this postponement period, the owners of time deposits and other savings as mentioned above shall not be imposed with any income tax on the interest received by them. The policy to grant tax relief shall not be applied for ever, as in principle according to Article 4 paragraph (1) letter f of the Law on Income Tax 1984, interest is an object of Income Tax. This tax relief is granted on the basis of the provisions in Article 4 paragraph (2) of the Law on Income Tax 1984, with the considerations as described above. If the state monetary or financial development in the future is considered as sufficiently strong, and the continuity of the development execution is therefore adequately secured, then this relief shall be re viewed.

Article 2.

Self explanatory.

SUPPLEMENT TO STATE GAZETTE OF THE REPUBLIC OF INDONESIA NO. 3266.

Appendix 32

THE PRESIDENT OF THE REPUBLIC OF INDONESIA
GOVERNMENT REGULATION OF THE REPUBLIC OF INDONESIA NO. 38 YEAR 1983 DATED DECEMBER 31, 1983

R E

IMPLEMENTATION OF LAW ON VALUE ADDED TAX 1984

THE PRESIDENT OF THE REPUBLIC OF INDONESIA,

Considering : that for the collection of the value added tax on goods and services and sales tax on luxury goods as referred to in the Law on Value Added Tax Law 1984 it is deemed necessary to further regulate said matters by a Government Regulation;

In view of :
1. Article 5 paragraph (2) of 1945 Constitution;
2. Law Number 6 of the Year 1983 re General Provisions and Procedure on Taxes (State Gazette Year 1983 No. 49, Supplement to State Gazette No. 3262);
3. Law No. 7 Year 1983 re Income Tax (State Gazette Year 1983, No. 50, Supplement to State Gazette No. 3263);
4. Law No. 8 Year 1983 re Value Added Tax on Goods and Services and Sales Tax on Luxury Goods (State Gazette Year 1983 No. 51, Supplement to State Gazette No. 3264);
5. Government Regulation No. 35 Year 1983 re Registration, Granting of Tax Payer Registration

Number, Submission of Tax Return, and Requirements for Proposing Objection (State Gazette Year 1983 No. 52).

HAS DECIDED :

To stipulate : GOVERNMENT REGULATION RE IMPLEMENTATION OF LAW ON VALUE ADDED TAX 1984.

CHAPTER I
GENERAL PROVISIONS

Article 1.

In this Government Regulation, the meaning of :

a. Importer shall be an Entrepreneur who within his business or work imports the Taxable Goods;

b. Indentor shall be a person or body within his/its business or work orders the Importer to import the Taxable Goods for and his/its behalf;

c. Exporter shall be an Entrepreneur within his business or work exports Goods;

d. Manufacturer shall be an Entrepreneur producing the Taxable Goods as referred to in Article 1, letters c and m of Law re Value Added Tax 1984, Including that of Real Estate and Industrial Estate;

e. Main Distributor or Sole Agent as referred to in Article 4 paragraph (1) letter a number 4 of Law re Value Added Tax 1984 shall be a person or body within his/its business or work, on the basis of the agreement with the manufacturer or Importer, having the right or authority to market the Taxable Goods produced or imported by said Manufacturer or Importer;

f. Patent Right or Trade Mark Holder as referred to in Article 4 paragraph (1) letter a number 5 of Law re Value Added Tax 1984 shall be a person or body possessing a right on the patent or trade mark of the Taxable Goods.

g. Patent Right and/or Trade Mark User as referred to in Article 4 paragraph (1) letter a number 5 of Law re Value Added Tax 1984 shall be a person or body on the basis of an agreement with the Patent Right Holder and/or Trade Mark Holder is granted right or authority to produce and/or market the Taxable Goods using the patent or trade mark possessed by the Patent Holder and/or Trade Mark Holder of said Taxable Goods;

h. Contractor shall be a person or body within his/its business or work conducts the construction, establishment, repair or rehabilitation of building or the other immovable goods, both for self interest and based on order, with or without written agreement. The definition of Contractor includes the Sub Contractor.

CHAPTER II
CONFIRMATION OF TAXABLE ENTREPRENEUR

Article 2.

The place for reporting the taxable Permanent Undertaking Form on the basis of Law re Value Added Tax 1984 to be confirmed as the Taxable Entrepreneur shall be the office of the Directorate General of Taxes the working area of which covers the domicile of the operation of said Permanent Undertaking Form.

Article 3.

The period of time for the Entrepreneur to report his business to the Directorate General of Taxes to be confirmed as the Taxable Entrepreneur as referred to in Article 3 paragraph (1) of Law re Value Added Tax 1984 shall be stipulated as follows :

a. for the Entrepreneur as referred to in Article 4

paragraph (1) letters a and d of Law re Value Added Tax 1984 who has or has not obtained the Tax Payer Registration Number and has commenced his business operation prior to July 1, 1984 shall be no later than August 1, 1984;

b. for the Entrepreneur as referred to in letter a who has or has not obtained the Tax Payer Registration Number and starts his business operation on or after July 1, 1984 shall be 30 (thirty) days after the commencement of thereof.

Article 4.

(1) The Entrepreneur can report his business to be confirmed as the Taxable Entrepreneur prior to the commencement of his business operation.

(2) The commencement of the business operation shall be the time of establishment or on obtaining the undertaking licence of the real commencement of the business operation.

Article 5.

(1) The Entrepreneur as referred to in Article 3 who shall report his business shall be obligated to fill in the Application Form to be confirmed as the Taxable Entrepreneur, provided by the Directorate General of Taxes.

(2) The Application Form as referred to in paragraph (1) can be filled out and signed on his own by the Entrepreneur or another person given special power of attorney for that purpose.

(3) The Application Form as referred to in paragraph (2) shall be submitted within the time as regulated under Article 3.

Article 6.

The Entrepreneurs opting to be confirmed as the Taxable Entrepreneur as referred to in Article 4 paragraph (1) letter b of Law re Value Added Tax 1984 can apply in writing to the office of the Directorate General of TAxes the working area of which covers the residence or domicile of the relative Entrepreneur by means of that regulated under Article 5.

Article 7.

(1) On the request as referred to in Article 5 paragraph (1), the Director General of Taxes shall issue a Decree on the confirmation as the Taxable Entrepreneur.

(2) The Decree of the Director General of Taxes as referred to in paragraph (1) shall be issued within 7 (seven) days after the receipt of the Application Form of the Entrepreneur as referred to in Article 5 paragraph (3).

(3) The Decree of the Director General of Taxes as referred to in paragraph (2) for the Entrepreneur opting to be confirmed as the Taxable Entrepreneur as referred to in Article 6 shall be effective for 3 (three) years.

CHAPTER III

TAX OBJECT AND OBLIGATION OF RECORDING

Article 8.

The type of service imposed with the Value Added Tax as referred to in Article 4 paragraph (2) letter b of Law re Value Added Tax 1984 shall be that conducted by the Contractor or Sub Contractor.

Article 9.

(1) The delivery of Goods or rendering of services constituting the taxable delivery or rendering shall be :

a. the delivery of Taxable Goods or Taxable Services to any party conducted by the Manufacturer, Main Distributor or Sole Agent, Importer, Indentor, Patent Right Holder, and/or Trade Mark Holder, Patent Right User and/or Trade Mark User of the Taxable Goods and the Service Provider as referred to in Article 8.

b. the delivery of Taxable Goods to the Taxable Entrepreneur as referred to in Article 4 paragraph (1) letter b of Law re Value Added Tax 1984.

(2) Every taxable delivery as referred to in paragraph (1) shall be imposed with tax according to Law re Value Added Tax 1984.

Article 10.

Excepted from the Import of Taxable Goods and Luxury Goods shall be :

a. importing and/or taking the Taxable Goods or Luxury Goods as the transferred second hand goods for the interest of own family;

b. passenger's bagage the value of which does not exceed that exempted from the import duty.

Article 11.

The activities such as harvesting, picking, cutting, cutting up finely, milking, and drying or preserving provisionally the agricultural, plantation, forestry, Livestock Breeding, and dairy, and fishery as well as the other oceanic products, including the definition of harvesting the agricultural produce and animal husbandry as referred to in Article 1 letter m of Law re Value Added Tax 1984, and they are therefore not taxable.

Article 12.

The recording and accounting as referred to in Article 6 paragraphs (1) and (2) of Law re Value Added Tax

1984, in addition to containing the acquisition price and delivery of Goods or Rendering of Services shall also include the description of goods and the unit (quantity) thereof.

CHAPTER IV
TAX TARIFF AND TAX CALCULATION METHOD

Article 13.

(1) The group of luxury goods imposed with the tariff of 10% (ten per cent) as referred to in Article 8 paragraph (1) of Law re Value Added Tax 1984 shall be :

a. non alcoholic beverages produced by means of automatic processing;

b. two-wheel motor vehicle;

c. luxury electric or gas appliances for the household and entertainment;

d. photographic equipment and the accessories thereof;

e. luxury sport equipment and the accessories thereof;

f. luxury sanitary.

(2) The group of luxury goods imposed with the tariff of 20% (twenty per cent) as referred to in Article 8 paragraph (1) of Law re Value Added Tax 1984 shall be :

a. alcoholic drinks;

b. race motor vehicle;

c. motor vehicle of sedan, station wagon, jeep and van;

d. cruise;

e. airplane and helicopter, except those used for public transport or the state interest;

f. video tape recorder and the accessories thereof;

g. electronic equipment for gambling, game and amusement;

h. air and fire arms except those used by the Armed Forces of the Republic of Indonesia and the other government agencies licenced therefor;

i. luxury mus. .al instruments;

j. household luxury ornamental goods.

(3) The type and kind of luxury goods included in the group as referred to in paragraphs (2) and (3) on the basis of the provisions under Article 8 paragraph (5) of Law re Value Added Tax 1984 shall be stipulated by the Minister of Finance.

Article 14.

(1) The Output and Input Taxes on the sales of the Taxable Goods which is returned can be deducted from the indebted tax in the Tax Period on the return of said Taxable Goods.

(2) The procedure of deducting the Output and Input Taxes on the sales of the returned Taxable Goods as referred to in paragraph (1) shall be stipulated by the Minister of Finance.

Article 15.

(1) The Taxable Entrepreneur who credits the Input Tax against the Output Tax in compliance with the provisions under Article 9 paragraph (2) of Law re Value Added Tax 1984 as the Tax Period thereof is not the same, can apply for creditting the Input Tax to the Director General of Taxes along with the reasons concerning the occurrence of the difference of the Tax Period.

(2) The Director General of Taxes can accept or refuse the application as referred to in paragraph (1).

(3) In case application as referred to in paragraph (1) is accepted, the Director General of Taxes shall inform hime together with the procedure of crediting thereof, and if refused, the reasons will be given.

Article 16.

In the case of export, the Input Tax creditable by the Exporter shall only amount to the Input Tax already paid on the acquisition of said exported goods.

CHAPTER V
TIME AND PLACE OF INDEBTED TAX AND TAX CALCULATION REPORT

Article 17.

(1) The time and place of the movable goods delivery shall be those of goods delivered to the buyer of the third party for and on behalf of the buyer, or at the time and place of goods delivered to the messenger, transport service entrepreneur, or tranporter.

(2) The time and place of immovable goods delivery shall be those of the signing of the document or agreement causing the transfer of right on said goods by the parties, or at the time and place of the goods symbolically or really delivered/submitted.

(3) In the case of import :

a. at the time and place of delivery from the import of the Taxable Goods shall be those of the goods imported to the Customs Area:

b. at the time and place the sea air transport

means entering the Customs Area by sailing or flying it, shall be those of the transport means registered to obtain the licence of domestic usage thereof.

(4) The time and place of the Taxable Services rendering shall be those of the signing of the contract or at the time and place of collection or payment on the reimbursement, or at the time or place of the Taxable Services activities.

Article 18.

(1) If a Taxable Entrepreneur has more than one business place, the indebted tax shall be paid where the Tax Invoice is made, except if the application for opting one business locations as the place for the indebted tax as referred to in Article 12 paragraph (2) of Law re Value Added Tax 1984 is approved by the Director General of Taxes.

(2) The Directorate General of Customs and Excises shall collect the tax according to the Law re Value Added Tax 1984 on the importation of the Taxable Goods simultaneously with the collection of import duty.

Article 19.

(1) As the receipt of the collection of Value Added Tax and Sales Tax on Luxury Goods, the Directorate General of Customs and Excises shall make a Tax Invoice according to the guideline stipulated by the Minister of Finance.

(2) The Directorate General of Customs and Excises shall deposit the already collected tax on the following working day, except if the collected tax on March 31 which should be deposited to the State Treasury on the very same day.

(3) The deposit as referred to in paragraph (2) shall be conducted by means of the deposit form stipulated by the Minister of Finance.

(4) One day after the deposit of the Value Added Tax and Sales Tax on Luxury Goods to the State Treasury, the Directorate General of Customs and Excises shall send the Tax Invoices and Tax Deposit Decuments to the Directorate General of Taxes with the way bill stipulated by the Minister of Finance.

(5) In case the tax collection on the importation of the Taxable Goods according to Law re Value Added Tax 1984 is postponed by the Directorate General of Customs and Excises due to the postponement of the collection of. Import Duty, the Input Tax can be credited in the Tax Period on the collection of the Input Tax.

Article 20.

(1) For every delivery of Taxable Goods or rendering of Taxable Services, the Tax Invoice shall be made.

(2) The Tax Invoice made by the Taxable Entrepreneur or the Directorate General of Customs and Excises shall constitute the legal evidence of collection.

(3) The Taxable Entrepreneur can apply in writing to the Director General of Taxes for making a combined tax invoice covering all deliveries of Taxable Goods or rendering of Taxable Services from the same buyer or recipient conducted in a Tax Period.

(4) The combined Tax Invoice as referred to in paragraph (3) shall be made in 10 (ten) days after the expiry of the Tax Period at the latest.

(5) The making of the combined Tax Invoice as referred to in paragraph (4) shall not affect the tax payment.

Article 21.

The making of the Tax Invoice on the receipt of the payment as referred to in Article 13 paragraph (2) of Law re Value Added Tax 1984 also covers :

a. the payment received on installments on the delivery of Taxable Goods;

b. the payment received on the Taxable Services work as referred to in Article 8 based on the stage of said work completion.

Article 22.

(1) The tax payment excess as referred to in Article 16 of Law re Value Added Tax 1984 shall be that of the Value Added Tax and Sales Tax on Luxury Goods included in the Decree on the Tax Payment Excess.

(2) The tax payment excess as referred to in paragraph (1) can be compensated by the other taxes which should be paid by the Taxable Entrapreneur, or can be reimbursed.

(3) The reimbursement of the tax payment excess as referred to in paragraph (2) shall be conducted within 1 (one) month as from the receipt of the application from the Taxable Entrepreneur.

(4) The payment excess on the export of the Taxable Goods as well as the Sales Tax on Luxury Goods shall be reimbursed within 1 (one) month as from the receipt of the application from the Taxable Entrepreneur.

(5) The application for the tax reimbursement as referred to in paragraph (4) shall be completed with the relative export evidences/documents.

CHAPTER VI
CONCLUDING PROVISIONS

Article 23.

Anything related to the implementation of this Government Regulation shall further be regulated by the Minister of Finance.

Article 24.

This Government Regulation shall come into force as from July 1, 1984.

For the public knowledge this Government Regulation shall be promulgated in the State Gazette of the Republic of Indonesia.

Stipulated in Jakarta
On December 31, 1983.

THE PRESIDENT OF THE
REPUBLIC OF INDONESIA

signed.

SOEHARTO.–

Promulgated in Jakarta
On December 31, 1983

THE MINISTER/SECRETARY
OF STATE OF THE REPUBLIC
OF INDONESIA

signed.

SUDHARMONO, S.H.

STATE GAZETTE OF THE REPUBLIC OF INDONESIA YEAR 1983
NO. 55.

Appendix 33

THE LAW ON TAX ON LAND AND BUILDINGS
(Law No. 12/1985 dated December 27, 1985)

BY THE GRACE OF ALMIGHTY GOD,
THE PRESIDENT OF THE REPUBLIC OF INDONESIA,

Considering :

a. that tax constitutes one of the most important sources of state revenues for the realisation and enhancement of national development as the implementation of Pancasila aimed at promoting the prosperity and welfare of the population, and it is therefore necessary to manage it by increasing public participation according to their capacities;
b. that land and buildings give advantage and/or a better social and economic position to individuals or organisations that have certain rights over them or obtain benefits from them, and it is therefore appropriate if such individuals or organisations are obligated to give up part of the benefits or comforts they obtain to the state through tax;
c. that in line with the message contained in the Broad Outlines of the State Policy of 1983 it is necessary to introduce a reform to the tax system, so that public participation and mutual assistance can be realised as a very great potential in national development;
d. that the tax system so far applied, especially the tax on goods and the property tax, has created the burden of double taxation on society, and it is therefore necessary to put an end to this condition by introducing a tax system which is simple, easy to implement, fair and ensures legal certainty;
e. that in order to achieve the above objective it is necessary to formulate the law on tax on land and buildings.

In view of : 1. Article 5 paragraph (1), Article 20 paragraph (1), and Article 23 paragraph (2) of the Constitution of 1945;

2. Law No. 5/1974 on the principles of regional administration (Statute Book of 1974 No. 38, Supplement to Statute Book No. 3037);

3. Law No. 6/1983 on general tax provisions and procedures (Statute Book of 1983 No. 49, Supplement to Statute Book No. 3262);

With the approval of
THE HOUSE OF REPRESENTATIVES OF THE REPUBLIC OF INDONESIA,
DECIDES:

By revoking:

1. The Household Tax Ordinance of 1908 (Statute Book of 1908 No. 13) as already several times amended, the latest by Provisional Law No. 19/1959 (Statute Book of 1959 No. 112, Supplement to Statute Book No. 1868) as stipulated into Law by No. 1/1961 (Statute Book of 1961 No. 3, Supplement to Statute Book No. 2124);
2. The Indonesian Land Rights Ordinance of 1923 (Statute Book of 1923 No. 425) as already several times amended, the latest by Algemeene Verordeningen Binnenelandsche Bestuur Java en Madoera (Statute Book of 1931 No. 168);
3. The Land Rights Ordinance of 1928 (Statute Book of 1928 No. 342) as already several times amended, the latest by Law No. 29/1959 (Statute Book of 1959 No. 74, Supplement to Statute Book No. 1882);
4. The Property Tax Ordinance of 1932 (Statute Book of 1932 No. 405) as already several times amended, the latest by Law No. 8/1967 (Statute Book of 1967 No. 18, Supplement to Statute Book No. 2827);

5. The Road Tax Ordinance of 1942 (Statute Book of 1941 No. 97) as already several times amended, the latest by algemeene Verordening Oorlogsmisdrijven (Statute Book of 1946 No. 47);
6. Article 14 letters j, k and l of Emergency Law No. 11/1957 on regional tax provisions (Statute Book of 1957 No. 56, Supplement to Statute Book No. 1287) as stipulated into law by Law No. 1/1961 (Statute Book of 1961 No. 3, Supplement to Statute Book No. 2124);
7. Provisional Law No. 11/1959 on tax on agricultural produce (Statute Book of 1959 No. 104, Supplement to Statute Book No. 1860) as stipulated into law by Law No. 1/1961 (Statute Book of 1961 No. 3, Supplement to Statute Book No. 2124).

To stipulate : THE LAW ON TAX ON LAND AND BUILDINGS,

CHAPTER I
GENERAL PROVISIONS
Article 1

Hereinafter referred to as:

1. Land shall be the surface of land and the body of land underneath.
2. Buildings shall be technical constructions which are planted or installed permanently on land and/or waters.
3. The sale value of the tax object shall be the average price obtained from transactions which take place properly, and in the absence of transactions, the sale value of the tax object shall be determined by comparing it with the price of another object of the kind, or the new acquisition value, or the sale value of the alternate tax object.
4. The report on the tax object shall be the letter used by the taxpayer to report data on the tax object according to provisions in this law.
5. The notification on tax due shall be the letter used by the Directorate General of Taxation to notify the amount of tax due to the taxpayer.

CHAPTER II
THE TAX OBJECT

Article 2

(1) The object of tax shall be land and/or buildings.

(2) The classification of the tax object as meant in paragraph (1) shall be stipulated by the Minister of Finance.

Article 3

(1) The tax object exempted from the tax on land and buildings shall be that which is:
   a. used solely for the purpose of public service in the fields of religious worship, social affairs, health, national education and culture, not meant for the purpose of profit making;
   b. used for graveyards, archeological relics, or the like;
   c. in the form of protected forests, nature reserves, tourist forests, national parks, pasture under village control, and state land to which no rights are yet reserved;
   d. used by diplomatic offices, consulates, based on the principle of reciprocity;
   e. used by organisations or representative offices of international organisations as determined by the Minister of Finance.

(2) the tax object which is used by the state for government administration shall be further subject to tax provisions based on a government regulation.

(3) The limit of the sale value of buildings exempted from tax shall be Rp 2,000,000 (two million rupiahs) per building unit.

(4) The limit of the untaxed sale value of buildings as meant in paragraph (3) shall be adjusted to the factor of adjustment as stipulated by the Minister of Finance.

CHAPTER III
THE TAX SUBJECT

Article 4

(1) The tax subject shall be individuals or organisations that actually have certain rights over land, and/or obtain benefits from land, and/or possess, control, and/or obtain benefits from buildings.

(2) The tax subject as meant in paragraph (1) that is subject to the obligation of tax payment shall become the taxpayer under this law.

(3) In the case of the tax subject for a certain tax object being unclear, the Director General of Taxation shall be allowed to determine the tax subject as meant in Article (1) as the taxpayer.

(4) The tax subject as determined according to paragraph (3) shall be allowed to submit a written statement to the Director General of Taxation declaring that he/she/it is not the taxpayer for the tax object concerned.

(5) If the statement submitted by the taxpayer as meant in paragraph (4) is approved, the Director General of Taxation shall cancel the stipulation of the taxpayer as meant in paragraph (3) within one month starting from the receipt of the aforesaid statement.

(6) If the statement submitted is not approved, the Director General of Taxation shall issue a decision on rejection along with reasons for such rejection.

(7) If after the period of one month starting from the date of receipt of the statement as meant in paragraph (4) the Director General of Taxation makes no decision, the statement submitted shall be considered approved.

CHAPTER IV
THE TAX RATE

Article 5

The rate of the tax imposed on the tax object shall be 0.5% (half a percent).

CHAPTER V
THE TAX BASE AND THE TAX CALCULATION METHOD

Article 6

(1) The tax base shall be the sale value of the tax object.

(2) The sale value of the tax object as meant in paragraph (1) shall be fixed every three years by the Minister of Finance, except certain areas for which it is fixed annually according to the developments in the areas concerned.

(3) The tax calculation base shall be the taxable sale value fixed at the minimum of 20% (twenty percent) and the maximum of 100% (one hundred percent) of the sale value of the tax object.

(4) The percentage of the taxable sale value as meant in paragraph (3) shall be fixed by a government regulation by taking into account the national economic condition.

Article 7

The amount of tax due shall be calculated by multiplying the tax rate by the taxable sale value.

CHAPTER VI
THE TAX YEAR, THE TIME AND PLACE TAX IS DUE

Article 8

(1) The tax year shall be the period of one calendar year.

(2) The time that determines the moment tax is due shall be according to the condition of the tax object on January 1.

(3) The place where tax is due:
   a. for the Jakarta area, in the Special Region of Jakarta;
   b. for other areas, in the second level regency or the second level municipality;

   in which the tax object is located.

CHAPTER VII
THE REGISTRATION OF, THE REPORT ON THE TAX OBJECT, THE NOTIFICATION ON TAX DUE, AND THE TAX ASSESSMENT LETTER

Article 9

(1) Within the framework of data collection, the tax subject shall register the tax object by filling out the report on the tax object.

(2) The report on the tax object as meant in paragraph (1) shall be filled out clearly, truthfully and completely, and signed and submitted to the Directorate General of Taxation whose operational area covers the location of the tax object, not later than 30 (thirty) days after the date of receipt of the report on the tax object by the tax subject.

(3) The implementation and procedure of registration of the tax object as meant in paragraph (1) and paragraph (2) shall be further regulated by the Minister of Finance.

Article 10

(1) Based on the report on the tax object as meant in Article 9 paragraph (1), the Director General of Taxation shall issue the notification on tax due.

(2) The Director General of Taxation shall be allowed to issue the tax assessment letter in the following cases:

a. if the report on the tax object is not submitted according to Article 9 paragraph (2) and after written warnings are issued the report is not submitted as required in the warnings;

b. if based on the result of examination or other information it turns out that the amount of tax due is bigger than the amount of tax calculated according to the report on the tax object submitted by the taxpayer.

(3) The amount of tax due in the tax assessment letter as meant in paragraph (2) point a. shall be the basic tax plus an administrative fine of 25% (twenty-five percent) calculated from the basic tax.

(4) The amount of tax due in the tax assessment letter as meant in paragraph (2) point b. shall be the difference between the tax due based on the result of examination or other information and the tax due calculated according to the report on the tax object plus an administrative fine of 25% (twenty five percent) calculated from the difference of the tax due.

CHAPTER VIII
THE PROCEDURE FOR PAYMENT AND COLLECTION

Article 11

(1) The tax to be paid based on the notification on tax due as meant in Article 10 paragraph (1) shall be settled not later than 6 (six) months starting from the date of receipt of the notification on tax due by the taxpayer.

(2) The tax to be paid based on the tax assessment letter as meant in article 10 paragraph (3) and paragraph (4) shall be settled not later than 1 (one) month starting from the date of receipt of the tax assessment letter by the taxpayer.

(3) The tax due which on the date of maturity is not paid or underpaid shall be subject to an administrative fine of 2% (two percent) per month, calculated from the date of maturity through the date of payment for a maximum period of 24 (twenty four) months.

(4) The administrative fine as meant in paragraph (3) plus the tax debt not yet paid or underpaid shall be collected with the tax collection letter, which must be settled not later than 1 (one) month starting from the date of receipt of the tax collection letter by the taxpayer.

(5) The tax due shall be paid at banks, post and giro offices, and other places as appointed by the Minister of Finance.

(6) The procedure for payment and collection as meant in paragraph (1), paragraph (2), paragraph (3), paragraph (4) and paragraph (5) shall be regulated by the Minister of Finance.

Article 12

The notification on tax due, the tax assessment letter, and the tax collection letter shall serve as the basis for tax collection.

Article 13

The amount of tax due based on the tax collection letter that is not paid on time may be collected with the distress warrant.

Article 14

The Minister of Finance shall be allowed to delegate the authority of tax collection to the Governor/Chief of the First Level Region and/or the Regent/Mayor/Head of the Second Level Region.

CHAPTER IV
OBJECTIONS AND APPEALS

Article 15

(1) The taxpayer shall be allowed to submit an objection letter to the Director General of Taxation against:

a. the notification on tax due;
b. the tax assessment letter.

(2) The objection letter shall be submitted in the Indonesian language by stating reasons clearly.

(3) The objection letter shall be submitted within 3 (three) months starting from the date of receipt of any of the letters as meant in paragraph (1) by the taxapayer, unless the taxpayer can show that the period is impossible to keep due to conditions beyond control.

(4) The note of receipt of the objection letter given by officials of the Directorate General of Taxation appointed for this purpose or the note of sending of the objection letter by registered mail shall serve as evidence on the receipt of the objection letter in the interest of the taxpayer.

(5) If requested by the taxpayer for the purpose of submitting the objection letter, the Director General of Taxation shall explain in writing the basis of tax imposition.

(6) the handing in of the objection letter shall not postpone the obligation of tax payment.

Article 16

(1) The Director General shall issue a decision on the objection within a maximum of 12 (twelve) months starting from the date of receipt of the objection letter.

(2) Before a decision is issued, the taxpayer may submit additional grounds or written explanations.

(3) The decision of the Director General of Taxation on the objection may grant part or the whole of it, reject it, or increase the amount of tax due.

(4) If the taxpayer submits the objection against the tax assessment as meant in Article 10 paragraph (2) point a., the taxpayer concerned shall be able to prove the inaccuracy of the aforesaid assessment.

(5) If after the period as meant in paragraph (1) the Director General of Taxation makes no decision, the objection letter submitted shall be considered granted.

Article 17

(1) The taxpayer shall be allowed to submit an appeal to the tax court against the decision issued by the Director General of Taxation as meant in Article 4 paragraph (6) and Article 16 paragraph (3) within 3 (three) months starting from the date of receipt of the decision by the taxpayer with a copy of the decision attached.

(2) The request for an appeal shall be submitted in writing in the Indonesian language.

(3) The handing in of the appeal request shall not postpone the obligation of tax payment.

CHAPTER X
DIVISION OF TAX RECEIPTS

Article 18

(1) Tax receipts shall belong to the state, which are divided between the central government and the regional administration to the extent of at least 90% (ninety percent) for the second level regional administration and the first level regional administration as the revenues of the regions concerned.

(2) The portion of receipts for the regional administration as meant in paragraph (1) shall for the greater part be allocated to the second level regional administration.

(3) The ratio of division of tax receipts as meant in paragraph (1) and paragraph (2) shall be stipulated by a government regulation.

CHAPTER XI
MISCELLANIES

Article 19

(1) The Minister of Finance shall be allowed to grant relief to the tax due:
  a. because of certain conditions of the tax object as related to the tax subject and/or owing to certain other causes;
  b. in the case of the tax object being hit by natural disasters or other extraordinary causes.

(2) Provisions concerning the granting of tax relief as meant in paragraph (1) shall be stipulated by the Minister of Finance.

Article 20

At the request of the taxpayer the Director General of Taxation shall be allowed to reduce the administraive fine due to certain causes.

Article 21

(1) Officials whose functions or tasks are directly related to the tax object shall:
  a. submit monthly reports on all mutations and developments of the tax object in writing to the Directorate General of Taxation whose operational area covers the location of the tax object;
  b. provide information needed at the request of the Directorate General of Taxation.

(2) The obligation to provide information as meant in paragraph (1) point b. shall also be valid for other officials having to do with the tax object.

(3) In the case of the officials as meant in paragraph (1) and paragraph (2) being obligated to maintain confidentiality, such an obligation shall not apply as far as the implementation of this law is concerned.

(4) The procedure for submitting reports and requesting information as meant in paragraph (1) and paragraph (2) shall be stipulated by the Minister of Finance.

Article 22

The officials who fail to carry out the obligations as meant in article 21 shall be liable to sanctions according to effective regulations.

Article 23

Matters that are not specifically regulated in this law shall be subject to the provisions in Law No. 6/1983 on general tax provisions and procedures as well as other relevant regulations.

CHAPTER XII
CRIMINAL PROVISIONS

Article 24

Whoever due to negligence:

a. fails to return/submit the report on the tax object to the Directorate General of Taxation;

b. submits the report on the tax object, but with false or incomplete contents and/or with false information attached;

which can inflict losses upon the state, shall be subject to a maximum detention at 6 (six) months or a maximum fine of twice the amount of tax due.

Article 25

(1) Whoever intentionally:

a. fails to return/submit the report on the tax object to the Directorate General of Taxation;

b. submits the report on the tax object, but with false or incomplete contents and/or with false information attached;

c. shows false or falsified letters or false or falsified documents as if they were true;

d. fails to show or submit letters or other documents;

e. fails to show data or provide information needed;

which inflict losses upon the state, shall be subject to maximum imprisonment of 2 (two) years or a maximum fine of 5 (five) times the amount of tax due.

(2) The acts as meant in paragraph (1) point d. and point e. committed by other than the taxpayer concerned shall be subject to a maximum detention of 1 (one) year or a maximum fine of Rp 2,000,000 (two million rupiahs).

(3) The punishment as meant in paragraph (1) shall be doubled if the tax criminal acts are repeated before 1 (one) year, starting from the end of part of or the entire imprisonment to be served, or starting from the payment of the fine.

Article 26

The criminal acts as meant in Article 24 and Article 25 shall not be prosecuted after 10 (ten) years have passed starting from the end of the tax year concerned.

Article 27

(1) The acts as meant in Article 24 and Article 25 paragraph (2) shall be misdemanours.

(2) The acts as meant in Article 25 paragraph (1) shall be felonies.

CHAPTER XIII
TRANSITIONAL PROVISIONS

Article 28

Regional development dues (Ipeda), the property tax (PKK), the tax on roads, and the household tax (PRT) that are due for the tax year of 1985 and previously shall be subject to provisions based on effective laws up to December 31, 1990.

Article 29

With the enforcement of this law, the existing rules for implementation in the field of regional development dues (Ipeda) based on Law No. 11/1959 on tax on agricultural produce, shall remain valid up to December 31, 1990 as long as they are not contradictory to and not yet regulated by new rules for implementation based on this law.

Article 30

The tax object in the field of crude oil and natural gas mining as well as in other mining areas, in connection with working contracts and production sharing contracts still effective upon the enforcement of this law, shall remain subject to regional development dues (Ipeda) based on provisions in the effective working contracts and production sharing contracts.

CHAPTER XIV

CLOSING PROVISIONS

Article 31

This law shall come into force as from January 1, 1986.

For public cognizance, this law shall be enforced by publishing it in the Statute Book of the Republic of Indonesia.

Enforced in Jakarta On December 27, 1985 THE MINISTER/STATE SECRETARY, sgd. SUDHARMONO, S.H.	Ratified in Jakarta On December 27, 1985 THE PRESIDENT OF THE REPUBLIC OF INDONESIA, sgd. S O E H A R T O

STATUTE BOOK OF THE REPUBLIC OF INDONESIA 1985
NUMBER 68

APPENDIX 34

THE LAW ON TAX ON LAND AND BUILDINGS
(Law No.12/1985 dated December 27, 1985)

ELUCIDATION
ON
LAW No. 12/1985
CONCERNING
TAX ON LAND AND BUILDINGS

I. GENERAL:

Within the Republic of Indonesia, where the livelihood of the population and the economy of the state are mostly agrarian in nature, land including waters and natural resources contained in it has a vital function in the development of a just and prosperous society based on Pancasila state philosophy and the Constitution of 1945. Therefore it is proper for the parties that obtain benefits from land and its natural resources, as they enjoy certain rights from the authority of the state, to give up part of the comfort they gain to the state through tax payment.

Before the enforcement of this law, land under the custom law was already subject to tax based on Law No.11/1959 and land under the western law was subject to tax based on the Indonesian Land Rights Ordinance of 1923, and the Land Rights Ordinance of 1928. In addition, there was also tax on land and buildings based on the Household Tax Ordinance of 1908 as well as other regional levies on land and buildings.

The tax system so far applied, especially corporeal and property tax, has caused taxes to overlap one another so that double taxation has posed a burden on society.

In line with the purport contained in the Broad Outlines of the State Policy, it is necessary to introduce a reform of the effective tax system by giving trust to taxpayers in executing their obligations and exercising their rights with regard to taxation, so as to expand and enhance the awareness of tax obligations, and ensure equitable distribution of income among the population.

It is therefore necessary to revoke the Household Tax Ordinance of 1908, the Indonesian Land Rights Ordinance of 1923, the Land Rights Ordinance of 1928, the Property Tax Ordinance of 1932, The Road Tax Ordinance of 1942, Article 14 letters j, k and l of Emergency Law No. 11/1957 on regional tax provisions, regional development dues (Ipeda), and other regulations on regional levies as far as land and buildings are concerned.

The other regulations, primarily those which have so far served as the basis for the imposition of levies in regions, such as especially the collection of tax on motor vehicles, remain effective.

By carrying out the tax reform through simplification involving various levies on land and/or buildings, tax rates and methods of payment, public awareness of tax obligations is expected to increase so that tax receipts will accordingly be bigger.

The tax object under this law covers land and/or buildings within the territory of the Republic of Indonesia.

In order to reflect public participation and mutual assistance in society in the financing of development efforts, all elements of the tax object are subject to tax.

In this law, land and/or buildings owned by the central government and the regional administration are taxable. The imposition of tax on land and buildings on the tax object used by the state for executing government functions, is to be further stipulated by a government regulation.

Receipts from this tax are directed towards the purpose of serving public interests in the regions concerned, hence the major portion of these tax receipts will be allocated to the regional administration.

The use of tax in this way by the respective regions will stimulate the public to fulfil their tax payment obligations, which at the same time reflects the spirit of mutual assistance on the part of the population in development financing.

Since the bulk of the tax on land and buildings will be used by the regional administration, it is deemed necessary to determine places of tax payment that are nearer and easier to reach, so that the regional administration concerned can readily utilise tax receipts to finance development efforts in the relevant region.

It is possible for taxpayers to enjoy relief in tax payments due to certain causes or in the case of the tax object being hit by natural disasters or other extraordinary developments, which render tax payers incapable of settling their tax debts.

II. ARTICLE BY ARTICLE

Article 1.

Point 1:

The surface of land covers soil and inland waters as well as the sea within the territory of Indonesia.

Point 2:

The definition of buildings covers:

- neighbourhood paths within a building complex such as a hotel, factory, and its yards, and others which constitute one unit with the aforesaid building complex;
- toll roads;
- swimming pools;
- luxury fences;
- sports grounds;
- shipyards, wharfs;
- luxury parks;
- oil, water and gas reservoirs/refineries, oil pipes;
- other facilities that bring benefits.

Point 3:

What is meant by:

- Price comparison with another object of the kind, shall be an approach/method of determining the sale value of a certain tax object by comparing it with another tax object of the same type, which is closely located and has the same function and whose sale price is already known.
- The new acquisition value shall be an approach/method of determining the sale value of a certain tax object by calculating the entire cost spent to obtain the object at the moment of assessment, deducted by depreciation based on the physical condition of the object.
- The alternate sale value shall be an approach/method of determining the sale value of a certain tax object on the

basis of the production resulting from the tax object.

Point 4: Sufficiently clear.

Point 5: Sufficiently clear.

Article 2.

Paragraph (1): Sufficiently clear.

Paragraph (2):

The classification of land and buildings shall be the grouping of land and buildings according to sale values and guidelines to facilitate the calculation of tax due.

In the classivication of land the following factors are taken into account:

1. Locations;
2. designations;
3. utilisation;
4. environmental conditions and so forth.

In the classification of buildings the following factors are taken into account:

1. the materials used;
2. engineering;
3. locations;
4. environmental conditions and so forth.

Article 3.

Paragraph (1):

Not for profit making shall mean that the tax object is used to serve public interests, and is really not aimed at profit seeking.

This can be seen among others from the statutes and internal rules of foundations/organisations engaged in religious worship, social affairs, health promotion, education, and national culture. Included in this defition are state owned tourist forests in line with Article 2 of Law No. 5/1967 on basic provisions concerning forestry.

Examples:
- Islamic boarding schools or the like;
- madrasah (Islamic schools);
- wakaf (ground for religious purposes);
- general hospitals.

Paragraph (2):

The tax object as meant herein shall be that which is owned/controlled/used by the central government and the regional administration in carrying out their executive functions.

Tax on land and buildings is tax imposed by the state which mostly constitutes regional revenue used among others for the provision of facilities that are also enjoyed by the central government and the regional administration.

It is therefore proper for the central government to join the financing of such facilities through the payment of tax on land and buildings.

With regard to land and/or buildings owned by individuals and/or organisations that are used by the state, the tax obligation depends on the agreements concluded.

Paragraph (3):

The limit of the untaxed sale value for the tax object in the form of buildings shall be Rp 2,000,000 (two million rupiahs) per building unit.

Examples:

1.	Sale value of a building	Rp	1,800,000.-
	Limit of untaxed sale value	Rp	2,000,000.-
	Sale value subject to tax	Rp	nil
2.	Sale value of a building	Rp	10,000,000.-
	Limit of untaxed sale value	Rp	2,000,000.-
	Sale value subject to tax	Rp	8,000,000.-
3.	Sale value of a building	Rp	500,000,000.-
	Limit of untaxed sale value	Rp	2,000,000.-
	Sale value subject to tax	Rp	498,000,000.-

Paragraph (4): Sufficiently clear.

Article 4.

Paragraph (1):

Documents on tax payment/settlement shall not constitute evidence on the possession of rights.

Paragraph (2): Sufficiently clear.

Paragraph (3):

This provision authorises the Director General of Taxation to determine the tax subject as the taxpayer, if the tax subject for a certain tax object is still unclear.

Examples:

1. Tax subject A obtains benefits from or makes use of land and/or buildings owned by another person named B not because of a certain right based on law nor because of a certain agreement, so that in this case A who gains benefits from or makes use of land and/or buildings as meant above shall be determined as the taxpayer.
2. A certain tax object is being disputed at court over its ownership, so that the individual or organisation who/which gains benefits from or makes use of the tax object shall be determined as the taxpayer.
3. A tax subject for a long time lives outside the area where a certain tax object is located, while an individual or organisation is empowered to maintain the tax object, so that the authorised individual or organisation can be appointed as the taxpayer.

   The appointment as the taxpayer by the Director General of Taxation shall not serve as evidence on the possession of rights.

Paragraph (4): Sufficiently clear.

Paragraph (5): Sufficiently clear.

Paragraph (6): Sufficiently celar.

Paragraph (7):

Based on the provision in this paragraph, if the Director General of Taxation fails to make any decision within 1 (one) month starting from the date of receipt of the taxpayer's statement, the determination as the taxpayer shall automatically be cancelled and a decision on revocation of the appointment be issued.

Article 5.

Sufficiently clear.

Article 6.

Paragraph (1): Sufficiently clear.

Paragraph (2):

Basically the sale value of the tax object is fixed every 3 (three) years. But for certain regions where the progress of development efforts causes a fairly big increase in the sale value of the tax object, the determination of the sale value shall be done annually.

In the fixation of the sale value, the Minister of Finance receives the suggestions of governors and takes into account the principle of self assessment.

Paragraph (3):

The taxable sale value (assessment value) shall be the sale value that serves as the basis for tax calculation, namely a certain percentage of the actual sale value.

Examples:

1. Sale value of a tax object= Rp 1,000,000.-
   Percentage of taxable sale value is e.g. 20% so that the sale value subject to tax = 20% × Rp 1,000,000.- = Rp 200,000.-
2. Sale value of a tax object= Rp 1,000,000.-
   Percentage of taxable sale value is e.g. 50% so that the sale value subject to tax = 50% × Rp 1,000,000,- = Rp 500,000,-.

Paragraph (4): Sufficiently clear.

Article 7.

The sale value of buildings before the application of the tax rate shall first be deducted by the limit of the untaxed sale value of buildings, viz. Rp 2,000,000,- (two million rupiahs).

Examples:

Taxpayer A has the following tax objects:

- Land measuring 800 m^2 with the sale price of Rp 300,000/m^2.
- A building measuring 400 m^2 with the sale value of Rp 350,000/m^2.
- A luxury garden measuring 200 m^2 with the sale value of Rp 50,000/m^2.
- Luxury fences 120 m in length and 1.5 m in average height with the sale value of Rp 175,000/m^2.

Percentage of taxable sale value is e.g. 20%.

The amount of tax due is as follows:

1. Sale value of land: 800 × Rp 300,000 = Rp 240,000,000.-

   Sale value of building:

   a. House and garage 400 × Rp 350,000 = Rp 140,000,000.-
   b. Luxury garden 200 × Rp 50,000 = Rp 10,000,000.-
   c. Luxury fence
      (120 × 1.5) × Rp 175,000 = Rp 31,500,000.-

   Rp 181,500,000.-

   Limit of untaxed sale value of building Rp 2,000,000.-
   Sale value of building = Rp 179,500,000.-
   Sale value of land and building = Rp 419,500,000.-

2. Amounts of tax on land and buildings due:

   a. On land = 0.5% × 20% × Rp 240,000,000.- = Rp 240,000.-
   b. On building = 0.5% × 20% × Rp 179,500,000.- = Rp 179,500.-

   Total of tax due Rp 419,500.-

Article 8.

Paragraph (1):

The period of 1 (one) calendar year shall be from January 1 through December 31.

Paragraph (2):

Since the tax year starts on January 1, the condition of the tax object on the date constitutes the moment tax is due.

Examples:

a. The tax object on January 1, 1986 is in the form of land and buildings.
   On January 10, 1986 the buildings catch fire, so the tax due remains on the basis of the condition of the tax object on January 1, 1986, i.e. the situation before the fire.
b. The tax object on January 1, 1986 is in the form of a plot of land without any buildings on it. On August 10, 1986 data on the land are recorded, and its turns out that a building is already erected on it, so the tax due for 1986 remains on the basis of the condition on January 1, 1986.

Paragraph (3):

The place where tax is due for the Batam municipality is in the first level provincial area concerned.

Article 9.

Paragraph (1):

For data collection, taxpayers will receive the report on the tax object (SPOP) to be filled out and returned to the Directorate General of Taxation. Taxpayers that have been subject to Ipeda (regional development dues) are not obligated to register their tax objects unless they receive SPOP, in which case they are required to fill out the report and return it to the Directorate General of Taxation.

Paragraph (2):

What is meant by clear, truthful and complete shall be:
Clear, which means that the supply of data in SPOP is done in such a way as to prevent misinterpretations that may bring losses to the state as well as taxpayers themselves. Truthful, which means that the data reported must be in conformity with the actual situation, such as the area of land and/or buildings, the year and price of acquisition and so forth must be in line with the columns/questions in SPOP.

Paragraph (3): Sufficiently clear.

Article 10.

Paragraph (1):

The notification on tax due (SPPT) is issued on the basis of the report on the tax object (SPOP), but in order to assist taxpayers, SPPT can be issued on the basis of data on the tax object already recorded at the Directorate General of Taxation.

Paragraph (2):

This provision authorises the Director General of Taxation to issue the tax assessment letter (SKP) to taxpayers that fail to fulfil their tax obligations properly.
According to paragraph (2) point a., the Director General of Taxation can issue the tax assessment letter by function, to taxpayers failing to submit the report on the tax object on

tax due (SPPT) based on the report on the tax object submitted by taxpayers.

Based on SPOP, SPPT is issued	= Rp 1,000,000.-
Based on examination, the tax that should actually due in the tax assessment (SKP) = Rp 1,500,000.-	
Difference	= Rp 500,000.-
Administrative fine 25% × Rp 500,000	= Rp 125,000.-
Total of tax due in SKP	= Rp 625,000.-

The amount of tax due worth Rp 1,000,000 as contained in SPPT, if not yet settled by the taxpayer concerned shall be collected based on the SPPT.

Article 11.

Paragraph (1):

Example:

If the notification on tax due in received by taxpayers on March 1, 1986, the date of maturity for payment shall be August 31, 1986.

Paragraph (2):

Example:

If the tax assessment letter is received by taxpayers on March 1, 1986, the date of maturity for payment shall be March 31, 1986.

Paragraph (3):

According to this provision, the tax due which on the date of maturity is not paid or underpaid, shall be subject to an administrative fine of 2% (two percent) per month of the amount unpaid or underpaid for a maximum period of 24 (twenty four) months, and part of a month is calculated as 1 (one) full month.

Example:

The notification on tax due for the tax year of 1986 is received by the taxpayer on March 1, 1986 with Rp 100,000 (one hundred thousand rupiahs) worth of tax due. The tax is paid by the taxpayer on September 1, 1986.

time, despite the issuance of written warnings which determine time limits. The assessment bears and administrative sanction as stipulated in paragraph (3).

According to paragraph (2) point b., if based on the result of examination or other information available at the Directorate General of Taxation the amount of tax due is bigger than the amount of tax in the notification on tax due calculated on the basis of the report on the tax object submitted by taxpayers, the Director General of Taxation by function issues the tax assessment letter. This assessment bears and administrative sanctions as stipulated in paragraph (3).

Paragraph (3):

This paragraph regulates the administrative sanction imposed on taxpayers failing to submit the report on the tax object as meant in paragraph (2) point a.; this fine is added to the basic tax, viz. 25% (twenty five percent) of the basic tax.

The tax assessment letter, based on data available at the Directorate General of Taxation, contains the determination of the tax object and the amount of tax due as well as the administrative fine imposed on taxpayers.

Article 12.

Sufficiently clear.

Article 13.

In case the tax due based on the tax collection letter is paid after the date of maturity already fixed, the collection is done by the distress warrant, which at present is pursuant to Law No.19/1959 on tax collection with the distress warrant.

Article 14.

The delegation of authority of tax collection to governors/chiefs of first level regions and/or regents/mayors/heads of second level regions does not involve collection affairs, but is only meant to act as tax imposition authorities, while the recording of data on the tax object and the determination of tax due remain under the authority of the Minister of Finance.

In case the amount of tax due as contained in the notification on tax due fails to conform to the actual condition of the tax object, the tax imposition authorities shall not be allowed to change the amount of tax due, but the matter must be reported to the Minister of Finance in this case the Director General of Taxation.

Article 15.

Paragraph (1):

Objection letters against the notification on tax due and the tax assessment letter shall each be submitted separately for every tax year.

Paragraph (2):

Sufficiently clear.

Paragraph (3):

This provision is meant to allow sufficient time to taxpayers for the preparation of objection letters along with their reasons.

If the 3 (three) month period cannot be fulfilled by taxpayers due to force majeure the extension of this limit can still be considered by the Director General Taxation.

Paragraph (4):

Sufficiently clear.

Paragraph (5):

Sufficiently clear.

Paragraph (6):

Sufficiently clear.

Article 16.

Paragraph (1):

Sufficiently clear.

Paragraph (2):

Sufficiently clear.

Paragraph (3):

Sufficiently clear.

Paragraph (4):

This provision necessitates taxpayers to prove the inaccuracy of the tax assessment, in case the taxpayers submit objections against the assessment by function. If they fail to prove the inaccuracy of the tax assessment by function, the objections are rejected.

Paragraph (5):

This provision is meant to give legal certainty to taxpayers, i.e. if within 12 (twelve) months starting from the date of receipt of the objection letter the Director General of Taxation makes no decision on the objection submitted, it means that the objection is accepted.

Article 17.

Paragraph (1):

This provision allows the opportunity for taxpayers still dissatisfied with the decision of the Director General of Taxation on their objections, to submit appeals to the tax court in this case the body currently existing for this purpose viz. the Tax Consultative Assembly.

Paragraph (2):

Sufficiently clear.

Paragraph (3):

Sufficiently clear.

Example:

Taxpayer A fails to submit the report on the tax object (SPOP).

Based on the available data, the Director General of Taxation issues the tax assessment letter (SKP) containing:

- the tax object with its area and sale value;
- the area of the tax object according to SPOP;
- the basic tax = Rp 1,000,000.-
- administrative sanction

  25% × Rp 1,000,000.- = Rp 250,000.-

  Total of tax due in SKP = Rp 1,250,000.-

Paragraph (4):

This paragraph regulates the administrative sanction imposed on taxpayers that fail to fill out the report on the tax object (SPOP) according to the actual situation as meant in paragraph (2) point b., viz 25% (twenty five percent) of the difference between the tax due based on the result of examination or other information and the tax due in the notification on

The taxpayer is thus subject to an administrative fine of 2% (two percent) viz. 2% × Rp 100,000 = Rp 2,000.-
The tax due on September 1, 1986 is:
basic tax + administrative fine = Rp 100,000 + Rp 2,000
= Rp 102,000.-

If the taxpayer pays the tax debt on October 10, 1986, the fine imposed is 2 × 2% of the basic tax, viz.:
4% × Rp 100,000 = Rp 4,000.-
The tax to be paid on October 10, 1986 is:
basic tax + administrative fine = Rp 100,000 + Rp 4,000
= Rp 104,000.-

Paragraph (4):

According to this provision the administrative fine and the basic tax as meant in the example of the explanation to paragraph (3), shall be collected by using the tax collection letter (STP), which must be settled within one month starting from the date of receipt of the STP.

Paragraph (5):

Sufficiently clear.

Paragraph (6):

Sufficiently clear.

Article 18.

Paragraph (1):

Sufficiently clear.

Paragraph (2):

Since the receipts from this tax are intended to serve public interests in the second level regions concerned, the bulk of the tax revenues are allocated to second level areas.

Paragraph (3):

Sufficiently clear.

Article 19.

Paragraph (1):

Point a.: Certain conditions of the tax object in relation to the tax subject and certain other causes, are in the form of very limited agricultural land, buildings controlled or owned by certain taxpayers for their own residence, land the sale value of which increases as a result of environmental changes and positive impacts of development, and land the utilisation of which is not yet in line with environmental designation.

Point b.:
- Natural disasters are earthquakes, floods, landslides.
- Other extraordinary causes:
  - fires;
  - droughts;
  - plant epidemics;
  - plant pests.

Paragraph (2):

Sufficiently clear.

Article 20.

This provision provides the opportunity for taxpayers to submit requests for reduction of the administrative fines as meant in Article 10 paragraph (3), Article 11 paragraph (3) and paragraph (4) to the Director General of Taxation.
The Director General of Taxation may reduce the aforesaid administrative fines partly or entirely.

Article 21.

Paragraph (1):

- Officials whose functions are directly related to the tax object are: district heads as officials authorised to issue deeds on land, notaries public as officials authorised to issue deeds on land, and officials authorised to issue deeds on land.
- Written reports on mutations of the tax object, among others e.g. transactions, grants, inheritance, shall be submitted to the Directorate General of Taxation whose operational area covers the location of the tax object.

Paragraph (2):

Officials having to do with the tax object as meant herein are among others e.g.: subdistrict heads or village heads, officials of the city planning service, officials of the building control service, officials of the agrarian service, officials of the inheritance office.

Paragraph (3):

Sufficiently clear.

Paragraph (4):

Sufficiently clear.

Article 22.

The regulations effective for the officials as meant in this article are among others: Government Regulation No.30/1980 on disciplinary rules for civil servants, Statute Book of 1860 No.3 on the function of notaries public.

Article 23

Other relevant regulations include Law No. 19/1959 on tax collection with the distress warrant.

Article 24

Negligence as meant in this article implies not being on purpose, inadvertence, and carelessness so that the acts inflict losses upon the state.

The report on the taxt object shall be returned/submitted to the Directorate General of Taxation not later than 30 (thirty) days starting from the date of receipt of the report on the tax object as meant in Article 9 paragraph (2).

Article 25

Paragraph (1):

The acts as meant in this paragraph, which are intentionally committed, belong to the category of felonies and therefore are subject to a more severe punishment.

Paragraph (2):

Those other than the taxpayer concerned as meant in this paragraph shall be officials whose functions are directly related to or have to do with the tax object, or other parties.

Paragraph (3):

To prevent the recurrence of tax crimes, on those who repeat the criminal acts as meant in para. (1) before 1 (one) year starting from the completion of serving part or the whole of the imprisonment sentenced or from the payment of the fine, a more severe punishment shall be imposed viz, by doubling the punishment as meant in paragraph (1).

Article 26.

The deviation from the provision in Article 78 of the Criminal Law is meant to make an adjustment to the obligation to keep tax documents for a period of 10 (ten) years.

Article 27.

Sufficiently clear.

Article 28.

Sufficiently clear.

Article 29.

Sufficiently clear.

Article 30.

The provisions in this law are effective for the tax object used under working contracts and production sharing contracts in the oil and gas mining sector and in other mining areas that are signed starting from the date of enforcement of this law viz. January 1, 1986, while for the existing working contracts and production sharing contracts the provisions contained in these working contracts and production sharing contracts shall remain valid.

Article 31.

Sufficiently clear.

APPENDIX 35

THE LAW ON STAMP DUTY
(Law No.13/1985 dated December 27, 1985)

THE PRESIDENT OF THE REPUBLIC OF INDONESIA

Considering: a. that national development demands the participation of the entire population in the accumulation of adequate funds for financing, especially originating from domestic sources, which constitutes a manifestation of civic obligation within the framwork of achieving national development objectives;

b. that stamp duty which so far has been imposed on the basis of the Stamp Duty Regulation of 1921 is no longer in keeping with the needs and developments of the situation in Indonesia;

c. that in connection with the above consideration, it is necessary to restipulate provisions concerning stamp duty which are simpler and easier for the public to implement;

d. that in order to achieve the above aim, it is necessary to issue a new law concerning stamp duty in place of the Stamp Duty Regulation of 1921;

In view of : 1. Article 5 paragraph (1), Article 20 paragraph (1), and Article 23 paragraph (2) of the Constitution of 1945;

2. Law No.6/1983 on general tax provisions and procedures (Statute Book of 1983 No. 49, Supplement to Statute Book No. 3262).

with the approval of
THE HOUSE OF REPRESENTATIVES OF THE
REPUBLIC OF INDONESIA,
D E C I D E S :

By revoking the Stamp Duty Regulation of 1921 (Statute Book of 1921 No.498) as already several times amended, lastly by Provisional Law No.2/1965 (Statute Book of 1965 No. 121), as already stipulated into law by Law No.7/1969 (Statute Book of 1969 No.38).

To stipulate: THE LAW ON STAMP DUTY.

CHAPTER I
GENERAL PROVISIONS

Article 1

(1) By the name of stamp duty, tax shall be imposed on documents as referred to in this law.

(2) Hereinafter referred to as:

a. Documents shall be papers which contain writing/print with meanings and purposes involving actions, situations or facts of certain individuals and/or parties concerned.

b. Stamp-duty matter shall be gummed stamps and stamped paper which are issued by the government of the Republic of Indonesia.

c. Signatures shall be those as normally used, including initials, imprints or stamps of signatures or stamps of initials, stamps of names or other marks used in place of signatures.

d. Post stamping shall be a method of stamp duty payment applied by the postal officials at the request of holders of documents of which the stamp duty is not yet properly settled.

e. Postal officials shall be those of the Post and Giro Public Corporation who are assigned to serve requests for post stamping.

CHAPTER II
OBJECTS, RATES, AND THE STAMP DUTY DUE

Article 2.

(1) Stamp duty shall be imposed on documents in the form of:
   a. agreements and other papers made out for the purpose of serving as instruments of evidence of actions, facts or situations of a civil nature;
   b. deeds of notaries public including their copies;
   c. deeds made out by authorised officials of deeds on land including their duplicates;
   d. papers mentioning amounts of money worth more than Rp 1,000,000 (one million rupiahs):
      1) which state the receipt of money;
      2) which declare the opening of bank accounts or keeping of money in bank accounts;
      3) which contain notifications on account balances at banks;
      4) which contain acknowledgements that money debts are already entirely or partly settled or calculated;
   e. certificates such as drafts, promissory notes, acceptances, and cheques with a nominal price of more than Rp 1,000,000 (one million rupiahs);

(2) The documents as meant in paragraph (1) points a, b, c, d, e and f shall be subject to stamp duty at the rate of Rp 1,000 (one thousand rupiahs).

(3) The Stamp duty rate of Rp 1,000 (one thousand rupiahs) shall also be imposed on documents that are used as instruments of evidence before court, namely:
   a. letters and household papers;
   b. papers that originally are not subject stamp duty based on their purposes, if used for other purposes or used by the other persons, not for the original purposes.

(4) The documents as meant in paragraph (1) points d, e and f which have a nominal price of more than Rp 100,000 (one hundred thousand rupiahs) but less than Rp 1,000,000 (one million rupiahs) shall be subject to the stamp duty rate of Rp 500 (five hundred rupiahs), and if the nominal price is not more than

Rp 100,000 (one hundred thousand rupiahs) no stamp duty shall be imposed.

Article 3

By a government regulation, rates of stamp duty and limits of nominal prices subject to stamp duty can be fixed, be annulled, be lowered, be increased to the maximum of six times on the documents as meant in Article 2.

Article 4

Stamp duty on the following papers shall be exempted:

a. documents in the form of:
   1) certificates of goods storage;
   2) bills of lading;
   3) certificates of passengers and goods transport;
   4) transfer notes written on the documents as meant in points 1), 2) and 3);
   5) letters of evidence on goods delivery and receipt;
   6) certificates of delivery of goods for sales at deliverers' own risk;
   7) other papers that can be considered the same as those as meant points 1) through 6);
b. all kinds of diplomas;
c. salary receipts, waiting fees, pensions, allowances, and other payments connected with working relations as well as the papers submitted obtain such payments;
d. letters of evidence on the receipt of State funds issued by the stated treasury, the regional treasury, and banks;
e. receipts for all kinds of tax and for other revenues considered the same as tax issued by the state treasury, the regional treasury, and banks;
f. receipts for money made out for internal organisational purposes;
g. documents that mention savings, payments of savings to depositors by banks, cooperatives, and other bodies engaged in this field;
h. pawn certificates issued by the State Pawnshop Corporation;
i. letters of distribution of profit or interest from securities, in whatever names and forms.

Article 5.

The moment stamp duty is due shall be determined as follows:

a. for documents made out by one party, it shall be the moment of delivery of the documents;
b. for documents made out by more than one party, it shall be the moment of completion of the documents;
c. for documents made out abroad, it shall be the moment the documents are used in Indonesia.

Article 6.

Stamp duty shall be paid by recipient parties or parties that obtain benefits from documents, unless otherwise determined by the party or parties concerned.

CHAPTER III
STAMP-DUTY MATTER, APPLICATION AND METHODS OF PAYMENT

Article 7

(1) The forms, sizes, colours of gummed stamps and stamped paper, as well as their printing, handling, sales, and examination of their legitimacy shall be stipulated by the Minister of Finance.

(2) Stamp duty on documents shall be paid by the following methods:
   a. by using stamp-duty matter;
   b. by using other means as stipulated by the Minister of Finance.

(3) Gummed stamps shall be fully stuck intact on documents subject to stamp duty.

(4) Gummed stamps shall be stuck where signatures are to be affixed.

(5) The affixing of a signature along with the relevant date shall be done in ink or the like, so that the signature is partly on paper and partly on a gummed stamp.

(6) Should more than one gummed stamp be used, the signature shall be affixed partly on all the stamps and partly on paper.

(7) Stamped paper which are already used shall no longer be used for the second time.
(8) If the contents of documents subject to stamp duty are too long to print on the sheet of stamped paper used, the remaining part may use unstamped paper.
(9) If the provisions as meant in paragraph (1) through paragraph (9) are not fulfilled, the documents concerned shall be considered unstamped.

Article 8

(1) The documents as meant in Article 2 whose stamp duty is not paid or not properly paid shall be subject to an administrative sanction of 200% (two hundred percent) of the stamp duty unpaid or underpaid.
(2) Holders of the documents as meant in paragraph (1) shall be obligated to settle the stamp duty due along with the fine by the method of post stamping.

Article 9

Documents which are made out abroad shall have their stamp duty paid at the time they are used in Indonesia by the method of post stamping.

Article 10

The post stamping as meant in Article 2 paragraph (3), Article 8 and Article 9 shall be done by postal officials according to the procedure laid down by the Minister of Finance.

CHAPTER IV
SPECIAL PROVISIONS

Article 11

(1) Government officials, judges, bailiffs, court secretaries, notaries public, and other officials in general in carrying out their tasks or functions shall not:
   a. receive, consider or keep documents with unpaid or underpaid stamp duty;

b. attach papers with unpaid or underpaid stamp duty to other related documents;
c. make photocopies, carbon copies, duplicates or quotations out of documents with unpaid or underpaid stamp duty;
d. give explanations or notes to documents with unpaid or underpaid stamp duty.

(2) Any violation of the provisions as meant in paragraph (1) shall be liable to administrative sanctions in line with the effective laws.

Article 12

The obligation to pay stamp duty and the administrative fine due according to this law shall no longer valid after five years have elapsed starting from the dates when documents are made out.

CHAPTER V
CRIMINAL PROVISIONS

Article 13

Whoever commits the following acts shall be subject to punishments according to the Criminal Law:

a. to produce imitations of or falsify gummed stamps and stamped paper or to imitate and falsify signatures required for the legitimacy of stamps;
b. to keep with the purpose of distribution or to bring into Indonesia stamps that are false, falsified or produced unlawfully;
c. to use, sell, offer, deliver, supply for sales or entry into Indonesia stamps whose marks, imprints, signatures, brands of legitimacy or dates have been removed to make them appear as if they were not yet used, and or to have other persons use them unlawfully;
d. to keep materials or apparatus known to be used for committing any of the crimes of producing imitations of and falsifying stamp-duty matter.

Article 14

(1) Whoever intentionally uses other means as meant in Article 7

paragraph (2) point b without the permission of the Minister of Finance shall be liable to maximum imprisonment of 7 (seven) years.

(2) The act as meant in paragraph (1) shall be a felony.

CHAPTER VI
TRANSITIONAL PROVISIONS

Article 15

(1) Documents with unpaid or underpaid stamp duty which were made out before the enforcement of this law shall remain subject to stamp duty according to the Stamp Duty Regulation of 1921.

(2) The implementation of the provision as meant in paragraph (1) shall be regulated by the Minister of Finance.

Article 16

Pending the issuance of provisions for the realisation of this law, implementation rules based on the Stamp Duty Regulation of 1921 that are not contradictory to this law and not yet revoked and replaced shall remain effective up to December 31, 1988.

CHAPTER VII
CLOSING PROVISIONS

Article 17

The implementation of this law shall be stipulated by a government regulation.

Article 18

This law shall come into force as from January 1, 1986.

For public cognizance, this law shall be published in the Statute Book of the Republic of Indonesia.

Enforced in Jakarta.
On December 27, 1985.
THE MINISTER/STATE SECRETARY,

sgd.

SUDHARMONO S.H.

Ratified in Jakarta
On December 27, 1985
THE PRESIDENT OF THE REPUBLIC OF INDONESIA,

sgd.

SOEHARTO

ELUCIDATION ON LAW No. 13/1985 CONCERNING STAMP DUTY

GENERAL:

The Republic of Indonesia as a law abiding country on the basis of Pancasila state philosophy and the Constitution of 1945 guarantees equal rights and obligations for all citizens to take part in national development.

One of the methods of realising the public role as meant above is by filling the obligation to pay stamp duty on the use of certain documents.

The provisions on the imposition of stamp duty so far applied as contained in the Stamp Duty Regulation of 1921 (Statute Book of 1921 No. 498) as already several times amended, lastly by Provisional Law No.2/1965 (Statute Book of 1965 No.121), as stipulated into law by Law No.7/1969 (Statute Book of 1969 No.38), are no longer in keeping with current needs and developments of the situation in Indonesia so that it is necessary to introduce simplification.

For this purpose, this law no longer stipulates stamp duty according to sizes of paper and proportional stamp duty, but instead only fixed rates of stamp duty, viz. Rp 1,000 (one thousand rupiahs) and Rp 500 (five hundred rupiahs).

For the sake of simplicity and facility in the payment of stamp duty, this can be sufficiently done by using gummed stamps and stamped paper, so that it is no longer necessary to visit the office of the Directorate General of Taxation to obtain letters of authorisation for payments.

The imposition of stamp duty is limited to documents as referred to in this law, which are used by the public in legal affairs.

In order to settle unpaid or underpaid stamp duty along with its fine (if any), the method of poststamping is applied.

ARTICLE BY ARTICLE:

Article 1.

Paragraph (1):

Sufficiently clear.

Paragraph (2):

Sufficiently clear.

Article 2.

Paragraph (1):

Point a : Holders of agreements or other papers as meant in this provision shall pay stamp duty on the agreements or papers they hold.

The other papers referred to herein shall be among others letters of authorisation, letters of grants, statements.

Point b : Sufficiently clear.

Point c : Sufficiently clear.

Point d, e, and f:

The amounts of money as well as nominal prices as meant in points d, e and f, shall also imply the amounts as well as prices in foreign currencies.

In order to determine their rupiah values, the amounts of money or nominal prices shall be multiplied by exchange rates as stipulated by the Minister of Finance that are effective at the moment the documents are made out, so as to ascertain whether or not these documents are subject to stamp duty.

Paragraph (2):

Sufficiently clear.

Paragraph (3):

This paragraph is meant to impose stamp duty on documents which originally were not subject to stamp duty, but since they are later used as instrument of evidence before court, they shall first be subject to post-stamping.

Point a : Ordinary letters as meant in point a of this paragraph are not intended to serve as evidence, for instance a person sends an ordinary letter to another

requesting the latter to sell an article.
This letter is not subject to stamp duty at the moment it is made out, but if later it is used as an instrument of evidence before court, it shall first be subject to post-stamping.

Household letters include for instance a price list. This list is not intended to serve as evidence, so that it is not subject to stamp duty. If later a dispute arises and the price list is used as an instrument of evidence, then this price list shall first be subject to post-stamping.

Point b: The documents as meant in point b of this paragraph are those which due to their purposes are not subject to stamp duty, but if the aims later change such documents shall be subject to stamp duty. For example, a letter of evidence on the receipt of money made out with the aim of meeting internal organisational requirements is not subject to stamp duty. If later the letter is used as an instrument of evidence before court, this letter shall first be subject to post-stamping.

Paragraph (4):

See the explanation on paragraph (1) points d, e, and f.

Article 3.

Sufficiently clear.

Article 4.

Point a:

Figure 1:

Sufficiently clear.

Figure 2:

Sufficiently clear.

Figure 3:

Sufficiently clear.

Figure 4:

Sufficiently clear.

Figure 5:

Sufficiently clear.

Figure 6:

Sufficiently clear.

Figure 7:

Referred to herein as other papers shall be documents that are excluded from figures 1 through 6 but owing to their contents and uses can be considered similar to the aforesaid documents, such as goods despatch certificates, warehouse warrants, passengers manifests, so that these papers are not subject to stamp duty, according to Article 4 point a.

Point b: Included in the meaning of all kinds of diplomas shall be certificats on completion of studies, certificates on passing examinations, certificates on completion of programs of education, training, courses, and upgrading courses.

Point c:

Sufficiently clear.

Point d:

Sufficiently clear.

Point e: The banks as meant herein shall be those which are appointed by the government to receive tax, duty and excise payments.

Point f:

Sufficiently clear.

Point g:

Sufficiently clear.

Point h:

Sufficiently clear.

Point i:

Sufficiently clear.

Article 5.

Point a: For documents belonging to point a, the moment stamp duty is due shall be the time when they are delivered to and received by the parties for whom they are made out, rather than the moment of signing, such as receipts, cheques, and so forth.

Point b: For documents belonging to point b, the moment stamp duty is due shall be the time when they are already completed, finished with the affixing of signatures of the parties concerned. An example is a transaction agreement. Stamp Duty is due at the moment the agreement is signed.

Point c:

Sufficiently clear.

Article 6.

In the case of documents being made out by one party, such as receipts, stamp duty shall be paid by recipients of the receipts.

In the case of documents being made out by 2 (two) parties or more, such as underhand agreements, each of the parties shall be subject to stamp duty on the documents received. If such agreements are made out with deeds of notaries public, stamp duty on both original sheets kept by notaries public and their copies for the parties concerned shall be paid by the parties obtaining benefits from the documents, viz. the parties concluding the agreements, according to this example.

If the party or parties concerned determine(s) otherwise, stamp duty shall be paid by the party or parties determined in the documents.

Article 7.

Paragraph (1):

Sufficiently celar.

Paragraph (2):

In general, stamp duty on documents is paid by applying stamp-duty matter according to the rates as stipulated in this law.

In addition, by a decree of the Minister of Finance other methods can be determined for the settlement of stamp duty, for instance by affixing imprints in place of stamp duty on documents with imprint-machines, according to the effective provisions stipulated for this purpose.

Paragraph (3):

Sufficiently clear.

Paragraph (4):

Sufficiently clear.

Paragraph (5):

Sufficiently clear.

Paragraph (6):

Sufficiently clear.

Paragraph (7):

This paragraph stesses that a sheet of stamped paper can only be used once, though it can happen that the writing or information contained in the stamped paper only covers part of the stamped paper.

If the blank part or the space without any writing or information is to be filled in with other writing or information, the filling of such writing or information shall be subject to separate stamp duty based on the rates as stipulated in Article 2.

If a sheet of stamped paper due some reason is not used and in this case not yet signed by the party concerned, while the stamped paper already bears several words or sentences that have not yet constituted a finished document, and then the writing on the aforesaid stamped paper is crossed out and new sentences or information are/is again rewritten, this stamp paper can be used without additional stamp duty.

Article 8.

Paragraph (1):

Sufficiently clear.

Paragraph (2):

Sufficiently clear.

Article 9.

Documents that are made out abroad shall not be subject to stamp duty as long as they are not used in Indonesia.

If the documents are to be used in Indonesia they shall first be subject to stamp duty based on the rates as stipulated in Article 2 by the post-stamping method without being fined. But if the aforesaid documents have their stamp duty settled only after being used, the post-stamping shall be imposed along with a fine of 200% (two hundred percent).

Article 10.

Sufficiently clear.

Article 11.

Sufficiently clear.

Article 12.

From the aspect of legal certainty the 5 (five)-year limit of expiration starting from the dates on which documents are made out shall be effective for all documents including receipts.

Article 13.

Sufficiently clear.

Article 14.

Paragraph (1):

Committing the act as meant in the explanation of Article 7 paragraph (2) without the permission of the Minister of Finance will bring benefits to owners or users of the devices and on the other hand inflict losses upon the State.

Therefore a criminal sanction shall be imposed in the form of imprisonment for the felony committed.

Paragraph (2): Sufficiently clear.

Article 15.

Paragraph (1): Sufficiently clear.
Paragraph (2): Sufficiently clear.

Article 16.

Sufficiently clear.

Article 17.

Sufficiently clear.

Article 18.

Sufficiently clear.

SUPPLEMENT TO STATUTE BOOK OF THE REPUBLIC OF INDONESIA NUMBER 3313